The Wages of Oil

The Wages of Oil

Parliaments and Economic Development in Kuwait and the UAE

Michael Herb

Cornell University Press
Ithaca and London

First published 2014 by Cornell University Press

Printed in the United States of America

Library of Congress Cataloging-in-Publication Data

Herb, Michael, 1966– author.
The wages of oil : Parliaments and economic development in Kuwait and the UAE / Michael Herb.
pages cm
Includes bibliographical references and index.
ISBN 978-0-8014-5336-6 (cloth : alk. paper)
1. Democratization—Kuwait. 2. Democratization—United Arab Emirates. 3. Kuwait—Politics and government. 4. United Arab Emirates—Politics and government. 5. Petroleum industry and trade—Political aspects—Kuwait. 6. Petroleum industry and trade—Political aspects—United Arab Emirates. 7. Economic development—Political aspects—Kuwait. 8. Economic development—Political aspects—United Arab Emirates. I. Title.

JQ1848.A91H47 2014
330.95357—dc23 2014022400

Cornell University Press strives to use environmentally responsible suppliers and materials to the fullest extent possible in the publishing of its books. Such materials include vegetable-based, low-VOC inks and acid-free papers that are recycled, totally chlorine-free, or partly composed of nonwood fibers. For further information, visit our website at www.cornellpress.cornell.edu.

Cloth printing 10 9 8 7 6 5 4 3 2 1

To Aqil and Yasmeen

Contents

Tables and Figures

Tables

Figures

Acknowledgments

This book has its genesis in several trips back and forth from Kuwait to Dubai in 2007 while I was in Kuwait on a Fulbright research fellowship. The trips were funded in part by a Research Initiation Grant from my home institution, Georgia State University. In Kuwait, I was hosted by the American University of Kuwait. An earlier version of some of the arguments in this book appeared in the August 2009 issue of the *International Journal of Middle East Studies.*

I have received invaluable help from many people in writing this book. I have had the opportunity to present various parts of this book at workshops, conferences, and lectures. Feedback from colleagues at these events has helped me sharpen my arguments and avoid mistakes. These events have included talks given at Kuwait University (organized by Khaled Al-Fadhel), at Yale University (Ellen Lust), Sciences Po (Steffen Hertog), the Center for Strategic and International Studies (Jon Alterman); the University of Olso (Bjørn Utvik and Jon Nordenson), Florida International University (Russell Lucas); the Project on Middle East Political Science at George Washington University (Marc Lynch), the Moulay Hicham Foundation, and the American University in Kuwait (Farah Al-Nakib). I presented a version of chapter 1 at the Gulf Research Meeting of the Gulf Research Center in July 2010; the workshop was organized by Steffen Hertog and Rola Dashti. Participants at the University of Chicago Comparative Politics Workshop read an early draft of chapter 3, and it is better as a result. Others who have helped include Abdulkhaleq Abdulla, Abdul Hamid al-Ansari, Hassan Mohammed Al Ansari, Mohammed Al-Dallal, Yousef Al-Ebraheem, Khaled bin Sultan Al-Essa, Ibtisam al-Ketbi, Mohammad Al-Moqatei, Odah Al-Rowaie, Anas

Al-Rushaid, Nasser Al-Sane, Khalid bin Jabor Al Thani, Ghanim al-Najjar, Mohammed Al-Rokn, Abd al-Rahim al-Shahin, Omar Al-Shehabi, Barbara Bibbo, Saad Bin Tefla, John Duffield, Hasan Johar, Shana Marshall, Jennifer McCoy, Pete Moore, Mary Ann Tétreault, and Sean Yom. Hamza Olayan of *al-Qabas* generously allowed me to consult the newspaper's archives. I am indebted to Steffen Hertog and Greg Gause for their extensive and extremely useful comments on a draft of the manuscript, and to Roger Haydon and the team at Cornell University Press. And thanks to Francis Cox for providing the cover photo.

My children, Aqil and Yasmeen, have been hearing about "the book" for a very long time—and here it is, at long last. I dedicate it to them. They mean the world to me. My wife Kathryn provided more support and encouragement than I can properly thank her for; she makes me happy.

Note on Transliteration

In transliterating the titles of Arabic sources, I have used a system based on that of the *International Journal of Middle Eastern Studies.* For place names, I have used the transliterations commonly in use on street signs and in other English language sources (thus, Shuwaikh, not Shuwaykh). For personal names, I have used the transliteration that appears to be favored by the individual him- or herself, as evidenced by websites, business cards, and the like.

Two Models

There are no accomplishments [of the National Assembly in promoting the private sector] because of a great imbalance lying in the nature of those who vote in elections. A majority of them are employees of the state or its enterprises. . . . The role of the deputy changes . . . to a role resembling that of a member of a union of government employees, and the National Assembly gradually becomes a large union for the employees of the government and its enterprises.
—Abdulwahab al-Haroun, former deputy in the Kuwaiti National Assembly

Not long ago, before oil, Kuwait and Dubai shared much in common; both were small trading ports on the Gulf littoral, dependent on pearling and trade, and ruled by Arab families under British tutelage. Both had thriving merchant communities and an economy oriented toward trade and the sea. Today they are very different places. Dubai is an internationally famous entrepôt, tourist destination, and showplace for ostentatious architecture. Partly because of its relatively limited oil wealth, Dubai has led the United Arab Emirates (UAE) in diversifying its economy beyond oil, building a vibrant entrepôt economy that attracts foreign visitors and residents from far and wide. Yet the UAE—in which Dubai is one of seven emirates—remains one of the least democratic countries in the world. Kuwait, by contrast, has none of the economic vitality of the UAE, but it has a parliament (the National Assembly) that is by far the most potent among the six Gulf monarchies. The Kuwaiti economy, however, remains almost entirely dependent on oil.

In this book, I offer an explanation for the divergent paths followed by Kuwait and the UAE. Explaining this puzzle is interesting in itself, but it also gives us a window on the underlying political economy of the Gulf. My goal is to set out a framework for understanding the distinctive politics and economics of the Gulf monarchies, one that explains how the often-competing interests of rulers, capitalists, citizens, and expatriates take shape in Gulf states with more or less political participation and in those with more or less oil rent per capita. I argue that:

- The Gulf rentiers should be divided into two groups. The first group is the extreme rentiers—Kuwait, the UAE, and Qatar—which enjoy the highest per capita rent incomes in the world. The second group is the not-quite-so-rich middling rentiers—Saudi Arabia, Oman, and Bahrain.
- The three extreme rentiers enjoy so much oil wealth that the state can employ nearly nine of every ten citizens who work for a wage, and the state can do this without imposing taxes on the private sector. This defines—and in a peculiar way—the class interests of a majority of citizens.
- Alone among the Gulf Cooperation Council (GCC) monarchies,[1] Kuwait has a strong parliament. This is largely due to an exogenous factor—the Iraqi threat to Kuwaiti sovereignty at independence and then again in the early 1990s.
- In Kuwait, the parliament gives the citizen majority a voice in determining economic policy. This results in a set of economic policies very different from those found in the UAE and Qatar.
- In the absence of a powerful parliament, the ruling families of the UAE are free to pursue their interests as the dominant local capitalists; at the extreme, the result is Dubai.

The contrast between Kuwait and the UAE today illustrates the vastly different possible futures facing the smaller Gulf states. If we extrapolate current trends, in some reasonably possible—even likely—future the northern emirates of the UAE will become a truly global business center, a megalopolis of many millions attracting immigrants in great waves from near and far. Kuwait, meanwhile, might just defy the odds (and the literature on the rentier state) and democratize. The great challenge faced by the richest Gulf rentiers is how to combine economic vitality and political participation, a feat that none appears likely to accomplish anytime soon, although Kuwait is perhaps better positioned than the UAE.

The Dubai Model and the Kuwait Model

At the height of the Dubai boom, Mohammed bin Rashid, the ruler of Dubai, dreamed big. He sought to build a world city, a thriving metropolis where, not so long before, there had been only a village. He planned a business district to

1. Bahrain, Kuwait, Oman, Qatar, Saudi Arabia, and the UAE.

rival Manhattan or Ginza, and he planned to build new cities on reclaimed land in the Gulf that would have a population upward of a million. He accomplished much before the real estate crash. Under his watch, Dubai came to have one of the busiest airports in the world and one of the busiest container ports, attracted a startling number of tourists, and made itself into a logistics and business hub for the Gulf and well beyond. Mohammed bin Rashid made Dubai into a brand known around the world. This was achieved in a place that not so long before had been not much more than a village. (In 1950, Dubai had a population of 53,000.[2] A British official described the Trucial Coast generally as having "many attractions for the traveler from the West who does not attach too much importance to his personal comfort."[3]) In 2006, Abdulkhaleq Abdulla, an Emirati scholar, said that Dubai was in the midst of its "moment in history."[4] The real estate and financial crash dented the growth of Dubai, but a few years after the crash, the economy was showing renewed vigor based on the strength of its logistics and tourism sectors.

All this business growth required—and still requires—people: laborers, renters, business owners, property purchasers, and more. By the middle of the 2000s Mohammed bin Rashid's dreams had long outgrown the available citizen population of his country, all of whom could live on the largest of his planned palms in the Gulf, with room to spare. By 2011, foreigners outnumbered citizens in the UAE by a ratio of nine to one.[5] This, understandably, left citizens feeling overwhelmed. It is as if 2.7 billion noncitizens lived in the United States alongside its 300 million or so citizens—with a billion or so having arrived in the past decade. This sort of comparison, of course, has its limits; scale matters. But we should take the comparison seriously before dismissing Emirati citizens' concerns about the demographic imbalance in their country as nativist xenophobia. The debate over demography should not be seen through the prism of the debates in developed democratic countries between those who want limited immigration and those who want none. The shaykhdoms on the Gulf littoral have always been cosmopolitan societies open to the rest of the world; many of the citizens of the UAE today see the question as one not of maintaining the traditional openness of their societies but, instead, of reducing their nation to a small caste of "nationals"[6] in

2. Government of Dubai, Dubai Statistics Center, "Population by Sex," www.dsc.gov.ae (accessed June 13, 2012). The original source of the population figure is a Kuwaiti mission sent to Dubai in 1953 (Hay 1959, 129).

3. Hay 1959, 129.

4. Abdulla 2006, 61, 84.

5. United Arab Emirates 2011.

6. In the UAE, citizens are typically called *nationals* in English. I prefer the term *citizens* here for clarity and to emphasize the differing legal status of citizens and expatriates.

a sea of foreigners. As one prominent Emirati intellectual put it, after pointing out that the progress of Dubai filled him with pride, "[we] fear that we may lose everything that we have built. This feeling comes from the fact that we are a small minority in a city that's full of foreigners. We are very scared."[7]

Kuwait, by contrast, has not experienced a Dubai-style boom. Instead, the distinction of Kuwait among the Gulf monarchies lies in its politics. Over the past few years, the National Assembly and the ruling family have competed for control of the government, and the ruling family has made substantial concessions. In recent years, the prime minister—also a member of the ruling family—has agreed to submit to votes of confidence in the National Assembly, admitting the principle that the government relies on parliamentary support. The opposition boycott of elections in late 2012 and in 2013 allowed the ruling family to regain its footing but not to reverse the institutional gains of the National Assembly. Unlike the other Gulf monarchies, Kuwait has made perceptible progress toward democracy, a point I make in more detail in chapter 2, where I also address the democracy scores of Kuwait and the UAE based on democracy rankings widely used by political scientists.

Despite the progress of Kuwait toward democracy, Kuwaiti capitalists today invest their money any place but in Kuwait, fleeing an investment environment that they increasingly view as hopelessly hostile (as evidenced, for example, by the dismal record of Kuwait in attracting foreign direct investment; see figure I.1). And Kuwaiti capitalists largely agree on whom to blame—the deputies in the National Assembly. Some go further and blame, in particular, the majority of Kuwaiti voters who rely on state oil riches for their paychecks and evince little interest in the sort of growth seen elsewhere in the Gulf. Most Kuwaitis who work for a salary are employed by the state or state-owned enterprises (SOEs) and thus rely directly on the oil wealth of the state for both their paychecks and for generous public services (this is also true of the citizens of the UAE, including those in the poorer emirates). Most private-sector development, as a direct consequence, does not benefit middle class Kuwaiti citizens; a tourist industry, for example, would employ very few Kuwaitis and generate little or no tax revenue. As a result of this dynamic, Kuwaiti politics is characterized by a surprisingly high level of outright class conflict between the publically employed middle class and the merchant capitalists. And this conflict is being won by the state employees via their influence in the popularly elected National Assembly.

7. Abdulkhaleq Abdulla, quoted in Hamza Hendawi 2008, "A Gulf State Grapples for Identity in Sea of Foreigners," Associated Press, May 1. For an excellent discussion of these issues, see Al-Shehabi 2012.

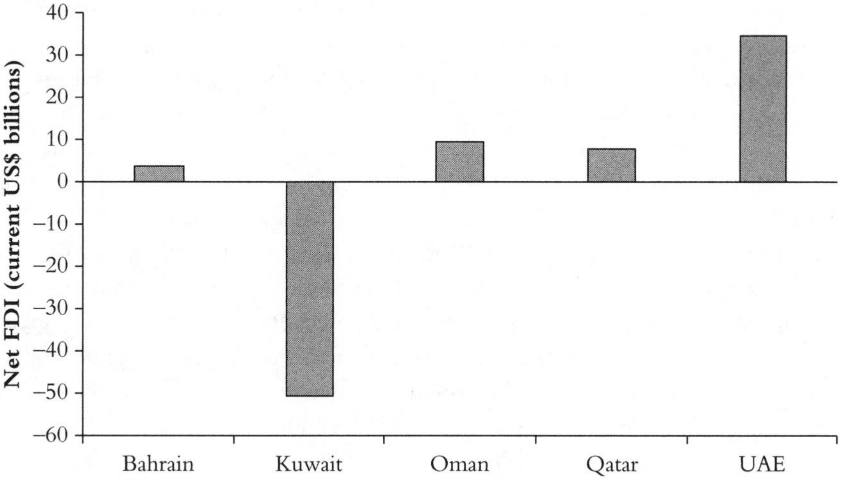

Fig. I.1 Net foreign direct investment flows ([inward FDI flows] minus [outward FDI flows]), 2000–2012. United Nations Conference on Trade and Development (UNCTAD), "Inward and Outward Foreign Direct Investment Flows, Annual, 1970–2012," http://unctadstat.unctad.org.

From the point of view of Kuwaiti citizens the absence of a Dubai-style boom has had at least one advantage: although Kuwaitis are a minority in their own country, the country's demographic structure is not nearly as unbalanced as that of the UAE (or Qatar). And the foreigners in Kuwait are mostly there to provide services to Kuwaitis rather than to ensure the profitability of the ruling family's real estate developments. A visitor to Kuwait feels the difference immediately; it is a city oriented toward satisfying the needs of its middle-class citizens. Dubai, by contrast, often feels like a city focused more on foreigners (especially those with money) than on its citizens, who can often be hard to find.

Of these two models, Kuwait and Dubai, it is quite clear which has been more influential in recent years in the Gulf—and it is not the Kuwaiti model of expanded political participation.[8] The ruling families of Abu Dhabi and Qatar are attracted to the economic diversification and international branding pioneered by Dubai.[9] These ruling families, once inclined to insularity, have in

8. On Dubai as a model see Hvidt 2009; Chorin 2010; Abdulla 2006, 64.

9. Hvidt 2011. Before the economic crisis of 2008, the (very influential) crown prince of Abu Dhabi said that "we see Singapore, and even Dubai, as being a step ahead of us, but it's good to have a challenge" (Oxford Business Group 2006, 19).

recent years made determined efforts to make their mark on the world. This is most evident in the many vanity projects embraced by the ruling families—such as the Abu Dhabi museum complex (Louvre Abu Dhabi and Abu Dhabi Guggenheim) and the Qatari plan to host the 2022 World Cup. It can also be seen in the Qatari ruling family's growing collection of contemporary art, of which it has been the largest purchaser in recent years.[10] What Qatar and Abu Dhabi do not share with Dubai is any shortage of capital. They can bail themselves out of their own mistakes. But their development models, like that of Dubai, rely on an abundance of foreign immigration; the Qatari demographic imbalance today rivals that of the UAE. The citizen populations of Abu Dhabi and Qatar simply are not numerous enough to create the glittering metropolises envisaged by their rulers. One solution, of course, is to offer citizenship to immigrants. But the Gulf monarchies have done little of this, and the logic of rentierism dictates that they will not start anytime soon. In a country with fantastic oil wealth, each additional citizen is one more person who gets a share of a fixed sum of oil wealth. In the next chapter, on Gulf labor markets, I explore this dilemma in more detail.

The problems of Kuwait have dimmed its attraction as a model for other Gulf states. In 1981, the merchant-owned Kuwaiti newspaper *Al-Qabas* could write on the eve of the first meeting of a newly elected parliament that "Today's celebration of democracy attracts the attention of all the peoples of the region, who look to Kuwait as a pioneer in various realms, first and foremost among them the realm of democracy."[11] In 2009, the same newspaper reviewed Gulf reactions to the political crisis of early 2009; a typical view was that "Instead of the Kuwaiti experience opening the door for other Gulf and Arab experiments, it has become a source of fear for some, while others exploit it to warn against following on the same path."[12] Before the same elections, Khalid Al-Dakhil, a prominent Saudi sociologist, said that the Kuwaiti model had not lost its influence but that its example "is a blow to the reformist current in the countries of the Gulf and Peninsula."[13] A

10. Sara Elkamel, "Qatar Becomes World's Biggest Buyer of Contemporary Art," *The Guardian*, July 13, 2011, http://www.guardian.co.uk/artanddesign/2011/jul/13/qatar-world-biggest-art-buyer; Robert Yates, "The Desert Blooms: Culture in Qatar," *The Guardian*, January 23, 2011, http://www.guardian.co.uk/world/2011/jan/23/qatar-film-festival-gulf-emirate.

11. *Al-Qabas* March 9, 1981, 1.

12. Hamza Olayan, "Kayfa qara'a ahl al-khalij wa al-nukhba hall majlis al-umma wa istiqala al-hukuma?" [How do the people and elites of the Gulf view the dissolution of the National Assembly and the resignation of the government?], *al-Qabas*, March 26, 2009, 13.

13. Quoted in Hussein Abdulrahman, "Kayfa tanazzar al-nukhba al-khalijiyya ila al-dimuqratiyya al-kuwaytiyya?" [How does the Gulf elite view Kuwaiti democracy?], *al-Qabas*, April 20, 2009, 24.

2007 first-page headline in *al-Qabas* summed up the view of Kuwaiti capitalists: "The Kuwaiti way of practicing democracy blocks development."[14]

But there are also other voices in Gulf society, voices less privileged and harder to hear, that have a different view of the Kuwaiti National Assembly. Gulf societies tend toward hierarchy, with the ruling families at the apex, prominent merchant families below them, citizens next, and unskilled foreign labor at the bottom. The Kuwaiti parliament gives a voice to citizens who otherwise would not have one; it does not empower the bottom of the hierarchy (the foreign laborers), but it does give the lower-middle-class citizens a voice. We can feel this viscerally when watching an interpellation of a member of the Kuwaiti ruling family, as the shaykh is "grilled" by members of the Kuwaiti parliament to the satisfaction of the assembled spectators. For a period in 2008, one of the most popular YouTube clips returned by a search for the "al-Sabah" (the Kuwaiti ruling family) was a clip of this exchange, in which a firebrand deputy (Musallam Al-Barrak) berated the shaykh; the clip was titled "The Difference between the Kuwait National Assembly and the Saudi Majlis al-Shura." In the comments section of the website, one viewer wrote, "I am from Saudi Arabia. Really I like this man [Musallam Al-Barrak] a lot. . . . As for the difference between the two assemblies it is large, and there is no basis for comparison. God bless." Another comment asked, "Where is the comparison? The Consultative Council in Saudi Arabia is only a decoration."[15]

The other three Gulf monarchies are not as rich (on a per capita basis) as Kuwait, Qatar, and the UAE. They cannot afford to hire all their citizens as state employees at generous wages. As a result, class politics in these societies is of the more conventional sort—some citizens must find employment in the private sector, and thus they have a stake in the private-sector generation of jobs. Nonetheless, up until the Arab Spring of 2011, the rulers of these countries seemed more intent on following the Dubai model than on providing jobs for their citizens. This had something to do, no doubt, with their desire to compete with the other Gulf ruling families; it also had something to do with the privileged access of members of the ruling families to real estate. This gave the shaykhs and princes an interest in the pell-mell Dubai model of growth. But there is at least some evidence that the Arab Spring—more than the 2008 world financial crisis—was a sobering reminder to the senior members of the ruling families of the risks of policies tilted too heavily in favor of capitalists. For the past several years, the Saudi and Omani

14. Safa'a Al Matari, Muhammad al-Atarbi, Marwan Badran, Hussayn Malak, Tamir Hamad, and Muhsin al-Sayyid, "Al-tariqa al-kuwaytiyya fi mumarasa al-dimuqratiyya ta'ttil al-tanmiyya" [The Kuwaiti way of practicing democracy blocks development], *al-Qabas*, May 19, 2007.

15. http://www.youtube.com/watch?v=AHJei1lsP1M (accessed July 7, 2008). The clip is no longer available.

regimes have pursued policies intended to provide jobs for their citizens—which is to say, they have defied the interests of capitalists with the sort of resolution that is driven by fear for the stability of their absolutisms. In 2011, in direct response to the Arab Spring, the Al Saud forced the Saudi private sector to hire more than 200,000 citizens, an increase of 35% accomplished in less than a year.[16]

Plan of the Book

In the remainder of this chapter, I discuss the literature on the resource curse, focusing on how it deals with class politics in really rich rentiers. (This literature is also often called the rentier state literature, and I use both terms here to describe the body of scholarship.)[17] In chapter 1, I explain the labor markets of Gulf rentiers and discuss their effects on class politics. I then turn to the issue of participation. In chapter 2, I show that the Kuwaiti National Assembly is, in fact, more powerful than the representative assemblies of the other Gulf monarchies; in chapter 3, I provide an explanation for this. There I delve into Gulf history; this history is crucial for the argument and it addresses issues crucial for understanding the current development trajectories of Gulf states.

In case studies of the UAE (chapter 4) and Kuwait (chapter 5), I combine the themes of the previous chapters. In chapter 4, I show what happens when an extreme rentier state has no parliament. In chapter 5, I show what happens when the citizen middle class in an extreme rentier has some political power. In the penultimate chapter I address the political science literature on the rentier state. In the final chapter I draw out implications for the future of the Gulf monarchies.

This is a work of historical institiutionalism in the sense that I explain the historical origins of an institution (the Kuwaiti National Assembly) and then trace the political and economic consequences of that institution.[18] I make causal arguments using several techniques. I employ a structured comparison of cases that are similar on many variables but differ on outcomes.[19] As David Collier, Henry Brady, and Jason Seawright recommend, I "juxtapose this comparative framing with carefully-executed analysis carried out within the cases."[20] I rely, in particular, on process tracing to establish causal linkages between causes and

16. Saudi Arabia, Ministry of Labor, "Nata'ij awwaliyya mubshira li-birnamij Nitaqat" [Promising early results of the Nitaqat program], *Nitaqat*, 2012, http://www.emol.gov.sa/nitaqat/pages/Activities_Act3.aspx (accessed September 12, 2012).

17. The word *state* in the term *rentier state* has been used by scholars both to refer to the political institution of the state and as a synonym for *country*. In this book, I use the term *rentier* (as a noun) to refer to a country that receives a good deal of rent income. I use *rentier state* to (1) refer to the state, as political institution, in a rentier, and (2) to describe the associated scholarly literature. See also Luciani 1990, 66.

18. Pierson and Skocpol 2002.

19. Hall 2003, 379–81.

20. Collier, Brady, and Seawright 2010, 10.

outcomes.[21] In this I employ "strategic narrative," which Jack Goldstone describes as differing from "straightforward narrative of historical events by being structured to focus attention on how patterns of events relate to prior theoretical beliefs about social phenomena."[22] Thus, I provide historical accounts that pay close attention to what we should find in the historical record if a specific factor caused the outcome in question. Throughout, I evaluate multiple possible explanations for outcomes to draw my conclusions about which casual explanation best fits the historical record. All research methods in comparative politics require trade-offs, especially between asking interesting questions and providing certain answers.[23] Here I am asking questions that are important for the future development of the Gulf monarchies—for both citizens and expatriates—and the methods I use are intended to make the most persuasive case I can muster in answering these questions.

The Resource Curse

Over the past two decades scholars have produced a voluminous literature on the resource curse, much of it in the form of large-n regressions. This work has helped to clarify the concepts and theoretical underpinnings of the resource curse. It has not, however, done much to resolve the issue of the causal impact of natural resource exports on democracy. Instead, the results of dueling studies have often hinged on finer points of methodological technique.[24] The descent into methodological wizardry is understandable in part: the topic is not one easily amenable to quantitative analysis, which is why issues of statistical technique loom so large.

A number of scholars have suggested that the causal impact of natural resource rents on outcomes varies in different contexts.[25] The impact of oil on democracy may be negative when rents are combined with one set of variables but positive when rents are combined with a different set of variables. Regression models typically assume that rents have the same causal effect on democracy across all countries, varying according to the magnitude of rentierism and holding other variables constant. There are ways to tweak this assumption by running regressions on subsets of all observations,[26] or with interaction variables, though the latter strategy has not often been used in quantitative work on the resource curse.

If this is systematically the case—and I think it is—then we can either design ever more complicated regression models, or we can pursue case studies that try to

21. George and Bennett 2005, chap. 10.
22. Goldstone 2003, 50. Goldstone cites Robin Stryker as the source of this term.
23. Gerring 2012, 32–36.
24. Haber and Menaldo 2011; Andersen and Ross 2013; Aslaksen 2010.
25. B. Smith 2004, 243; 2007, 7–9; Yom 2011, 219; Smith 2007, 7–9; Hertog 2010b, 6–7.
26. Dunning 2008; Andersen and Ross 2013.

trace the causal impact of natural resource rents in specific contexts. In this book, I do the latter. My conclusions have lessons for the study of rentierism elsewhere in the world, and I discuss these in the penultimate chapter. But I do not claim that the causal mechanisms that I identify operate in all rentiers. This is, I think, a strength and not a failing. If in fact the causal impact of rentierism varies according to context, we will learn much more through close examination of specific contexts than through the pursuit of general mechanisms that probably do not exist. Put differently: if context matters, and there are many indications that it does matter in ways that are very hard to capture in a regression model, then understanding the resource curse requires close attention to the varying contexts in which natural resource wealth is present. This book does just that, for the handful of countries in the world with the highest per capita rent revenues.

Extreme Rentiers, Middling Rentiers, Poor Rentiers

Not only do the causal effects of natural resource exports vary according to context, but they also vary according to the degree of rentierism. The impacts of natural resource rents are not only greater when there are more rents, but they are also of a different kind.

The measurement of rentierism has been the subject of much debate in the literature, and there is no wide agreement on just which cases have high values of rentierism. The foundational works on the theory of the rentier state measured what Annika Kropf calls *resource dependence;* these studies used measures in which rentierism is expressed as a fraction of something else. In recent years, in response to problems with these measures, scholars have increasingly used per capita measures of rentierism. Kropf usefully calls these measures of *resource abundance*, as distinguished from the earlier measures of resource dependence.[27] While measures of resource dependence are expressed as a percentage, measures of resource wealth are expressed in units of production, value of production, or something similar. Taking oil exports as an example, a measure of resource dependence is calculated as follows:

Resource dependence = value of natural resource exports ÷ GDP

Jeffrey Sachs and Andrew Warner use this measure in their seminal 1995 work on natural resources and economic growth. Giacomo Luciani, in his early 1990

27. Kropf 2010, 110. Dunning (2008, 19–21) uses the same terms in a different way. For him, *all* rentier states are resource abundant (rentier states have a high ratio of rent revenues to all government revenues). Resource dependent countries are a subset of rentier states; they are those rentier states in which rents make up a high share of the entire economy. If there is a substantial non-rent economy, but rent revenue looms large in state finance, the country is a non–resource dependent rentier state.

chapter, uses a similar measure, defining a rentier state as a country that receives at least 40% of its government revenues from the export of oil or a similar source of rents.[28] By contrast, a measure of resource abundance is expressed in per capita terms. Using again the example of oil export revenues:

Resource abundance = oil export revenues ÷ population

The increasing popularity of resource abundance in the literature—instead of resource dependence—is a result of serious problems with the role of GDP in the measure of resource dependence.[29] A country in which natural resource income accounts for the bulk of GDP may have a great deal of natural resource wealth (say, Qatar) or it may have a much more modest amount of resource wealth per capita, but even less GDP from other sources (Angola). If this measure is said to *cause* a political outcome, it is entirely unclear whether the outcome is caused by resource wealth or by non-resource poverty. This creates a particularly tangled causal thicket. The only real solution is to attempt, as far as possible, to make the measure of rentierism independent of the size of the non-oil economy. The measure of resource abundance provided above does this, for the most part.[30]

There is a second reason to prefer measures of resource abundance over measures of resource dependence. Countries can have a high value on measures of rent dependence if they have a lot of rents *or* are very poor (or both): Qatar and Angola can have similar values on the variable. If we think about how we would expect rents to have causal impacts on political outcomes, however, this does not work. Qatar has enough

28. Luciani 1990, 72; Sachs and Warner 1995, 2, 8. Ross (2001, 338) uses a similar measure, and I have done it myself (Herb 2005).

29. Wright and Czelusta 2004, 7–8. In a related context, Ross (2004, 36) raises this concern, and he discusses it in more detail in a later *American Political Science Review* article (2008, 121). For some of the pitfalls of using measures of dependence, see Birdsall and Subramanian 2004, 77.

30. A perfect measure of rentierism, true to the original causal intuition of the rentier state theory, is hard to come by. Figures for hydrocarbon reserves are influenced by the level of investment in exploration, which in turn is endogenous to levels of development. Figures for reserves, even more problematically, are also political. As one scholar writes, "Mineral geologists scoff at reserve numbers, and no one believes that they really represent comprehensive measures of 'resource endowments.'" (Stijns 2001, 10.) If we instead use production figures, rather than reserves, we run up against the problem that these figures do not distinguish between resources consumed domestically and those exported, while the causal mechanisms of the theory rest on the receipt of revenues from abroad. But if we use figures for exports rather than production, we find a different difficulty—exports are deeply affected by level of development. Richer countries use more of their oil production; some countries simply grow out of being oil exporters as domestic demand increases. For example, Iran produces less oil per capita than the United States consumes (U.S. Central Intelligence Agency, *The World Factbook,* www.cia.gov, accessed August 26, 2012). In short, there is no silver bullet, no available perfect measure of rentierism. That said, some measures are better than others, and measures of rent abundance are less laden with problems than are measures of rent dependence. This is especially true of the extreme rentiers of the Gulf, where most production is exported despite high levels of domestic consumption, and where the importance of oil in the economies is not merely a symptom of non-oil poverty.

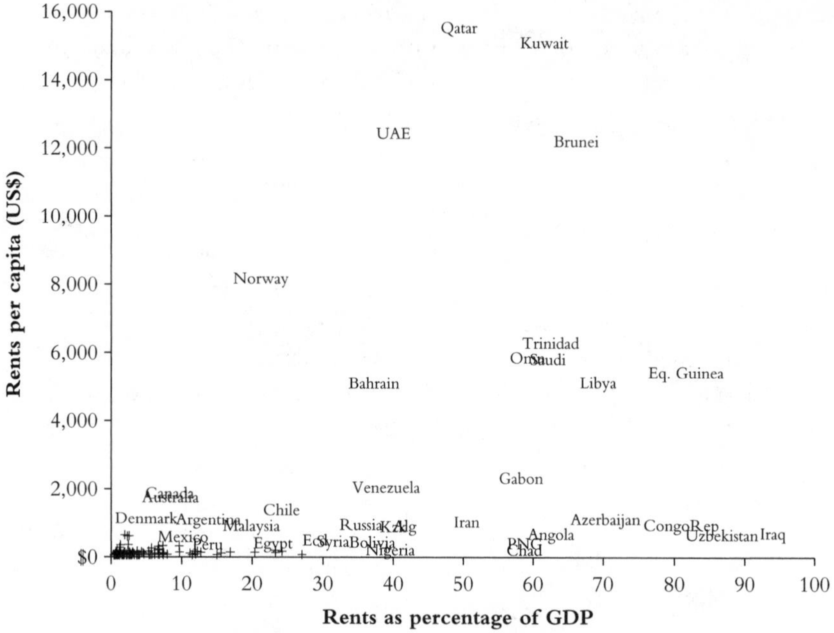

Fig. I.2 Rent abundance versus rent dependence, 2006. The most recent year with data available for all extreme rentiers is 2006. Values are calculated using rent, GDP, and population data from the World Bank. The rent data series in the *World Development Indicators* is "total natural resource rents (% of GDP)." This data series is an estimate of all rents derived from natural resources, including coal, timber, minerals, natural gas, and oil. The value for Turkmenistan is inexplicably large, at 161% of GDP, and it has been omitted from the chart. Countries appear by name in the figure if they have a high value on one measure; otherwise, they are represented by a "+." World Bank, 2012, *World Development Indicators,* http://data.worldbank.org; Hamilton and Clemens 1999; Bolt, Matete, and Clemens 2002.

rent wealth to make its citizens quite prosperous. Angola does not. Measures of resource abundance capture this difference, but measures of resource dependence miss it.

Measures of resource abundance produce a set of cases that differs quite distinctly from the set produced by measures of resource dependence. This point has not been appreciated in the literature on rentier states and the resource curse. Some countries, of course, are both rent abundant *and* rent dependent. But other countries are one but not the other. Figure I.2 allows us to see this clearly. The scatterplot shows rent abundance graphed against rent dependence (specifically, rent income per capita against rents as a percentage of gross domestic product, GDP). Figure I.3 uses a different dataset, the World Trade Organization data on exports of minerals and fuels.[31]

31. See also Ross 2012, 20–22, table 1.1.

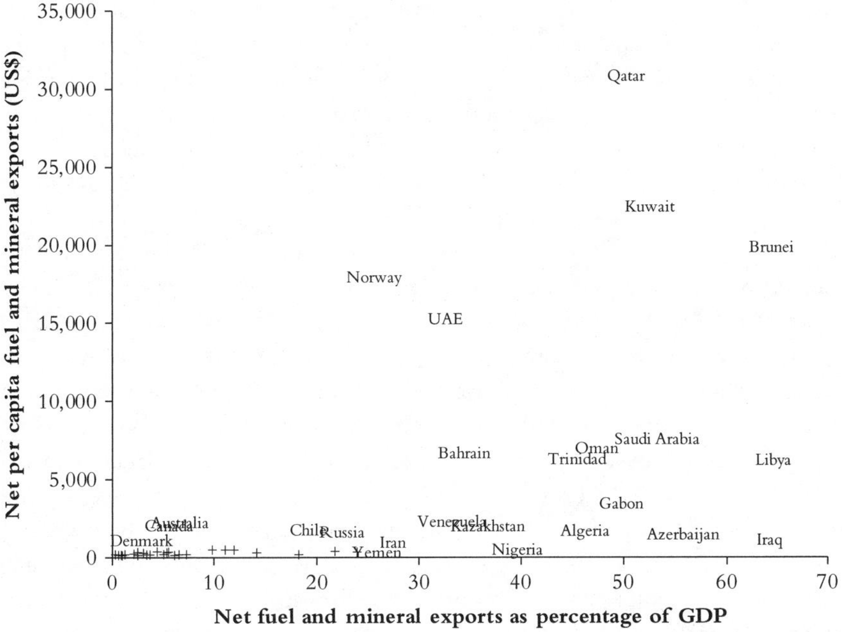

Fig. I.3 Rent abundance versus rent dependence, fuel and mineral export data, 2006. Data include Standard International Trade Classification (SITC) categories 3, 27, 28, and 68. Net exports are calculated by subtracting total imports from total exports; negative values are set to zero. Dollars are current. Countries appear by name in the figure if they have a high value on one measure; otherwise, they are represented by a "+." Data for fuel and mineral exports are from the World Trade Organization *Statistics Database http://stat.wto.org/StatisticalProgram/WSDBStatProgramSeries.aspx* (accessed April 13, 2012). Data on population and GDP are from World Bank, 2012, *World Development Indicators*, http://data.worldbank.org.

A group of countries along the bottom center-right of figures I.2 and I.3 are rent dependent without being rent abundant. When we use measures of rent dependence, these countries look just as much like rentiers as Kuwait or Qatar. But when we use measures of rent abundance, they differ; their rentierism is mostly a symptom of their underlying poverty. Figures I.2 and I.3 highlight the awkward fact that there are fewer countries that are unusually rent abundant than there are countries that are unusually rent dependent. We find several countries that have a reputation for being rentiers in the bottom right of the scatterplots, including all the countries that Benjamin Smith calls the "big four" of rentierism studies: Iran, Algeria, Venezuela, and Nigeria.[32] These countries are demoted from full rentierdom when we use

32. Smith 2007, 4, 36–37. Terry Lynn Karl (1997, 17–18) calls these "capital-deficient oil exporters."

measures of rent abundance; their levels of rent abundance resemble that of Canada or Australia, countries not usually thought of as rentiers. The upper-left part of the scatterplots, however, offers few new countries that are rent abundant without being rent dependent, apart from the well-known case of Norway. The overall effect is to winnow down the overall number of cases with a high measure of rentierism.[33]

Only a few countries around the world are truly rent abundant. These countries include all six GCC monarchies, Brunei, Norway, Trinidad and Tobago, Equatorial Guinea, and Libya. Even among these cases, the countries with the highest per capita exports stand out: the three extreme rentiers of the Gulf—Qatar, Kuwait, and the UAE—and Brunei. Even then, figures I.1 and I.2 arguably understate the degree of rentierism in the Gulf monarchies because these figures include all residents of these countries, not just citizens. In the extreme rentiers of the Gulf, expatriates outnumber citizens by large margins, and a good argument can be made for measuring rents per citizen rather than per resident. Citizens have a privileged claim on rent revenues in the Gulf states, and the states spend much more on their citizens, per capita, than on foreigners. Household servants make up a sizable share of the population of all three monarchies, and pretending that they are anything other than minor beneficiaries of the oil wealth of their host countries does not help us understand the full effects of oil wealth on the political economies of these countries. Figure I.4 shows rents per citizen and per resident for the richest rentiers, using the World Bank rent data. Again Qatar, the UAE, and Kuwait lead the world by a large margin, followed by a second group of rentiers that includes Saudi Arabia, Oman, Bahrain, Norway, Trinidad, and Libya. Brunei falls between these two groups.

In short, the literature on rentier states (and the resource curse) mixes together three distinct types of rentiers:

- Extreme rentiers: Kuwait, Qatar, the UAE, and Brunei.
- Middling rentiers: Norway, Saudi Arabia, Oman, Bahrain, Trinidad, Libya, and Equatorial Guinea.
- Poor rentiers: countries in which rents are prominent only because the economy produces little other wealth; these include Nigeria, Angola, and Iran.

33. If a logarithmic transformation is applied to the data, the extreme rentiers look less extreme, and the differences among the poorer rentiers look more substantial. Whether or not it is appropriate to transform the data depends on one's theory about how rents affect outcomes, and a logarithmic transformation makes sense in some contexts. But one cost of transforming the data is that it obscures outliers that perhaps should, instead, be explained. My argument here is that, in terms of the real-world consequences of rent wealth, the extreme rentiers really are outliers—they are a lot richer than poor rentiers and even middling rentiers, not just somewhat richer, and this matters politically and economically.

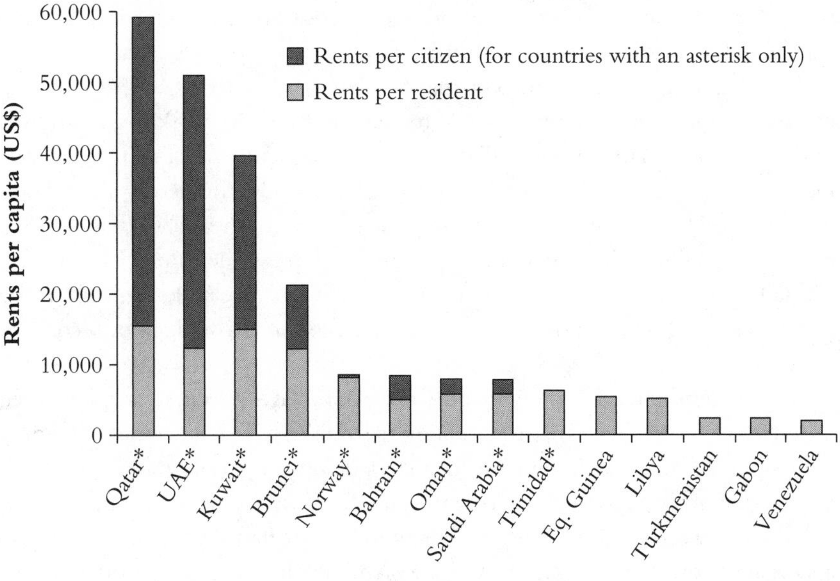

Fig. I.4 Rents per citizen in the richest rentiers, 2006. Countries marked with an asterisk distinguish citizens from noncitizens in the overall population. No good data are available for the number of foreigners in Libya or Equatorial Guinea, although the number is nontrivial. World Bank, 2012, *World Development Indicators*, http://data.worldbank.org.

This set of cases is different from what we are accustomed to. The universe of extreme rentiers consists of three Gulf monarchies and Brunei, followed by fewer than a dozen middling rentiers. When we measure rentierism using measures of rent abundance, poor rentiers fade into the background; they are remarkable only for their rent dependence, not their rent wealth. Yet in poor countries the receipt of even a modest amount of rents may have political consequences. To be sure, these consequences are very difficult to sort out from the negative consequences of poverty, but they still exist. There is, at the same time, little reason to think that the causal consequences of poor rentierism will resemble those of rents in extreme rentiers—the differences are likely to be differences of kind, not of degree.

Labor Markets and Class Conflict in Rentiers

Extreme rentierism has one clear, unambiguous, and (relatively) easily measured economic consequence: the public sector employs the lion's share of citizens who work for a wage. This creates an unusual class structure in these societies. A large majority of citizens depend for their paychecks on oil revenues, not on taxes levied on the private sector, and capitalists in these countries, for their part, employ foreigners rather than citizens. This breaks a crucial link between capitalists and wage employees found in other capitalist societies.

My portrayal of class politics in the Gulf rentiers departs from the existing literature on the class consequences of rentierism. In earlier works on rentierism, scholars tend toward the view that rentierism alleviates class conflict. Jacques Delacroix, for example, argues that the absence of production leads to the disappearance of class politics, at least among citizens.[34] Another scholar argues that rentierism "eliminat[es] economically motivated pressure groups. . . . But at the same time it leads to the emergence of culturally and ideologically based groups such as Islamist movements, for whom economic issues are of secondary importance."[35]

More recently, Thad Dunning and Carles Boix have employed analyses based on class politics to argue that rich rentiers are unlikely to democratize. Dunning argues that in some cases, rent wealth makes democracy more (rather than less) likely. Specifically, he argues that democracy leads to the distribution, or redistribution, of wealth from the rich. In countries that have both rent wealth and a substantial non-rent private sector, the rich have less to fear from democracy because democracy will lead to the distribution of rent wealth, not the distribution of the wealth of the private sector, to the poor. In a country with only rent wealth—but no substantial non-rent private sector—the only game in town is rent wealth, and the elites have no resources to fall back on if democracy leads to the distribution of rent wealth toward the less fortunate. In countries entirely dependent on rents, then, elites will be much more resistant to democracy. Venezuela inspires the model. Dunning cites the Gulf monarchies as examples of the second type of rent-dependent countries.[36] His implicit prediction is clear: oil has a pro-democratic effect in a country such as Venezuela but not in Kuwait; to the extent that the private sector of a country diversifies beyond the hydrocarbon sector, the country will be more likely to democratize.

Carles Boix argues that two main factors determine the likelihood that a country will be democratic: its level of equality and the degree to which the capital owned by the rich is mobile. More equality and more mobility are better for democracy.[37] The rich know that under democracy the poor will redistribute capital because it is immobile. The rich, fearing this redistribution and unable to threaten to flee with their capital—oil wells are immobile—tenaciously resist

34. Delacroix 1980, 17–18. See also Luciani 1990, 77–78.

35. Shambayati 1994, 307.

36. Dunning 2008, 7–18, 27, 87.

37. Boix 2003, 12. Acemoglu and Robinson (2006) make an argument in a generally similar vein but do not discuss rich rentier states.

democracy.[38] Boix makes unequivocal predictions; his model, he says, "predicts that high-income countries that base their prosperity on fixed natural resources, such as oil, should remain authoritarian in spite of their wealth. To avoid expropriation of their fixed assets, the owners will systematically crush any democratic movement."[39] He predicts that the odds of democratization in a country dependent on oil are exactly zero.[40]

These studies recognize that there are class politics in oil states and attempt to trace outcomes that apply across a very diverse set of cases. The theories, however, give us little traction in understanding the political economy of the Gulf monarchies and, specifically, Kuwait. The models predict unrelenting, unrelieved authoritarianism in Kuwait, and this does not exist. Of course, it is not reasonable to expect these theories to explain every case. But anomalous cases can teach us a great deal, especially if they are easy cases for the theory. This is true of Kuwait: it is extraordinarily rich in rents. It is notable that Dunning's theory emerged from an effort to find an explanation for another anomalous case—Venezuela—in another part of the world. Dunning, in this and other works, suggests that the effects of rent are not constant across cases and vary according to the existing political context.[41] Class politics can be important in rentiers, but there are multiple causal pathways through which rents can affect political outcomes. Dunning's model captures the Venezuelan case, but it is very hard to devise a single model that captures the complexities of the causal impacts of rent (and interactions with other variables) across the universe of cases—or even across all rentiers in the world today. In this work I am unapologetic about not trying to come up with a model that applies across all cases of rentierism. Following what Sean Yom has called the "revisionist trend" in resource curse scholarship, I instead show how rents interact with the existing political and economic context in the Gulf to shape the future of the Gulf monarchies.[42]

38. Boix 2003, 43. It is not entirely clear, however, that the poor do in fact redistribute wealth under democracy (Timmons 2010).

39. Boix 2003, 43.

40. Ibid., 85, 87.

41. Dunning 2005, 474.

42. Yom 2011, 219.

Chapter 1

Labor Markets and Class Politics

The most distinctive quality of the political economies of the Gulf rentiers is their extraordinary labor markets. In the extreme rentiers of the Gulf, the vast majority of citizens who work for a wage work in the public sector for high wages set largely by government edict. Foreigners work in the private sector (or sometimes in the public sector) for wages set by the market. These labor markets have profound political consequences, especially on the class politics of citizen society.[1]

The three extreme rentier states of the Gulf— Kuwait, the UAE, and Qatar— have built elaborate welfare states that include free health care, free education through university, marriage grants, subsidized utilities, and sizable housing grants (or interest-free loans). Taken together, these programs are generous, there can be no doubt. But by and large they do not put cash directly into the pockets of citizens. To do this, the state gives citizens public-sector jobs (or private-sector jobs with paychecks subsidized by the state). As a consequence, public-sector employment in the rich rentiers has an uncomfortable dual nature. In one sense, public-sector jobs are a standard exchange of labor for pay;

1. Any analysis of Gulf labor markets faces the problem of serious deficiencies in the nature and quality of the data reported by the Gulf states. Qatar and the UAE, for example, shy away from reporting data on the relative size of their foreign and citizen populations. Important data series suffer from unexplained jumps in direction, or the data from one official source differs substantially from data from another official source. Thus, for example, Onn Winckler (2008) concludes that odd discrepancies in the Saudi data can best be explained by systematic inflation of the citizen population estimates in the censuses before 2004. Marc Valeri (2009, 206) bemoans the imprecision in the official Omani statistics. See also Hertog 2010b, 187.

in another, many citizens see these jobs as their monthly payments from what amounts to the national oil trust fund. As a Kuwaiti researcher put it, "[f]or the ruling family, the bureaucracy serves as a respectable, and apparently modern means of distributing part of the 'loot', which replaces the traditional method of straightforward handouts. . . . The creation of new jobs in the bureaucracy became an objective in its own right, with little regard to what new appointees should or could do."[2] In this light, generous pay for little labor is not a violation of market rationality—or featherbedding—but, instead, a birthright of citizenship. This point is critical to understanding the political economy of Gulf labor markets and Gulf politics.

In Kuwait, the process of distributing state jobs is highly centralized. Citizens register their names with the Civil Service Commission (CSC), which has a website for this purpose.[3] After a wait of some time, the CSC nominates most of those who apply for positions in the public sector. Local newspapers publish lists of those who receive employment in state offices and the office to which they have been appointed.[4] This centralized system was put in place to increase transparency and to discourage favoritism.[5] The tradition of more or less guaranteeing a state job to every graduate, however, goes back to the 1960s.[6] Published reports indicate that most of those who apply for a job are offered one; from the inception of the system in 1999 to the end of 2006, some 98,000 eligible Kuwaiti citizens applied for and 78,000 received positions.[7] More detailed figures on who did and did not receive positions (from 1999 to 2003) reveal that all but a few hundred of those who did not receive a position were women with a high school education or less. Almost all women with college degrees and men with secondary school degrees and higher received a position.[8] Citizens can register their names again if they leave state employment or are released as being "unsuited" for their original appointment.[9] The

2. Al-Ghazali 1989, 316. See also Al-Dekhayel 1990, 267–68.

3. Civil Service Commission, Kuwait, www.csc.net.kw. For an historical perspective, see Al-Ghazali 1989, 327–69.

4. For an example see Yusuf al-Mutayri, "Al-Gharib: Diwan al-khidma al-madaniyya yarashshih 868 lil-'amal lada al-jihat al-hukumiyya: 'Alayhim maraji'a jihat al-'amal al-murashshahin laha mubasharatan" [Al-Gharib: The CSC nominates 868 for positions in government offices: They must report to their assigned workplaces immediately], *al-Qabas*, May 3, 2007.

5. Wajdi 2004, 21–25, 124–25.

6. Al-Dekhayel 1990, 263–66.

7. Zaynab Malallah, "20 alf muwatin wa muwatana la yazalun b-intizar al-tawzif: Al-batala al-muqanna'a tatadhakham fi al-jihat al-hukumiyya wa al-intajiyya sifr" [Twenty thousand citizens still wait for positions: Featherbedding in government agencies swells while productivity is zero], *al-Qabas*, March 13, 2007.

8. Wajdi 2004, 126, 127, 145, 146.

9. Ibid., 45–46, 60–61, 99.

other two extreme rentiers—Qatar and the UAE—similarly give a public-sector job to most citizens who want one. The Qatari state provides an implicit guarantee of a position in the public sector to secondary school and university graduates.[10]

The number of new state employees is driven by the number of new graduates rather than by any demand for additional employees on the part of the state bureaucracy. Thus, many employees have very little to do. There is a great deal of what in the Gulf is called "masked unemployment" (*al-batala al-muqanna'a*), by which is meant the existence of positions filled by occupants who do no productive work—that is, featherbedding. The phenomenon is not new—the Kuwaiti parliament undertook its first investigation of the problem in 1963.[11] Stories circulate in Kuwait about new employees showing up for a new job and finding neither any work to do nor a desk to do it from.

Working conditions in the public sector are hardly onerous. In Kuwait, government employees are typically expected to be at work seven hours per day, five days per week (many arrive at 7:30 a.m. and leave at 2:30 p.m.).[12] Expatriates who work in the private sector, by contrast, often work six days per week and also work a second shift that starts in the late afternoon. In 2006, Sheikha Lubna, UAE minister of economy, estimated that the average number of working days in the government sector was 180, while it was 275 in the private sector.[13] Other factors, in addition to short workdays, make public-sector employment attractive to citizens. Dismissal is a remote possibility. Qatari nationals who lose their jobs in the state receive their salaries until they find a new one.[14] Throughout the Gulf, citizens can typically retire from the public sector after twenty years of service, with generous pensions subsidized by rent revenues.[15]

Pay packages for citizens in the public sector are set relative to state oil income rather than overall productivity in the economy. According to a World Bank report discussed in *Al-Qabas*, the average pay for a Kuwaiti government employee was 827 dinars per month in 2007–2008, which amounts to something on the order of $36,000 annually.[16] This income is tax free, and the government

10. Stasz, Eide, and Martorell 2007, 2, 19.

11. Al-Ghazali (1989, 291).

12. Kuwait News Agency (KUNA) 2005.

13. Robert Ditcham, "Emiratisation Needs Private Sector to Succeed, Says Lubna," Gulfnews.com, June 8, 2006, http://gulfnews.com/business/economy/emiratisation-needs-private-sector-to-succeed-says-lubna-1.240001.

14. Stasz, Eide, and Martorell 2007, 19.

15. Fasano and Goyal 2004, 7.

16. This is total pay, including base salary and various supplements and allowances. Foreigners working for the Kuwaiti government, by contrast, received an average pay of 390 dinars monthly, or approximately $1,700. Mubarak al-Abd al-Hadi, "64% ziyadat al-rawatib khilal 7 a'wam" [64% increase in salaries in 7 years], *al-Qabas*, March 14, 2008.

subsidizes costs that in richer nonrentiers would be paid by citizens from their own pockets. A newly minted college graduate in the UAE was paid around $26,000 annually in 2005, whereas a foreigner with a university degree earned $8,000 less.[17]

Not surprisingly, most citizens gravitate toward public-sector employment. In a 2001 survey, 80% of UAE college students reported that they hoped to find work in the public sector.[18] A class of Kuwaiti students taught by the author at the American University in Kuwait in 2007 intended to seek government jobs on graduation. And, in point of fact, about 90% of all economically active citizens of the richest rentiers work in the public sector, including SOEs. Exact figures can be hard to come by because of the often sorry state of labor-force statistics in the Gulf rentiers, where basic demographic data are often treated as a state secret. This is especially true when it comes to figures for employment in the military and police (where many male citizens work) or, in some cases, simply for the number of foreigners present in the country. Nonetheless, the Qatar government reports that in 2010, 92% of Qataris worked in the public sector or in SOEs.[19] In the UAE in 2008, 88% of citizens worked in the public sector. In Kuwait, the number of citizens in the private sector was higher, around 20%, in large part because the state pays the salaries of many citizens working in the private sector.[20] In 2013, the cost of these subsidies was expected to amount to US$1.6 billion; the total wage bill in 2011–2012 (including foreigners working for the government) was US$18.4 billion. The ostensible success of Kuwait in moving citizens into the private sector does not mean that all these citizens depend on the private sector for their paychecks. Many, perhaps most, receive much of their pay directly from Kuwaiti oil revenue.[21]

In recent years, citizens have responded to the availability of public-sector jobs by increasing their participation rates in the labor force. That said, this is from a relatively low starting point; early retirement ages, the legacy of the virtually complete absence of women in the salaried workforce in the early days of oil, and

17. International Monetary Fund (IMF) 2005a, 38.

18. Ibid., 28, note 19.

19. It is not clear whether this included the military and police. If not, the percentage of Qataris working in the public sector was even higher than 92%. State of Qatar 2010b, table 83.

20. State of Kuwait 2013b, 8. These figures do not include those employed in the military or National Guard (although they do appear to include the police). The number of citizens employed by the state was thus adjusted using figures for the Kuwaiti military and paramilitary forces. State of Kuwait 2012b, 17; Cordesman, Shelala, and Mohamed 2013, 124.

21. State of Kuwait 2013a, 7; Yusuf al-Mutayri, "Mufaja'a fi khittat al-tanmiya: Da'm al-'amala qanbala mawquta" [Suprise in the development plan: Wage support is a time bomb], *al-Qabas*, June 9, 2013, 1.

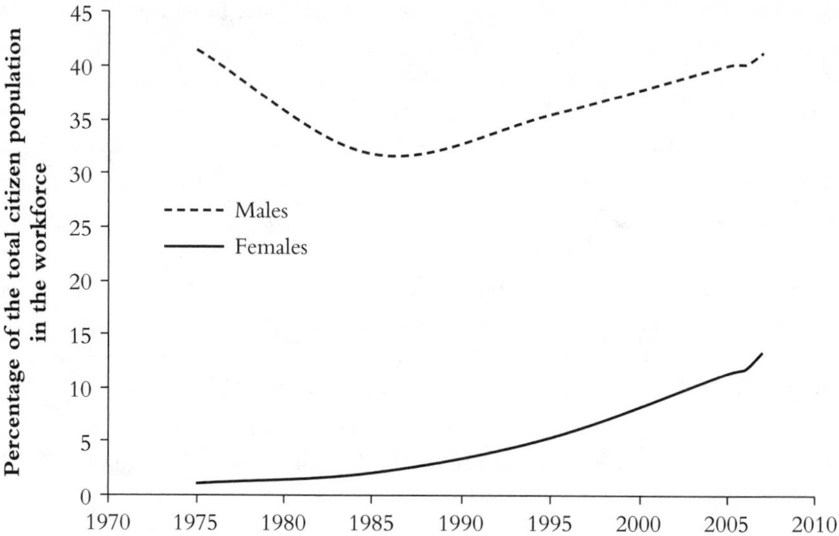

Fig. 1.1 Percentage of UAE citizen men and UAE citizen women in the labor force, 1970–2010. These data are the percentages of the entire population, not of the population ages fifteen and above, and thus are not comparable to the standard measures of the labor-force participation rate. United Arab Emirates 2010b, 14; 2009, 12.

stipends for university attendance keep many out of the workforce (see figure 1.1 for changes in labor force participation over time).[22] In the UAE, for example, 28% of citizen women ages fifteen and older participated in the workforce in 2008, whereas 63% of citizen men participated.[23] By way of comparison, the averages for Organization for Economic Cooperation and Development (OECD) countries are 53 and 70% for women and men, respectively, and the averages for the Middle East and North Africa (MENA) are 26 and 74%.[24] Historically, it appears that oil led to an initial decline in workforce participation as citizens abandoned the private sector and then to an increase as state policies moved citizens into the public sector, replacing the expatriates who initially had staffed the state bureaucracy. In the UAE, citizen women with university degrees are *thirty-five times* more likely to hold a job than illiterate citizen women (see figure 1.2). The growth in female labor-force

22. The data source for Figure 1.1 gives the percentage of the entire population in the workforce, not the more standard percentage of the population above 15 years of age. The figures in the text, which are for recent years, use the standard measure.

23. United Arab Emirates 2010a, chart 3.43.

24. World Bank, 2009, "Labor Force Participation Rate," *World Development Indicators* (http://data.worldbank.org). The denominator is the 15+ population.

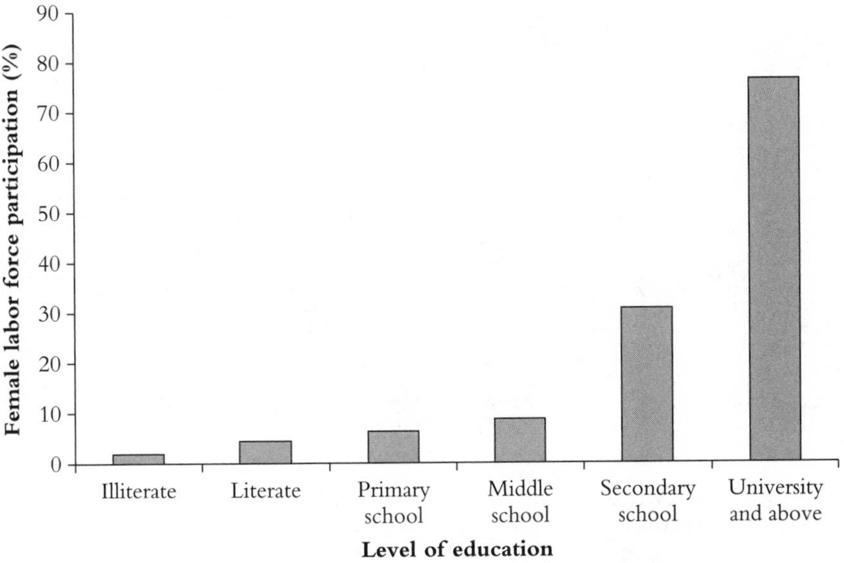

Fig. 1.2 Female UAE citizen labor-force participation by level of education, 2008. United Arab Emirates 2010a, worksheet 3.43.

participation is a direct consequence of female education, and especially female university education, which is, in turn, paid for by oil wealth.[25]

Despite the generous employment policies of the richest rentiers, not every citizen receives a job. It appears that those with little education, especially women, are most likely to be denied a public-sector position. Because these citizens are also very uncompetitive in the private-sector job market, failure to secure a public-sector job typically results in unemployment; their "reservation wage" is above the market wage.[26] In 2008, most unemployed citizens in the UAE had never held a job.[27] From one perspective, this unemployment is the result of unrealistic expectations on the part of citizens; they could find jobs if they were willing to lower their reservation wage. A perspective more sympathetic to these citizens (mostly women) would observe that (1) they are not directly receiving their share of the oil wealth through public-sector employment and (2) the wages in the

25. Compare this to Michael Ross (2008) on women and oil. In Kuwait, which has experienced extreme rentierism longer than Qatar and the UAE, women made up 42% of the employed citizen workforce in 2011 (State of Kuwait 2012a, 94).

26. Fasano and Goyal 2004, 7.

27. United Arab Emirates 2008b, 25.

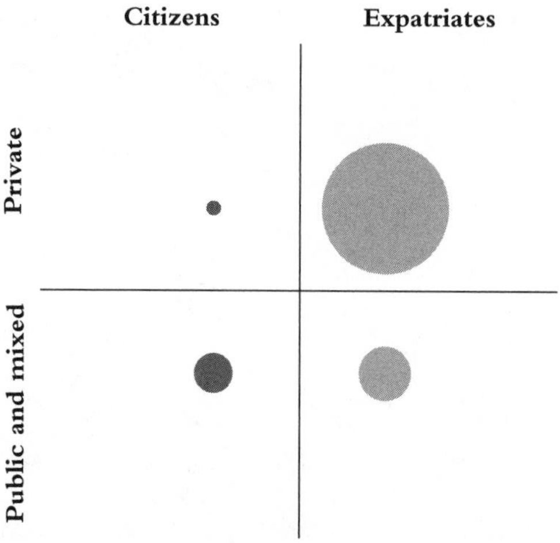

Fig. 1.3 UAE workforce by citizenship and sector, 2008. Circle size is proportional to the number of workers. United Arab Emirates 2008b, 23; 2009, worksheet 4; 2010a, worksheet 3.35.

private sector are very low precisely because government policies encourage the importing of labor from very low-cost countries, pushing down the free-market cost of labor to very low levels, especially for less-skilled labor.

Citizens make up only a small part of the labor market in the extreme rentiers. In the UAE and Qatar, for every one citizen in the workforce there are nine expatriates (see figures 1.3 and 1.7). Within the private sector itself, the imbalances are even more overwhelming. For every Emirati who works in the private sector, there are eighty-one foreigners.

This vast army of expatriate workers ensures that there is no labor scarcity of the sort that would drive up the price of imported labor to anything approaching the pay levels enjoyed by citizens in the public sector (where, indeed, pay scales explicitly differentiate between citizens and noncitizens; citizens typically are paid more than foreigners for the same work).[28] It is not an accident that the bulk of this labor comes from very poor countries; Bangladeshi labor has been especially prominent in the Gulf in recent years.[29] To give an example from the bottom end of the job

28. In Kuwait, a 1971 reform formally introduced divergent wage scales for foreigners and citizens who occupied the same grade in the civil service. This occurred on the occasion of a substantial pay increase, which went primarily to citizens Al-Dekhayel 1990, 278–80.

29. In Kuwait, the largest expatriate communities in 2011 were from (in declining order) India, Egypt, Bangladesh, the Philippines, Syria, Pakistan, Sri Lanka, Ethiopia, Jordan, Nepal, Iran, Lebanon, Indonesia, and Afghanistan. Muhammad Ibrahim, "Al-'amala al-wafida fi al-bilad taraja'at 17%" [Foreign labor in the country falls 17%], *al-Qabas*, September 21, 2011, 6.

market, in 2007 employment agencies in Kuwait suggested a salary of 40 KD (about $142) per month for live-in household help.[30] In the UAE, the average wage in the construction sector was something like $175 per month.[31] The easy availability of foreign labor has led to what McKinsey (the consulting firm) calls a "downward spiral" in productivity rates across the Gulf, accompanied by a fall in real wages of up to 25% in the private sector from 1994 to 2003.[32] Instead of increasing the productivity of labor, the Gulf private sector has sought out cheaper sources of labor.

The extremely low cost of labor, fed by an enormous influx of labor from poor countries, has rendered unskilled citizen labor uncompetitive in the private-sector labor market. In the richest three rentiers, hardly any citizen will—or can—compete with expatriates for less-skilled positions at the market wage absent government subsidies or state-imposed market distortion. The private sector will not hire citizens for these positions unless forced to by the state (and thus at a higher than market wage). It is not surprising that a strong social norm has emerged that makes it inappropriate for Gulf citizens in the richer rentiers to engage in unskilled labor usually undertaken by expatriate labor.

At the more skilled end of the labor market, citizens can sometimes compete directly with foreign labor. A citizen with a degree from a U.S. university and work experience in the West (and a work ethic shaped by that experience) can often offer a private-sector employer as much or more than a Western expatriate, given the citizen's better understanding of the culture and politics of his or her society. Data on pay for citizens in the public and private sectors provide evidence for this, although it is difficult to make direct comparisons.[33] According to a World Bank study, reported in *al-Qabas,* citizens with a secondary school education between twenty-one and twenty-five years old were paid twice as much working in the public sector than their compatriots working in the private sector. The wage differential narrowed for citizens toward middle age and then widened into a chasm for those in their late fifties. By contrast, Kuwaitis with a degree beyond secondary school and employed in the private sector were paid more, in some middle-age groups, than those employed in the public sector.[34]

30. Falah al-Fadhli, "90% min mashakil al-khadam sababha 'adam daf'a rawatibhum" [90% of the problems of servants are caused by failure to pay their salaries], *al-Qabas,* March 17, 2007, 16. Almost half of all expatriates in the private sector (which does not include household labor) earned less than 120 KD (around $425) per month. Yusuf al-Mutayri, "Al-wafidun fi al-khass: 92% thukur" [Expatriates in the private sector: 92% male], *al-Qabas,* September 3, 2012, 12.

31. Human Rights Watch 2006, 23.

32. Al-Kibsi, Benkert, and Schubert 2007, 22–23.

33. On the difficulties of making such comparison, see Nelson 2004, 19–20.

34. Mubarak al-Abd al-Hadi, "Qararat al-ta'yin tukhda' li-'tibarat ijtima'iyya akthar min al-ta'limiyya" [Decisions to hire subject to social more than educational considerations], *al-Qabas,* March 14, 2008, 6.

Capitalists and Public-Sector Employees

The distorted labor markets of the extreme rentiers produce two main classes among citizens: capitalists and public-sector employees. Public-sector employees rely very largely on oil revenues to fund both their paychecks and the public services on which they depend. This breaks the usual link between capital and labor. Among citizens, only capitalists (and some highly skilled professionals) have a strong investment in the success of the private sector. The more modestly skilled citizen middle class does not depend on the private sector for employment, nor are their public services paid for by taxes levied on the private sector. The result is a divorce between the private sector and the bulk of the citizenry, leaving most citizens without a strong reason to care about the level of profits in the private sector. This undermines the class compromise that Adam Przeworski argues underlies modern capitalism. As Helmut Schmidt, German Social Democratic leader, once said, "The profits of enterprises today are the investments of tomorrow, and the investments of tomorrow are the employment of the day after."[35] In this class compromise, labor relies on capital for jobs and for the tax revenues that fund public services. In the richest rentiers of the Gulf, however, the basis for this class compromise does not exist, at least not for citizens; the "employment of the day after" is offered instead to expatriates.

The class interests of expatriates are defined by their reliance on private-sector employment. Expatriates, rather than citizens, benefit from job creation by the private sector. And many expatriates also own and operate businesses. Indeed, in the UAE household-income survey, expatriate families were substantially more likely than citizen families to have a head of household who owned a business.[36] For the expatriate middle class, Przeworski's class compromise emphatically is in effect. These expatriates are content to let the ruling families earn their untold billions in exchange for the opportunity to build a better life, and this cannot happen without a thriving private sector.

The relative size of the two classes—the citizens primarily dependent on wage income from oil and the group primarily dependent on the private-sector economy—is not always clear. There is no doubt that the percentage of citizens who receive a substantial income from the private sector increases as the non-oil economy grows. Taken to the extreme, it is possible to imagine an economy in which a small caste of citizens lives off taxes levied on a productive, mostly non-oil economy, although this is not yet the case in any of the Gulf rentiers.

35. In Przeworski 1985, 42–43.
36. United Arab Emirates 2008a, 4.

How Many Citizens Depend on Public-Sector Jobs?

Citizens with a stake in the private-sector economy include not only large capitalists but also smaller property rentiers who receive income from renting to expatriates. If this were a substantial percentage of the citizenry, it would give a wider swath of the citizen population a stake in private-sector diversification. A UAE household-income survey in 2007 and 2008 provides some evidence on this point. The survey found that employment makes up the largest share of income for Emirati families; in 2007–2008, the wage income was 64% of all current income. Given that the overwhelming majority of Emirati wage-earners work in the public sector, this income comes very largely from the state. Transfers—state pensions and the like—amounted to an additional 9% of household income.[37] Two items—rents (20% of income) and self-employment income (5%)—derive from the private sector, but these are likely to be much more unevenly distributed among citizens than wage and transfer income.[38] (In contrast, the data for Qatar suggest that Qataris earn more income from the private sector.[39]) Fewer Emiratis than might be imagined owned businesses. Of Emirati citizens participating in the workforce in 2008, only 2.6% owned business and employed others, an additional 1% were self-employed, and the balance worked for a wage.[40] In short, in the UAE citizens rely on the state for the bulk of their income.

Do Taxes Levied on the Non-Oil Economy Fund Public-Sector Jobs?

It may be that taxes on the private sector fund the wage bill for a substantial number of jobs in the UAE public sector, particularly as a consequence of the economic diversification led by Dubai. This would tend to reestablish a basis for Przeworski's class compromise between capital and citizen labor. (In contrast, in Kuwait and Qatar public-sector salaries are clearly paid from hydrocarbon revenues.) In the UAE, there is not, to be sure, any need to pay public-sector salaries

37. Ibid., 11, 12. Overall, the average income of citizen families was around $120,000 annually.

38. The Al Nahyan ruling family of Abu Dhabi has long had a program in place to provide real estate to citizens of the emirate, and a great deal of the rental income accruing to UAE citizens is probably received by citizens of Abu Dhabi and not of the poorer emirates such as Ras al-Khaimah or Fujairah (Abu-Baker 1995, 170).

39. In Qatar "net income from businesses and free enterprises" in 2007 made up 33% of citizen income, wages 57%, and transfers from the government only 6%. Six years earlier, in 2001, wages made up 73% of citizen income. The enormous increase in income from businesses and free enterprises is not explained (State of Qatar 2011, 21).

40. United Arab Emirates 2008b, 19. According to the Household Income and Expenditure Survey of 2007–2008, among heads of household, 3.6 were business owners, 1.4 self-employed, 67.2 worked for a wage, and 27.8 were not employed (many of these were presumably retired) (United Arab Emirates 2008a, 4).

from non-oil revenue; the UAE receives most of its government revenue from oil, and it runs a surplus (from which comes its huge sovereign wealth fund). In 2011, 85% of the consolidated UAE government revenue came from hydrocarbons (or investment profits), and 9% came from customs, fees and charges, profits, and taxes.[41] The wage bill for all of the UAE (excluding the military) amounted to just less than 9% of hydrocarbon revenue.[42] The degree that non-oil revenue is used to pay the public-sector wage bill in the UAE is a choice made by the rulers.

Despite the availability of oil revenue in Abu Dhabi that is easily sufficient to pay all public-sector salaries in the UAE, a fairly large number of UAE citizens are employed in Dubai and are paid from the resources of that emirate. In 2010, the Dubai emirate government employed 25,600 citizens (including police). Various semi-government institutions—Dubai World, Emaar, the aluminum company, Emirates Group—employed an additional 4,166 Emirati citizens, for a total of about 30,000.[43] Two years earlier, the total public- and mixed-sector employment in the UAE amounted to about 200,000 citizens.[44] In short, Dubai Inc. employed perhaps 15% of Emiratis who worked in the public sector.

The revenue of Dubai is not entirely generated by the non-oil economy. In 2003, hydrocarbons accounted for more than one-third of the Dubai government revenues; this fell about one-quarter in 2008 and fell even further in subsequent years—however, in these years transfers from Abu Dhabi (derived, of course, from oil) amounted to more than one-quarter of the revenue.[45] We can conclude that non-oil revenue from Dubai Inc. pays the salaries of a significant but still small minority of public-sector employees in the UAE. This percentage will grow over time if the Dubai—and the UAE—non-oil economy continues to grow. In the long run it could make Emirati citizens dependent upon the private sector, but not directly: citizens would rely on taxes levied on the (expatriate-staffed) private sector to fund their privileged positions in the public sector.

How Long Can It Last?

The ability of the extreme rentiers to offer the vast majority of their citizen graduates a public-sector job, funded through oil revenues, will not last forever. There are three main threats to this policy: a fall in the price of oil, a rise in the number of employed

41. The balance, 5.6%, was from "other" sources. These percentages are IMF estimates (IMF 2012d, 29).
42. It might be double that if the military wage bill were included (IMF 2012b, 29).
43. Government of Dubai, Dubai Statistics Center, *Statistical Yearbook—Emirate of Dubai 2010*, figs. 3.5 and 3.9, http://dsc.gov.ae/ (accessed June 6, 2013).
44. United Arab Emirates 2008b, 23; 2010, worksheet 3.35; 2012, 9.
45. IMF 2011b, 34.

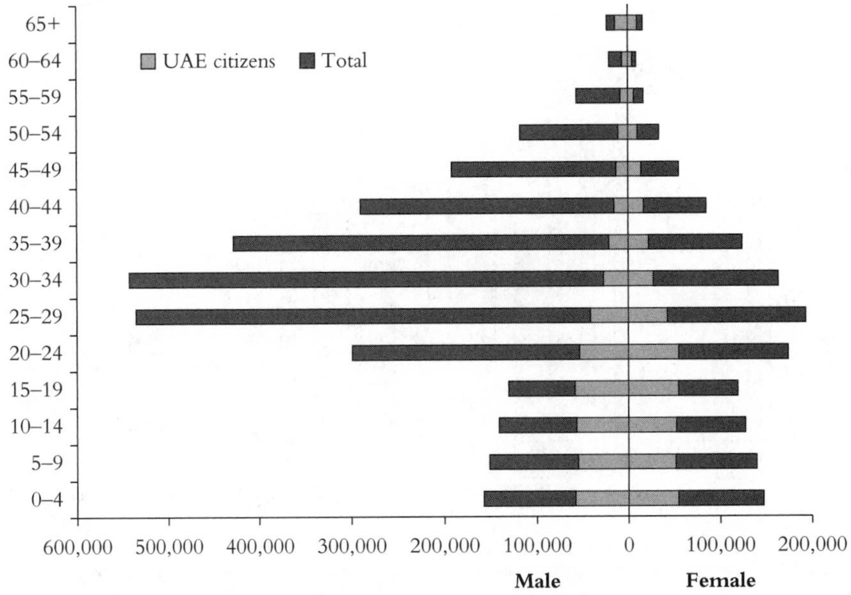

Fig. 1.4 UAE population pyramid, 2007. United Arab Emirates 2009, 4.

citizens, and the drying up of oil and gas reserves. Anticipating the day that some combination of these three things will happen, citizens might do well to support the growth of the non-oil economy—and perhaps with more enthusiasm than many show now.

There are, however, several factors that make citizens less inclined to take the long view. First, the citizens of Gulf monarchies, like the rest of humanity, tend to impose a fairly steep discount on future income. Second, the oil will not run out soon. The published figures for oil reserves are widely suspect, but reserves in Kuwait and the UAE should last for roughly another one hundred years[46] (although the Kuwaiti reserves may be only half of the published amount[47]). Qatar sits on the world's third largest reserves of natural gas, and at current production rates, these reserves will last centuries.[48] Third, population growth will continue for some time, but census data suggest that the Gulf states have gone through a demographic transition and that the citizen populations will level out (figure 1.4),

46. United States, Energy Information Administration, "Country Analysis Briefs: Kuwait," July 2011, http://www.eia.gov (accessed September 17, 2012).; United States, Energy Information Administration, "Country Analysis Briefs: United Arab Emirates," January 2011, www.eia.gov (accessed September 17, 2012).

47. "Oil Reserves Accounting: The Case of Kuwait," *Petroleum Intelligence Weekly*, January 30, 2006.

48. United States, Energy Information Administration, *Country Analysis Briefs: Qatar*, January 2011, http://www.eia.gov (accessed September 17, 2012).

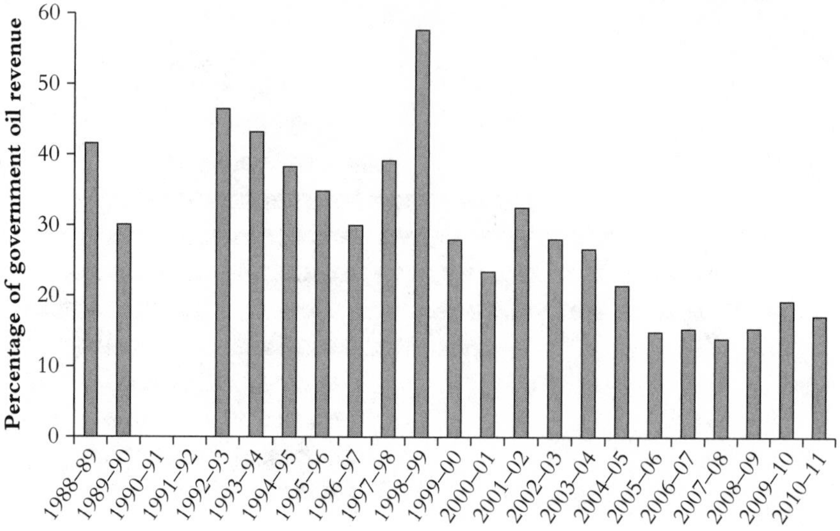

Fig. 1.5 Wages paid to government workers as a percentage of government oil revenue in Kuwait, 1988–2011. Central Bank of Kuwait, "Quarterly Statistical Bulletin," http://www.cbk.gov.kw/ (accessed October 14, 2011), table 26, Q4 1995, Q4 1999, Q4 2004, Q2 2011.

although, to be sure, there are still large cohorts of young citizens who will be looking for jobs in the future and the leveling out is less pronounced in Kuwait.[49] The share of the budget going toward salaries in Kuwait, surprisingly, has not shown a strong upward trend; however, this is only because oil revenues are growing faster than the state can spend them on salaries (see figure 1.5). Fourth, all three of the rich rentiers currently save a substantial portion of their oil earnings in sovereign wealth funds. In 2010, the Kuwaiti fund held a balance approaching $300,000 per citizen, and the Abu Dhabi sovereign wealth fund held well over $600,000 per Emirati citizen (or some millions per Abu Dhabi citizen).[50] Finally, promotion of the non-oil economy creates jobs, but today almost all of these jobs go to foreigners, further exacerbating the demographic imbalance in these societies. Creating private-sector jobs for *citizens* in anticipation of a decline in rent revenues requires much deeper changes in the economy than merely creating, for example, a tourist industry.

49. State of Kuwait 2012a, 49.

50. Calculated from figures provided by the Sovereign Wealth Fund Institute, www.swfinstitute.org (accessed September 17, 2012).

None of this changes the fact that, someday, these states will not be able to offer all their graduates a public-sector job. In Kuwait, the likely result is that citizens will have to find employment in the private sector, at market wages. When that happens, Kuwait is likely to wind up with labor markets that resemble those of its less-rich Gulf neighbors: Saudi Arabia, Bahrain, and Oman. In the UAE, a different, dystopian future is possible. As the diversified economy grows (and, someday, oil revenues fall), citizens could become a small privileged caste of public-sector workers living not only from oil revenues but from taxes levied on the noncitizen majority.

Labor Markets and Class Politics in the Middling Rentiers

Bahrain, Oman, and Saudi Arabia are not as rich as the other three GCC states, and this has a direct effect on the structure of their labor markets and the nature of class politics. A comparison of figures 1.6 and 1.7 illustrates the difference between Bahrain, a more ordinary rentier, and Qatar, an extreme rentier. In both Qatar and Bahrain, expatriates in the private sector make up a substantial majority of the

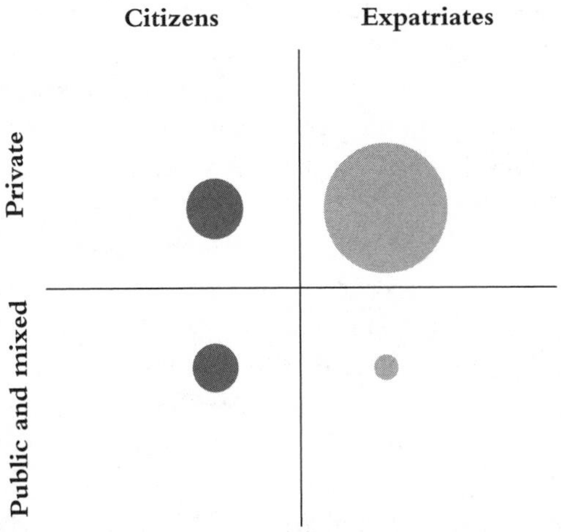

Fig. 1.6 Bahraini workforce by citizenship and sector, 2009. Circle size is proportional to the number of workers. Published labor market figures for Bahrain exclude the military and security services. I estimated these as 20,000 and added them to the figures for the public sector. Most are very probably foreign by birth, but many have been granted citizenship; I estimated that 75% were citizens. Labour Market Regulatory Authority (LMRA), Kingdom of Bahrain, based on data from *Bahrain Labour Market Indicators,* http://www.lmra.bh/blmi (accessed June 26, 2009); International Crisis Group 2005, 2, 8, note 51; Bahrain Independent Commission of Inquiry 2011, 15–16; Cordesman, Shelala, and Mohamed 2013, 148; Bahrain Center for Human Rights.

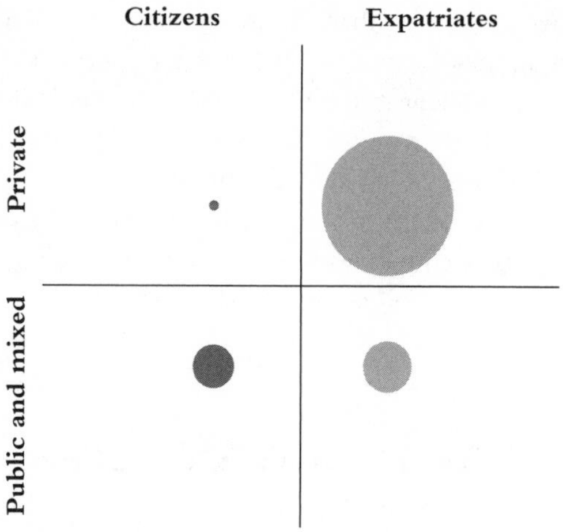

Fig. 1.7 Qatari workforce by citizenship and sector, 2007. Circle size is proportional to the number of workers. International Monetary Fund 2009b, 9.

total workforce. In Qatar, very few citizens work in the private sector. In Bahrain, by contrast, most citizens work in the private sector, often in jobs—such as taxi driver or hotel employee—that Kuwaitis or Emiratis would not take.[51] In Qatar, expatriates outnumber citizens even in the public sector, while in Bahrain, citizens virtually monopolize the scarce public-sector jobs that are available, largely shutting out expatriates (except in the security forces, where the regime hires foreigners for political reasons but also—reportedly—gives them citizenship to increase the number of Sunni citizens).

The presence of Bahraini citizens in the private sector, however, does not mean that businesses show much eagerness to hire citizens.[52] Figure 1.8 shows expatriate wages as a percentage of Bahraini national wages at various educational levels. Bahrainis with little education are paid several multiples of what foreigners are paid, and this compromises their desirability from the point of view of employers (a similar situation prevails in Saudi Arabia[53]). Moreover—and to illustrate the fundamental problems in the Bahraini labor market—the wage for the median government employee is almost double that of the median Bahraini private-sector

51. Kapiszewski 2001, 80.

52. Ramady (2005, 361) has a particularly useful list of the reasons for this.

53. Kingdom of Saudi Arabia, Central Department of Statistics and Information, "Employment and Earnings Study for the Year 1421 (2000)," www.cdsi.gov.sa (accessed June 29, 2009).

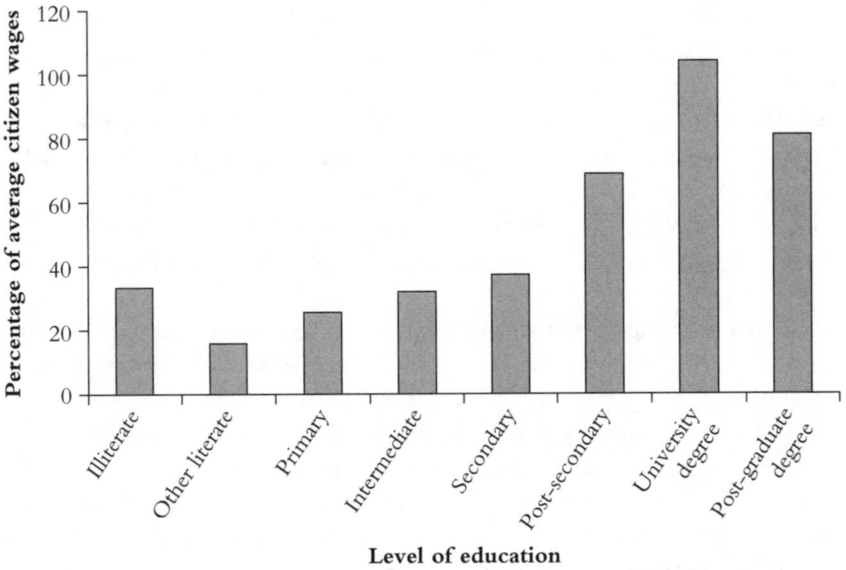

Fig. 1.8 Average expatriate wages as a percentage of average Bahraini citizen wages, by educational level, March 2009. Labour Market Regulatory Authority (LMRA), Kingdom of Bahrain, based on data from Bahrain Labour Market Indicators, http://www.lmra.bh/blmi (accessed June 28, 2009).

employee.[54] Citizens who find state jobs make up a privileged group in Bahraini society.

The situation in Oman probably resembles that of Bahrain, except that citizens rather than foreigners staff the military and security services. Despite this, many citizens must find employment in the private sector. Unfortunately, however, there are no publically available data that allow us to draw firm conclusions. Detailed data on government employees omit not only the military but also the police. Without these two categories, there are about as many Omanis employed in the formal private sector as in the public sector, at just under 160,000 each in 2009, and the International Institute for Strategic Studies estimates that the number employed in the military comes to another 42,000. As in all the other Gulf rentiers, expatriates make up by far the largest share of private-sector employment.[55]

54. Based on data from Labour Market Regulatory Authority (LMRA), Kingdom of Bahrain, "Bahrain Labour Market Indicators," www.lmra.bh/blmi (accessed June 28, 2009).

55. Central Bank of Oman, 2011, 24; Cordesman, Shelala, and Mohamed 2013, 161.

The Saudi job market appears to lie somewhere between that of Bahrain and the richer rentiers, although again there are serious data problems. It is clear that Saudis have largely pushed expatriates out of the public sector and that expatriates dominate the private sector.[56] But, until very recently, the concentration of Saudi workers in the public sector approached the level found in the three richer rentiers; it appears that about 80% of employed Saudis work in the public sector.[57] This is in part due to very low rates of female employment; in 2009, 9% of Saudi women above the age of 15 were employed. Employment was 33% for men and women together.[58]

Because many citizens of the middling rentiers (especially Oman and Bahrain) must find work in the private sector, they have a far stronger immediate interest in private-sector growth than do citizens of the richest rentiers. Ghazi al-Qusaybi, the noted poet who also served as the Saudi minister of labor, was asked if he was waging war on the private sector by pursuing Saudization efforts. He responded by reiterating Przeworski's social contract: "the private sector, in the years and decades and centuries to come, will be the main employer of citizens, and it is not in anyone's interest to harm it or restrict its activities."[59] The problem in Saudi Arabia, and the one that generated al-Qusaybi's problems, was that the private sector still prefers to hire expatriate labor. Class politics in these countries revolves around the degree of pressure applied on the private sector to employ citizens rather than expatriates. The private sector wants access to cheap foreign labor, while citizens want protection from pressure on wages caused by massive immigration. The recent expulsion of hundreds of thousands of immigrant workers from Saudi Arabia, much to the consternation of business owners, suggests that the Saudi regime, at least, thinks that the threat of unemployment trumps the needs of the business class.

Finally, this discussion of the role of foreigners in the Gulf labor markets inevitably leads to comparisons with the role of foreigners in the labor markets—and societies—of rich nonrentier economies. Studies of the effects of immigration on citizens' wages in highly productive nonrentier societies suggest that immigration has a modest impact on wages and that this impact is generally positive.[60] This literature is convincing for the cases it addresses, and I certainly am not arguing that

56. On Saudi labor force statistics, see Flynn 2011, 580–82; Kingdom of Saudi Arabia, n.d.

57. Saudi Arabian Monetary Agency (SAMA), 2012, 186; Central Department of Statistics and Information, Kingdom of Saudi Arabia, "Saudi Labour Force (15 Years and Over) by Sex," 2013, http://www.cdsi.gov.sa.

58. IMF 2012b, 23.

59. In "Ghazi Al Gosaibi: Al-najumiyya al-'ilamiyya laysat abadiyya" [Ghazi al-Qusaybi: Media stardom is not eternal], *Elaph*, December 4, 2007, www.elaph.com.

60. Ottaviano and Peri 2012.

"as a theoretical matter, immigration *has* to lower the wages of natives."[61] Nevertheless, the Gulf rentiers are very different from productive nonrentier economies, both in the volume of immigration and in the maintenance of juridical distinctions between citizen and expatriate labor that makes citizen and noncitizen labor not easily substitutable. In the rentiers, we see very persistent evidence that immigration tends to drive citizens out of the private-sector labor market and—even more to the point—clear evidence that private-sector employers avoid hiring citizens whenever possible. Falling productivity in the Gulf economies is another indication of the effect of immigration on wages, and businesses in the UAE, for example, have adapted business models built on low-cost labor.[62]

Class Consequences of Labor Market Reforms

The status quo in Gulf labor markets, in both the extreme and middling rentiers, is extraordinarily expensive. Citizens worry about the demographic imbalance resulting from the lopsided ratios of foreign residents to citizens. Expatriates resent their second-class status and its accompanying insecurity. The foreign business community distrusts the unorthodox and unfamiliar character of the Gulf labor markets, and especially the privileged position of unproductive citizens. And across the spectrum, many complain about the consequences of breaking the link between pay and productivity for citizens in the public sector, including its corrosive effect on the work ethic of the average citizen. These concerns have generated a variety of efforts to cajole, bribe, or strong-arm citizens into taking private-sector jobs. All these strategies have winners and losers. An examination of the strategies provides a window on the class politics of the Gulf monarchies, and it illustrates the forces that will shape any future changes to the class structure of Gulf societies.

Naturalizing Expatriates

One obvious way to rapidly increase citizen participation in the private sector is to give citizenship to long-term residents. This, however, happens rarely in the Gulf monarchies today. The first reason is a straightforward matter of numbers

61. Card 2012, 211. See also Ottaviano and Peri 2012; Council of Economic Advisers 2007.

62. For a really excellent discussion of low-wage production in Dubai, see Paul Downs, "Can We Compete with a Factory in Dubai?" *New York Times,* You're the Boss Blog, August 1, 2012, http://boss.blogs.nytimes.com/2012/08/01/middle-east-journal-assessing-a-factory-in-dubai/.

and identity; naturalizing long-term foreign residents would utterly transform the basic Arab identity of the three extreme Gulf rentiers. The second reason grows from the political economy of extreme rentierism; each additional citizen of Kuwait or the UAE becomes a burden on the public fisc—one more citizen added to the set of people among whom the fixed resource of oil revenues (in the form of public-sector jobs, free health care, housing subsidies, free education, and so on) must be divided. At the same time, each new citizen will not pay taxes and is unlikely to contribute more than he or she consumes to national income. By contrast, in a country (such as the United States or Germany) that does not have a rentier economy, the typical immigrant who becomes a citizen pays taxes; better educated-immigrants tend to consume fewer state services and generate more tax revenue.[63] Thus, xenophobia is not necessary to explain the restrictive citizenship policies of the Gulf. These policies are, instead, a response to very concrete economic realities.

How then do we explain the naturalizations that have occurred in the Gulf states in the past, such as the granting of citizenship to thousands of *bedu* (bedouin) by Kuwait in the 1960s and 1970s? Typically these naturalizations were imposed by the ruling families and were designed to alter the demographic makeup of the citizen society in a way that made the power of the ruling families more secure, despite the burden on the fisc. The Bahraini regime continues to grant citizenship for precisely this reason. As the citizen middle class has gained influence in Kuwait, naturalizations of this sort have ended.

Cutting Public-Sector Salaries and Denying Public-Sector Jobs to Citizens

Capitalists in the Gulf, local and foreign, often advocate policies that would push citizens into the private sector by lowering public-sector salaries and reducing the number of jobs given to citizens. The foreign business community is, if anything, more enthusiastic about this strategy than are local capitalists, typically because foreign business people fail to understand the role of state employment in distributing oil wealth or do not sympathize with it. The International Monetary Fund (IMF), although recognizing the political problems, recommended in 2005 that the UAE more or less freeze citizen salaries to bring them into line with private-sector salaries, and it recommended that the UAE issue "a public statement that government employment is not guaranteed for every national. . . ."[64]

63. Edmonston and Smith 1997, 11–12; Council of Economic Advisers 2007.
64. IMF 2005a, 31.

The costs of this strategy, of course, are borne almost entirely by the citizen middle class. Most citizens, not surprisingly and quite accurately, see this strategy as a mortal threat to their livelihoods. When a Kuwaiti parliamentary deputy who represents a better-off constituency suggested that Kuwaitis were spoiled and that public-sector wages ought not to be raised, a deputy from a relatively poorer district responded, "most Kuwaitis are chained to car and house payments, and other payments, and inflation—by the admission of the government—consumes everything, and despite that when they request an increase in their salaries . . . there comes one who doubts their need and desire to live a dignified life from the wealth of their country."[65]

The reference to the "wealth of the country" goes to the heart of the issue. For most Kuwaitis (or Emiratis or Qataris), public-sector employment is their main access to their national oil riches. Cutting public-sector salaries or denying jobs to citizens amounts to taking away their share of the oil wealth and giving it to someone else.[66] To the extent that this benefits later generations, there might be some rationality to the argument from the point of view of citizen public-sector employees. If the redistribution were to the private sector in the form of contracts or to the ruling families, then there would be very little indeed to recommend such a policy for citizens. It would amount to taking money from the citizen middle class and giving it to the rich.

While the three richest rentiers have done little to limit the growth of public-sector employment (and salaries), citizens of the middling rentiers have been less fortunate. Their states have not been able to provide the bulk of citizens with a public-sector job (though this is not quite as apparent in Saudi Arabia as it is in Bahrain and Oman). The consequence has been a sharp division in the fortunes of citizens: some citizens find well-paying, secure public-sector jobs, and others work in private-sector positions that typically are much less well paid. Although some citizens have responded to the lack of public-sector jobs by going to the private sector, other citizens have simply stayed out of the workforce, relying on other family members and state support for income.

Educating Citizens

While unskilled Gulf citizens cannot compete with unskilled expatriate labor in the private sector, highly educated Gulf nationals can compete with better-educated expatriates. Thus economic reformers, the IMF, and the international

65. In Mish'al al-Salama, "Al-hasad fi 'uyun . . . Baqir" [Envy in the eyes of . . . Baqir], *al-Rai*, June 9, 2007, www.alraialaam.com (accessed June 10, 2007).

66. Sometimes even governments see public-sector salaries as "a form of sharing the hydrocarbon wealth with the population at large . . ." (IMF 2008, statement by A. Shakour Shaalan [attached to the end of the document], 2).

business press frequently recommend state investments in citizen education to increase the number of citizens in the private sector. The regimes also find the idea attractive; it is a strategy that creates few losers and is thus not politically contentious. The Qatari regime has famously invested billions in importing foreign universities to Doha. Mohammed bin Rashid, the ruler of Dubai, sees education as a key component of the Dubai development model and the UAE government strategy documents put a very heavy emphasis on educating citizens.[67]

But this approach alone will not solve the overall problem. Only a small citizen elite today is competitive in the private-sector job market. These citizens tend to come from well-off backgrounds, earn degrees from Western universities, work for a period abroad, and display an abundance of ambition and intelligence by any standard. They would form a small elite in any society. Most citizens face an incentive structure that does not reward this sort of educational achievement. As long as public-sector jobs are freely provided to citizens, the safest (and certainly the least arduous) strategy for most citizens is to educate themselves only to the standard required for these state jobs, and that is often a low standard. It is notable that students at universities in Kuwait, despite a great deal of talk about private-sector jobs, by and large aspire to work for the state. And these are many of the best Kuwaiti students (except for those who go abroad). If these students want jobs, it is clear that it is easier—and far more certain—for those with fewer skills to seek out a public-sector job on graduation from secondary school.

Increasing the Cost of Expatriate Labor

A fourth way of encouraging citizens to take up private-sector jobs is to raise the cost of expatriate labor. Capitalists would bear the costs of this strategy, and in no small part for this reason, it has not implemented with any particular vigor in the three richest rentiers. The result is that unskilled and moderately skilled labor have a very low cost, and the international business community recognizes this as a key advantage to the business climate in the richer rentiers. Thus, an international company that monitors business conditions praised the "open-border foreign labour policy" of the UAE, which has enabled "the private sector to recruit expatriate labour at internationally competitive wages."[68] The IMF writes warmly of the UAE that

> The flexible labor policy adopted thus far in the U.A.E. has been an important contributing factor behind the diversification of the non-oil economy. Such a

67. United Arab Emirates Cabinet, "Highlights of the U.A.E. Government Strategy 2011–2013: Putting Citizens First," www.uaecabinet.ae.

68. Business Monitor International (2007, 28, 31). Unusually among foreign observers, the McKinsey Company outright recommends restrictions on foreign labor (Al-Kibsi, Benkert, and Schubert 2007, 20).

> policy has allowed the U.A.E. to have access to abundant supply of labor at internationally competitive wages. About 90 percent of the labor force in the U.A.E. are expatriates and work mainly in the private sector. This labor policy has been a key contributor to maintaining the competitiveness of the non-oil economy.[69]

In addition to local and international capitalists, ordinary citizens in the richest rentiers benefit directly from inexpensive labor. Middle-class citizens employ foreign labor in their homes. Increasing the cost of expatriate labor across the board would hit the average citizen directly in the wallet.

Nonetheless, this strategy is a very obvious way of addressing the labor market imbalances in the Gulf rentiers, and to some extent, all the monarchies have made efforts to increase, at least marginally, the cost of foreign labor. There are three main ways that this can be done:

- Set a minimum wage.
- Limit supply at the border, thus increasing wages by forcing employers to bid for a limited supply of labor.
- Impose a tax on employers who employ expatriates.

Increasing private-sector wages would create a rent in the form of the gap between the market cost of foreign labor and the actual cost paid by employers. Who gets this rent varies according to the method used. Setting a minimum wage gives the rent to employed expatriates. And because this is not a politically powerful group, this is not an approach extensively used. The Bahraini Labour Market Authority (LMRA)—which, to its credit, has examined the problem intelligently and in great detail—explicitly notes that the benefits would go to expatriates when rejecting the option of imposing a minimum wage on expatriates as a means of increasing the number of Bahrainis working in the private sector; the LMRA calculated that 80% of the increase in wages would go to expatriates.[70] It would require a very large increase in the minimum wage, affecting much of the expatriate labor force, to bring expatriate wages up to a level that would make citizens attractive to private sector employers. As a result of these issues, the minimum wages that exist in the Gulf tend to be low, and the UAE, in practice, has no minimum wage at all.[71]

The more common method of raising the cost of migrant labor in the Gulf is to restrict immigration by limiting the supply of work visas. If this policy were

69. IMF 2005a, 13–14.

70. Labour Market Regulatory Authority, Kingdom of Bahrain, 2010, "Why Isn't Enforcing a Minimum Wage a Superior Alternative to the Proposed Reforms?" February 17, http://portal.lmra.bh/english/faq/question/28.

71. Human Rights Watch 2006, 56–57.

implemented according to the letter of the law, the rents would go to those expatriates lucky enough to secure a visa. Instead, citizen brokers with privileged access to the bureaucracy sell the visas to foreigners, capturing part of the rent. These brokers also charge the employers because employers often lack the necessary political connections to easily import labor. Steffen Hertog estimates that the average cost of a visa, charged to a future migrant worker, ranges from $2,000 to $4,000.[72]

The third way to raise the cost of migrant labor is to impose a tax on each immigrant worker, paid by employers. The proceeds of the tax go to the state, which determines the recipient of the rent. Bahrain implemented such a tax in July 2008, charging employers 10 Bahraini dinars (BD) per month for each expatriate (about US$26 per month).[73] (Singapore, by way of comparison, imposes a tax of well over US$100 per month on each domestic laborer and a tax that can go above US$350 for some unskilled workers.[74]) The proceeds of the Bahraini tax were to go to a fund intended to train Bahrainis for private-sector jobs, encourage private-sector growth, and so forth.[75] The Bahraini tax, by design, falls hard on the employers of less-skilled expatriate labor (it shares this with the Singaporean labor policies that were its inspiration),[76] and for that reason, the tax has proven to be highly unpopular among some Bahraini businessmen.[77] The LMRA was also associated with the crown prince, a moderate within the ruling family, and the benefits of the program were perceived to go primarily to the Shi'i population of Bahrain. The events of 2011 resulted in the defeat of the main patron of the LMRA reform efforts.

In Saudi Arabia, the Arab Spring had an opposite effect. The regime imposed a monthly tax on companies that had more foreigners than Saudis on the payroll. These companies pay US$50 per month per worker for each foreign worker above the number of Saudis employed by the firm. Although the tax met with substantial opposition, the state appears not to have relented.[78]

72. Hertog 2010c, 299. See also Human Rights Watch 2006, 26–29.

73. "Bosses Plan Fees Protest," *Gulf Daily News* (Bahrain), August 28, 2010, http://www.gulf-daily-news.com/NewsDetails.aspx?storyid=285664.

74. Singapore Ministry of Manpower, "Foreign Worker Levy Rates," 2010, http://www.mom.gov.sg/; Human Rights Watch 2010, 18.

75. Al-Kibsi, Benkert, and Schubert 2007, 27.

76 . Market Reform Affect Bahrain's Competitiveness in the Region?" February 17, portal.lmra.bh/english/faq/question/22.

77. "Bosses Plan Fees Protest," *Gulf Daily News* (Bahrain), August 28, 2010, http://www.gulf-daily-news.com/NewsDetails.aspx?storyid=285664.

78. "Saudi's Expat Worker Levy Hits Construction Profits," *Arabianbusiness.com*, September 12, 2013, http://www.arabianbusiness.com/saudi-s-expat-worker-levy-hits-construction-profits-517964.html.

Quotas and Reserved Professions

An alternative strategy, one whose costs also fall mostly on capitalists, is the imposition of quotas on the private sector. All the Gulf states, to some degree, require that a minimum percentage of the employees of some firms be citizens. These quotas typically vary by industry. Thus, the UAE has had quotas in banking (4% of the workforce), insurance (5%), and trade (2% for larger companies).[79] Or entire job categories can be reserved for citizens. For example, Saudi Arabia has mandated that only citizens can sell jewelry. And the Omani government has closed a number of professions to non-Omanis, including customs expediters, plow operators, water-truck drivers, fishermen, taxi drivers, and real estate agents; in contrast to the quotas in the UAE, many of these are less-skilled positions.[80] In the relatively poorer UAE emirate of Ras al-Khaimah, the ruler announced that the fish trade would be reserved for Emiratis, although the actual cleaning of fish could still be done by foreigners.[81] These policies do nothing to get rid of the sharply divided job markets in the Gulf states; instead, they move the fence that divides citizen and expatriate labor into the private sector itself.

The costs of these quotas fall primarily on businesses. Citizen employees hired to meet quotas "are often perceived as a burden, and companies consider the salaries paid to them as a form of tax."[82] It is widely understood that many Kuwaiti citizens employed in the private sector do not do any work at all. Their employer pays them purely to meet the requirements for Kuwaitization, and their salaries are treated as a cost of doing business that has been imposed by the government (unless, of course, the state actually pays the salaries). The private sector, not surprisingly, puts a great deal of time and effort into avoiding this tax. The IMF has welcomed the UAE lack of "wide-ranging employment quotas" for citizens on the grounds of the "significance of expatriate labor's contribution to growth and to maintaining the competitiveness of the economy."[83]

Because these policies impose serious costs on businesses, they are often enforced with a notable lack of vigor, especially in the three richer rentiers. In 2006, during one of the many efforts to encourage the private sector to hire Emiratis, an official reported that "There are 796 private companies that have a zero per-

79. Business Monitor International 2007, 28.

80. PRS Group, "Oman: Labor Conditions" (via Lexis-Nexis), July 1, 2006 (accessed June 6, 2007).

81. Nasouh Nazzal, "RAK's Fishing Industry to Undergo Emiratisation," *Gulf News,* January 25, 2007, gulfnews.com/news/gulf/uae/general/rak-s-fishing-industry-to-undergo-emiratisation-1.156441.

82. Nabil Ali al-Yousuf, of the Dubai School of Government, quoted in Ellen Knickmeyer, "Gulf States Try to Steer Jobs to Citizens; Employers Resent Efforts Intended to Fight Unemployment and Radicalization," *Washington Post,* August 25, 2008.

83. IMF 2005b, 21.

cent emiratisation rate, however 632 of these are considered cooperative as they are taking serious steps in this regard." Serious steps, it seems, need not include actually hiring any Emiratis.[84]

The quota system also gives businesses a strong incentive to seek out special treatment from the bureaucracy. As the Bahraini LMRA succinctly describes the ills of the system, "The current Bahrainisation regime, for instance, has differential targets not only by industry sector, but in effect by company. The result has been a system that is non-transparent, highly discretionary, hard to understand for the average employer, and open to inappropriate influence."[85] In Oman, a Western consultancy points out that the requirements for Omanization are best dealt with by knowing a member of the ruling Al Said family or someone else in a position of authority who can get the requirements waived.[86]

Despite these problems, however, the strategy does offer some promise for moving citizens into the private-sector job market, particularly in the middling rentiers. Quotas can move citizens into the workforce without bankrupting the state or upending the economic and political status quo. These policies are more palatable to capitalists because they do not affect the overall cost of expatriate labor; the costs of the policy are limited to the specific positions affected. By contrast, policies that raise the cost of expatriate labor across the board (via taxes, restrictions on entry, or a minimum wage) have much more pervasive effects, particularly if the cost is raised enough to make citizen labor attractive to employers.

Quotas and reserved professions work best when the barrier between jobs reserved for citizens and those open to citizens is well defined, when the state is able to resist private-sector efforts to undermine the system, and when citizens find private-sector positions attractive. Banking, in particular, is a relatively highly skilled industry with a workforce that includes far more citizens than is the norm in the Gulf. In the UAE, about one-third of the employees in the banking sector are said to be Emiratis; Qatar National Bank claims a Qatarization level of 41%; and many Bahrainis work in the banking sector of their country.[87] The (highly

84. In Wafa Issa, "Firms Faltering in Emiratisation to Be Blacklisted," *Gulf News*, June 11, 2006, http://gulfnews.com/news/gulf/uae/employment/firms-faltering-in-emiratisation-to-be-blacklisted-1.240467.

85. Labour Market Regulatory Authority, Kingdom of Bahrain, "Why Aren't the Proposed Labour Fees Segmented by Sector or Skill Level?" February 17, 2010, portal.lmra.bh/english/faq/question/26.

86. PRS Group, "Oman: Most Likely Regime Scenario" (via Lexis-Nexis), January 1, 2007 (accessed June 6, 2007).

87. Randeree 2012, 11; Qatar National Bank n.d., 35. UAE banks, however, fudge the numbers by outsourcing operations to contractors and the free zones. On Saudi Arabia, see Ramady (2005, 359). Even in the banking industry, however, the private sector must compete with the public sector on hours, wages, and working conditions, and this produces friction between employers and citizen employees. Bassma Al Jandaly, "'Give Us the Chance to Prove Ourselves'," *Gulf News*, January 30, 2007, gulfnews.com/news/gulf/uae/employment/give-us-the-chance-to-prove-ourselves-1.152906.

regulated) mobile phone companies also hire citizens. In the UAE, Etisalat and du (both majority owned by the state) have achieved Emiratization rates of 35 and 23%, respectively.[88] In Kuwait, the stores of the mobile phone companies are one of the very few places where citizens work in customer service positions.

Quotas are even more popular in the middling rentiers. In 2011 the Saudi regime, jolted by events in Egypt and Tunisia, dusted off this policy and started to enforce it with a renewed vigor. Under a plan dubbed "Nitaqat," companies were to be ranked in terms of their performance in hiring citizens, with those ranked in the "red" category unable to renew the visas of their existing foreign workers and those in the highest category able to bring in additional workers.[89] This, of course, was not the first such plan to be seen in the Gulf, and it will not be the last. Unlike other similar plans, however, Nitaqat had some immediate and concrete consequences in the form of a rush by Saudi firms to hire citizens.[90] The ministry of labor claimed that the number of Saudis employed in the private sector jumped from 707,000 to 955,000 in under a year.[91] The costs of this reaction of the regime to the Arab Spring were borne, of course, by Saudi capitalists, who faced a substantial new cost to doing business in the kingdom.

Subsidizing Private-Sector Employment of Citizens

Finally, some Gulf states simply pay the salaries of citizens employed in the private sector. For example, in Kuwait the state pays a number of "allowances" to citizens employed in private-sector positions. These allowances (some of which are tied to family size and marital status) are also paid to public-sector workers and effectively form a part of a citizen worker's pay package whether employed in the public or private sector. In Kuwait in 2012, the state subsidy for a married male private-sector employee started at around $3,000 per month, a sum large enough to call into doubt the notion that these citizens are in a real sense employed by the private sector.[92] Later in 2012, the Kuwaiti government gave a raise

88. Georgina Enzer, "Etisalat, Du Aim for Greater Emiratisation," *ITP.net*, January 25, 2011, http://www.itp.net/583681-etisalat-du-aim-for-greater-emiratisation.

89. Ministry of Labor, Kingdom of Saudi Arabia, "Limatha Nitaqat alan?" [Why Nitaqat now?], *Nitaqat*, 2012, http://www.emol.gov.sa/nitaqat/pages/WhyNow.aspx (accessed September 22, 2012).

90. Siraj Wahab, "Nitaqat a Boon for Saudi Job Seekers," *Arab News*, August 23, 2011, http://www.arabnews.com/node/388442; Dudley 2012, 38–39.

91. Saudi Arabia, Ministry of Labor, "Nata'ij awwaliyya mubshira li-birnamij Nitaqat" [Promising early results of the Nitaqat program], *Nitaqat*, 2012, http://www.emol.gov.sa/nitaqat/pages/Activities_Act3.aspx (accessed September 22, 2012).

92. Yusuf al-Mutayri, "Al-da'm al-hukumi li-muwazzafi al-khass: 456–790 dinaran lil-a''zab wa 884–1248 lil-mutazawwij" [Government support for private-sector employees: 456–790 dinars to bachelors and 884–1248 to married men], *al-Qabas*, May 10, 2012, 4; Tony Blair Associates 2009, 203.

to private-sector employees in an effort to discourage the movement of citizens from the private sector to the public sector.[93]

The cost of these policies is borne almost entirely by the fisc, and their high cost means that they are available, in a serious way, only to the three richer rentiers. Business owners suffer no harm, and citizens receive jobs. Perhaps the best way to think of the payments are as disbursements from the national oil trust fund that require that the recipient, as a condition of receiving the payment, be employed (or pretend to be employed). This maintains (or attempts to maintain) the link between the distribution of oil wealth and employment.

As with other efforts to push citizens into private-sector positions, the policy is open to abuse by citizens and employers. For example, in 2008 the Kuwaiti government went looking, during work hours, for 800 private-sector employees collecting government allowances and found only 181 of them actually at work. Some were thought to be living abroad.[94] It appears that these citizens were hired for the purpose of collecting their government allowances, with the connivance of their employers. One Kuwaiti businessman complained that other business owners hired their wives and relatives—without expecting them to actually work—to claim the government allowances.[95]

★ ★ ★

The Gulf labor markets are exceedingly distinctive, in both the middling and the extreme rentiers. Capitalists seek to drive down the price of (noncitizen) labor by encouraging immigration of expatriate labor while the political economic logic of rentierism closes off the possibility that these immigrants will gain citizenship. Citizens flee to jobs in the public sector, where oil revenue makes it possible for the state to pay them wages well above those set by the market. The overwhelming concentration of citizens in public-sector jobs in the extreme rentiers breaks the usual connection between citizen labor and the private sector, which in nonrentier capitalist economies takes the form of jobs and redistributed tax revenues.

The political consequences of the absence of the usual capitalist social contract between labor and capitalists vary in the extreme rentiers. In Kuwait, where citizens have a voice, the effects are most pronounced. In the UAE, where capitalists are supreme, the results are distinctive in their own way. In the next two chapters, I turn to the issue of political participation, explaining how and why Kuwait gives its state-employed middle class a much greater voice in setting public policy than do the UAE and the other Gulf monarchies.

93. Yusuf al-Mutayri, "Hijra 12 alf mawatin min 'al-khass' ila 'al-hukumi'" [Migration of 12 thousand citizens from the private sector to the public sector], *al-Qabas*, July 25, 2012, 8.

94. Ahmad Al-Khaled, "Protest over Alleged 'Ghost Employment,'" *Kuwait Times*, June 24, 2008.

95. Munir Yunus and Ahmad Bumara'i, "Al-Ayyar: Yartakibun jarima fi haqq al-kuwayt wa mustaqbalha" [Al-Ayar: They are committing a crime against Kuwait and its future], *al-Qabas*, August 21, 2011, 46.

Chapter 2

Participation

Although the extreme rentiers of the Gulf share similar labor markets, Kuwaitis can hold their rulers accountable, while citizens of the other Gulf monarchies cannot. Even so, it is not universally conceded that the Kuwaiti parliament is qualitatively stronger than any other GCC parliament. In this chapter, I examine the constitutional structures of the monarchies to show what makes the political institutions of Kuwait different from those of the other Gulf monarchies.

Most models of democratization are derived from the experiences of republics rather than monarchies, and thus they usually do a poor job of capturing the dynamics of democratization in monarchies. Democracy, as it is typically conceived by political scientists, minimally requires that the leaders of the legislative and executive branches be elected by the people in fair elections. In the prototypical case of modern democratization in republics, free and fair elections to one branch of government usually are also accompanied, within a reasonably short period of time, by free and fair elections to the other branch. Thus, free and fair elections to either the executive or the legislature typically mark the crucial onset of democratization, and democratization is signaled by the first free and fair elections that are respected by the incumbent authoritarian regime.

In monarchies, by contrast, free and fair elections to a national parliament can be held repeatedly over the course of years, or even decades, without any transition to democracy. This is because two very different principles of authority determine selection of the legislative and executive powers. The legislature may be elected whereas the leading officers of the executive branch are appointed by the monarchy.

In monarchies of this sort—and this includes Kuwait—the crucial issue is thus not elections (or elections alone) but, instead, control over the appointment of the prime minister and the formation of the government. Democratization is achieved when parties in the parliament, rather than the monarch or the ruling family, appoint the prime minister and form the government. When this occurs, a monarchy becomes a parliamentary democracy of the sort found in democratic monarchies around the world today.

The gradualist path to democracy, as it took place in the monarchies of northwestern Europe, can reasonably be said to have three stages. The first is absolutism; this is a monarchical system that lacks a constitution (written or unwritten) that constrains and defines the powers of the monarch and also lacks an elected parliament. In the second stage, once called constitutional monarchy, a written or unwritten constitution calls for elections to a parliament but also explicitly provides for the office of the monarch and gives that office some potential authority. In practice, the power of the monarchy can range from virtually absolute to very limited, with the degree defined less by the provisions of the constitution than by political practice. In monarchies that took a gradualist path to democracy, the election of a parliament typically preceded the achievement of parliamentarism by several decades. The third stage is parliamentarism, in which political parties in the parliament appoint the prime minister and the other ministers, and the political power of the monarchy becomes nominal. Note that there is nothing inevitable about the movement from one stage to the next. Some monarchies historically moved from the first stage, through the second, and to the third. Others vacillated among the three stages, and many never made it past the first stages before being overthrown.[1]

When we measure the Gulf constitutions according to whether they give citizens the ability to substantially influence policy, the constitutions of the Gulf fall into two groups. The constitution of Kuwait provides for free elections to a parliament that has real power; the other Gulf monarchies (1) lack free elections, (2) lack a parliament with more than advisory powers, or (3) lack both. Free and fair elections to a national assembly that has no real powers do not empower citizens. Free and fair elections to a parliament with real influence vis-à-vis the ruling family do empower citizens, at least to the degree that the elections are fair, the constitutional powers are substantial, and the constitution is respected. While the Kuwaiti constitution is flexible enough to provide a path forward toward democracy, the constitutions of the other Gulf states are not.[2] In these states, unlike Kuwait, the first task of serious political reform is to rewrite their constitutions. Table 2.1 summarizes the differences among the Gulf state constitutions.

1. Herb 2004.
2. For another view, see Parolin 2006, 55.

TABLE 2.1.
National representative assemblies in the Gulf monarchies

	Bahrain	Kuwait	Oman	Qatar	Saudi Arabia	UAE
Name	National Assembly	National Assembly	Majlis Oman	Consultative Council	Consultative Council	Federal National Council (FNC)
Houses	Upper: Consultative Council Lower: Council of Deputies	Unicameral	Upper: State Council Lower: Consultative Council	Unicameral	Unicameral	Unicameral
Lower house	40 elected members	50 elected members; up to 15 appointed members	Variable: 1 deputy for small *wilayats* (under 30,000 residents), 2 deputies for larger districts; 84 elected members	Currently: 35 appointed members Under new 2004 constitution: 30 elected and 15 appointed members	150 appointed members	20 elected members; 20 appointed members
Upper house	40 appointed members	—	Appointed: number of members equal to or less than number in lower house	—	—	—
Can a majority of elected members remove confidence in ministers?	No Requires a two-thirds majority of all members of the lower house	Yes Requires an absolute majority of the elected members (except elected deputies in government who cannot vote)	No	Currently: No Under 2004 constitution: No Requires a two-thirds majority of entire council	No	No

(*Continued*)

TABLE 2.1.
(Continued)

	Bahrain	Kuwait	Oman	Qatar	Saudi Arabia	UAE
Legislative powers of the assembly	When the two houses disagree, the two houses vote together on legislation by simple majority of those present; two-thirds majority of both houses required to overturn king's veto	Legislation is passed by majority of all deputies; veto override requires absolute majority (or two-thirds majority if immediate)	Upper and lower house pass laws separately; if there is a disagreement, they meet together and vote by majority	Currently: Consultative only Under 2004 constitution: Consultative council has legislative powers, but they are sharply limited	Consultative only	Consultative only
Clearly identified, nontribal blocs within the assembly?	Yes	Yes	No	No	No	No
Full (or nearly full) suffrage for citizens?	Yes	Yes	Yes	Naturalized citizens and their descendants cannot vote under 2008 electoral law	No elections to the Majlis al-Shura	No; the rulers select the members of the electorate
Government manipulation of the process of counting votes?	Accusations of fraud in recent parliamentary elections	None reported in recent decades	None reported	None reported (municipal elections)	None reported (municipal elections)	None reported

Malapportionment and gerrymandering?	Severe gerrymandering and malapportionment with the goal of reducing Shi'i representation	Some traditional malapportionment; overrepresentation of urban *hadhar* voters	Malapportionment generally favoring rural areas and smaller *wilayats*	?	Not applicable	Malapportionment as result of federal system
Freedom of speech during campaigns?	Limited	Generally, candidates are free to take a range of positions on important issues	Limited, although improving over time	Limited	Limited	Limited
Process by which constitution was written	Issued by decree for the most part	Drafted by a constitutional council of 20 elected members and 12 appointed members; issued by the ruler	Issued by decree	Drafted by an appointed committee; ratified in popular referendum, issued by emir.	Issued by decree	Issued over signature of rulers
Process by which constitution is amended	Amended by a two-thirds vote of each of the two houses	Amended by two-thirds vote of all members of the Assembly; approved by emir.	Amended by decree	Amended by two-thirds vote of consultative council, approved by emir	Amended by decree	Council of Rulers requests amendment; approved by two-thirds vote in FNC

Despite these differences in constitutions and legislative power, the measures of democracy often used by political scientists—such as by Freedom House and Polity—do not register a particularly large difference in the level of democracy (or, more precisely, its absence) in the rankings of Kuwait and the UAE. In 2012, Kuwait averaged a 5 on the Freedom House scale (from 1 to 7, where 1 is the most free) and the UAE averaged 6. On the Polity scale (from 10 to −10, where 10 is the most democratic), Kuwait gets a −7 and the UAE a −8. The scores for the UAE on these measures are not unreasonable; it is an authoritarian regime. But the scores for Kuwait do not capture its combination of democratic and authoritarian institutions very well. This is, no doubt, because the form of monarchical rule in Kuwait is uncommon in the modern world; a regime type in which an elected legislature has some authority over a mostly authoritarian executive is not a constellation that occurs frequently. That said, the failure of the Polity score to capture this is much more complete than that of Freedom House.

Kuwait

The crucial power enjoyed by the Kuwaiti National Assembly—the power that makes it qualitatively more powerful than the representative assemblies of any other Gulf monarchy—is the power to remove confidence in individual ministers or (in effect) the prime minister. Only elected members of the National Assembly, and of these, only those who do not serve in the government, can vote on motions of confidence. This gives a majority of the elected members the ability to remove confidence in individual ministers or, in effect, the prime minister (and, thus, the government as a whole). No minister has ever lost a vote of confidence, but a number have resigned immediately before a vote was to be taken, anticipating defeat. In December 2009, the first vote of confidence in the prime minister took place. He won handily, but the vote itself further established the idea that the government survives only on the basis of a majority of the elected members of the National Assembly, and not on the authority of appointment by the emir alone.

All members of the National Assembly can vote on regular legislation, which passes with a majority vote. The unicameral Kuwaiti National Assembly is composed of two groups of deputies: (1) elected deputies, at least one of whom must also serve in the council of ministers, and (2) appointed members of the council of ministers who serve, ex officio, as members of the National Assembly. There are fifty elected members of the Assembly and up to fifteen appointed members.[3]

3. Articles 56 and 80 of the Constitution of Kuwait.

The National Assembly also has the power to override the emir's vetoes with a simple majority vote; given that the assembly includes up to fifteen appointed members who usually vote as a bloc, the elected members of the assembly must gather together a supermajority to pass legislation or to override a veto against the opposition of the government. On occasion, the National Assembly manages this feat. At the same time, the government does not always need a majority vote of the elected members of the National Assembly to pass legislation. This was most notably the case with the 2005 vote to allow women to vote.[4]

The constitutional powers of the National Assembly would not matter much if the government regularly stole the elections, as has been the case in many monarchies outside the Gulf.[5] In Kuwait, elections have been fair (with the exception of the 1967 election), with few complaints about the process of counting ballots (though the details of the electoral system have been the subject of continual disagreement).[6] Women gained the right to vote in 2005. The elections, to be sure, are not perfect; districts are malapportioned (although this is more by tradition than by government manipulation), and the opposition boycotted the December 2012 elections to protest changes in the electoral system imposed by the emir and designed to discourage voting by blocs. The change, in essence, was a shift to the single non-transferrable vote (SNTV) system.[7] Overall, however, electoral flaws have not prevented opposition victories in recent elections (when the opposition has competed), suggesting that the government has limited ability to shape the outcome of elections. In institutional terms, the question of democracy in Kuwait today is more about the role of the ruling family (and the National Assembly) in appointing the government than about the quality of elections.

United Arab Emirates

The contrast between the UAE and Kuwait is stark. The UAE does not have serious elections, and its federal assembly—the Federal National Council (FNC)—lacks serious powers. Until 2006, the FNC was entirely appointive, with the ruler of each emirate having the authority to select the representatives from his emirate. In 2006, elections of a sort were held for twenty of the forty seats on the unicameral council. In these elections, the rulers hand-picked the electorate, which

4. Michael Herb, "Women's Political Rights 2005," Kuwait Politics Database, May 2005, http://www2.gsu.edu/~polmfh/database/positions20.htm.

5. Herb 2004.

6. O'Grady et al. 2008.

7. Herb 2013.

numbered fewer than 7,000 citizens across the seven emirates. In the 2011 elections, the regime expanded the electorate to 130,000, but turnout was very low.[8] Reports on the winners of the elections did not discuss anyone who might be identified as a reformer, even though a few deputies who won in 2006 did use the FNC as a platform to raise somewhat sensitive issues.

The FNC has few powers under the 1972 constitution. Article 110 makes it clear that the government can pass legislation even against the opposition of the FNC. Legislation must go through the FNC, and it can be amended, but if the government rejects the amendments (or if the FNC rejects the bill outright), the president can still issue the law after approval from the Council of Rulers. Abd al-Rahim al-Shahin, noted Emirati constitutional scholar, points out that, in substance, the FNC is a consultative council. It can discuss issues, but the Council of Ministers can decide that its decision is against the national interest.[9]

Even so, in practice the FNC sometimes plays a role in Emirati politics by virtue of its ability to raise issues in a public forum. In 1986, the FNC amended a law on state security, and its amendments were accepted by the government and the rulers following wide discussion among the public.[10] In 2004, an Emirati academic wrote that the "FNC acted as a channel through which popular views were transmitted to leaders."[11] Yet the FNC sometimes struggles to play even this role. After the December 2006 elections, the FNC asked the government to follow the constitutional provision and bring laws to the FNC for advice before issuing them.[12] This complaint was echoed in 2012, when a member of the FNC asked why the annual budget was not being submitted to the FNC for discussion, as required by the constitution.[13]

Some of the seven individual emirates that compose the UAE have their own representative assemblies, but none are freely elected or have real legislative powers. Abu Dhabi has had its own Consultative Council since 1971. It is entirely appointed and has no legislative powers; its membership is broadly representative of Abu Dhabi tribes.[14] In Sharjah, an appointive council with limited legislative

8. Al-Suwaidi 2011, 46; "Turnout in UAE's Second Election Low at 28 Percent of Handpicked Voters," *Al Arabiya News*, 2011, http://www.alarabiya.net/articles/2011/09/24/168394.html (accessed September 25, 2012).
9. Al-Shahin 1997, 281.
10. Al-Rokn 1991, 260–62.
11. Al-Sayegh 2004, 115.
12. "UAE Laws Approved without FNC Debate Need to Be Reviewed," *Khaleej Times*, March 28, 2007.
13. "Al-majlis yu'akkid ahammiyya munaqasha mashru' al-mizaniyya al-sanawiyya lil-dawla" [The FNC confirms the importance of debating the draft annual budget of the state], *Al-Ittihad*, January 4, 2012, http://www.alittihad.ae/details.php?id=1195&y=2012 (accessed September 25, 2012).
14. Davidson 2009, 125.

powers has been in place since 1987; elections were promised in 2005, but nothing came of it.[15] Dubai lacks a representative assembly of any sort, despite occasional discussions about setting one up.[16]

In short, UAE citizens have little political influence through representative institutions. In the next two chapters, I explain how this came about and how efforts in the 1970s to make the UAE constitution more like the Constitution of Kuwait came to naught.

Qatar

In one sense, the status of the Qatari national representative assembly is complicated; the current assembly operates under the provisions of an old constitution, despite the new constitution having come into force in 2005. In other respects, it is simple; under both constitutions, the assembly has little authority.

The new Permanent Constitution of Qatar was approved in a referendum in 2003, ratified by the emir in 2004, and finally published in the official gazette in 2005.[17] It calls for a partially elected Consultative Council, but as of 2013 no elections had been held to this body, despite repeated promises that elections were going to be held (promises spanning a decade and more). The final article of the new constitution specifies that, until elections are held, the Consultative Council will operate under the provisions of the Basic Law, the precursor to the current constitution.[18] Under the Basic Law, the Consultative Council has thirty-five members, all of them appointed by the emir. The powers of the council are pretty much summed up in the provision that it will "express its opinions as recommendations."[19]

Under the new constitution, the Consultative Council would have—if elections were held—thirty elected and fifteen appointed members. The council would

15. Consultative Council of Sharjah, "Ikhtisasat al-majlis al-istishari" [Competencies of the Consultative Council], http://www.ccsharjah.gov.ae/ (accessed September 26, 2012); Consultative Council of Sharjah, "Tashkil al-majlis" [Composition of the majlis], http://www.ccsharjah.gov.ae/ (accessed September 26, 2012); Eman Al Baik and Nada S. Mussallam, "Sharjah Elections Move Wins Wide Applause," *Khaleej Times*, February 27, 2005; Davidson 2005, 198.

16. Davidson 2008, 159.

17. Kapiszewski 2006, 116–17; State of Qatar, Ministry of Justice, "The Permanent Constitution of the State of Qatar," Al-Meezan: Qatar Legal Portal, 2014, http://www.almeezan.qa/ (accessed 23 March 2014).

18. Articles 77 and 150 of the Permanent Constitution of the State of Qatar.

19. Article 40 of the Permanent Constitution of the State of Qatar. At times, the Basic Law has called for elections, but these have not been held. See Nakhleh 1980, 171–72; Al-Kuwari 2011. See also Ehteshami and Wright 2007, 921; Kamrava 2009, 417–18.

be able to remove confidence in ministers, but only with a two-thirds vote of the membership of the council.[20] Overriding the emir's veto of legislation would also require a two-thirds majority of the Consultative Council, but even then the emir could suspend the law "to serve the higher interests of the country."[21] Although the council would be able to refuse to pass legislation, the emir would have generous powers to issue laws by decree in the absence of the council, and these could only be overturned by a two-thirds majority.[22] All these provisions of the 2004 constitution are clearly designed to work together, with the overall goal of depriving the elected members of the council—if and when there are in fact any elected members—from imposing any real constraints on the power of the emir and his government.

The history of Qatari elections is confined to the municipality. Elections may (or may not) have been held in 1963, following a period of unrest.[23] Elections were held in 1999 to the Municipal Council, then again in 2003, 2007, and 2011.[24] Across these elections there have been few or no complaints of government manipulation of the process of counting ballots. Candidates, however, have not been allowed to speak on the entire range of policy issues in their campaigns or to form ideologically oriented groups. And the new elections law issued in 2008, which is intended to govern elections to the Consultative Council under the 2004 constitution, restricts voting rights and the right to run as a candidate to Qatari citizens with "first-class" citizenship.[25] Under Qatar's citizenship law, "first-class" citizens are those who were in the country before 1930 and their descendants. The 2008 elections law thus disenfranchises something like one-third of the (already very small) citizen population.[26]

Oman

Oman holds elections that are increasingly free and fair. The representative assembly, however, has few powers. Over the past two decades, the sultan of Oman has taken a long series of small steps to expand political participation in Oman.

20. Article 111 of the Permanent Constitution of the State of Qatar. The Constitution (article 77) specifies that the 15 appointed members be chosen from "among the ministers and others," leaving open the possibility that many of the appointed members would vote as a bloc by virtue of being members of the government, as occurs in the Kuwaiti National Assembly.

21. Article 106 of the Permanent Constitution of the State of Qatar.

22. Articles 70, 90, and 104 of the Permanent Constitution of the State of Qatar.

23. Bahry says elections were held, Al-Kuwari says they were planned but not held. Bahry 1999, 119; Al-Kuwari 2011, 35.

24. Kamrava 2009, 416–17.

25. "Al-shura yuwafiq 'ala mashru' qanun al-intikhabat" [Shura approves election law draft], *Al-Rayaa* (Doha), May 20, 2008.

26. Al-Kuwari 2012, 15. See also Partrick 2009, 20–21.

Before 2011, reform dealt almost entirely with the quality of elections. The first assembly, in 1991, was essentially appointed; local notables nominated candidates, and the regime made the final selection. Universal suffrage was introduced in the 2003 elections, but campaigning was very restricted; posters, advertising, and public gatherings were all prohibited.[27] The 2007 elections were somewhat freer, but candidates still were constrained from staking out clear positions on issues. The minister of information opined that all candidates have "one campaign program and that is Oman."[28] Newspaper advertisements by candidates were allowed for the first time but required prior approval by the ministry of the interior.[29] Marc Valeri points out that the structure of the ballot and the inability of candidates to differentiate themselves on policy lines led to voting along tribal lines. He argues that this also has produced a particular apathy about these elections among the urban and nontribal parts of the Omani citizenry.[30] Malapportionment in the electoral system—which is weighted against cities—contributes to this problem. Half the deputies (forty-two) are elected by only 25% of the population, and only eight deputies are elected by the urban districts, which contain another 25% of the population.[31] It was not until the 2011 elections that press coverage of election results clearly indicated the ideological leanings of winning candidates. Three "protesters" won seats; these were men who participated in the protests that were the manifestation of the Arab Spring in Oman. One of these three has been arrested during the protests. By Kuwaiti standards, this was a small step, but in the Omani context, it was a substantial change.[32]

These elections are now to the lower house of a bicameral representative assembly. All members of the lower house (the Consultative Council) are elected, while the upper house is entirely appointed. But these elected members enjoy few actual powers. Up until the reforms prompted by the Arab Spring, the Omani Basic Law

27. Valeri 2006, 196–99.

28. Basim Al-Bakur and Muhammad Sayf Al-Rahbi, "Al-intikhabat al-'umaniya: Iqbal kathif wa hudhur lil-mar'a iqtira'an wa tamthilan" [Omani elections: High turnout and a female presence in voting and running for office], *Al-Hayat*, October 28, 2007.

29. Muhammad Sayf Al-Rahbi, "12 imra'a yuwajihna 632 murashshahan al-sabt al-muqbil . . . Intikhabat al-shura al-'umani tabda' al-yawm kharij al-saltana" [12 women face 632 male candidates this Saturday . . . Elections to the Omani council begin today outside the Sultanate], *Al-Hayat*, October 20, 2007.

30. Valeri 2006, 203.

31. Ibid., 199. Figures calculated using population figures from the Omani Ministry of the Economy's *Statistical Yearbook 2009* http://www.ncsi.gov.om/NCSI_website/book/SYB2009/index.htm (accessed April 8, 2014>.

32. Sunil K. Vaidya, "One Woman, Three Activists Get Elected in Oman's Shura Council," *Gulf News*, October 16, 2011, http://gulfnews.com/news/gulf/oman/one-woman-three-activists-get-elected-in-oman-s-shura-council-1.893059.

of 1996 gave the elected lower house of parliament no powers whatsoever, simply specifying that the powers of the council were determined by law. That law, in turn, was not generous in its grant of powers. As the *Gulf News* (a Dubai newspaper) put it in its coverage of the 2007 elections, "while candidates say they have been asked [by the government] not to make promises in their campaigns, some point out that there is no use in making promises that cannot be kept. . . . The consultative council, they point out, is just that, and has no legislative powers."[33]

The events in other Arab countries in spring 2011 sparked protests in Oman and prompted the sultan to promise additional political reforms. The changes came in the form of a decree, issued by the ruler, that revised the Basic Law of 1996. (The Basic Law was issued as a decree and is amended by decree.) The 2011 amendments required that new laws proposed by the Council of Ministers be sent first to the Majlis Oman for approval or amendment. Should the two houses—one appointed, the other elected—disagree, their differences are to be resolved in a joint session and by majority vote.[34] The appointed upper house can have as many members as the elected lower house, and thus the provision for a joint session sharply limits the authority of the elected members of the Majlis Oman.[35] The Council of Ministers, however, no longer has the power to decide that laws should be sent directly to the sultan, bypassing the Majlis Oman, as it did under the previous law.[36] The new reforms also gave the elected Consultative Council the right to interpellate "service" ministers, who are in charge of ministries that deliver services to citizens, such as the ministry of health (in Gulf usage the ministries of sovereignty, by contrast, include defense, foreign affairs, and interior). Following the interpellation, the Council sends its conclusions to the sultan. There is no provision for a vote of confidence.[37] In no small part, the 2011 amendments merely moved powers already granted by law (in the law pertaining to the

33. Abbas Al Lawati, "Residents Say Tribal Voting Is Ideal for Representation," *Gulf News*, October 27, 2007, http://gulfnews.com/news/gulf/oman/residents-say-tribal-voting-is-ideal-for-representation-1.208020. For a more optimistic view, see Jones and Ridout (2005, 384), who write that "in practice, it does exercise powers although none are constitutionally prescribed."

34. Sultan Qaboos bin Said, "Marsum sultani raqm 99/2011 bi-ta'dil ba'dh ahkam al-nizam al-asasi lil-dawla" [Sultani decree number 99 of 2011 amending some of the provisions of the Basic Law of the state], October 19, 2011.

35. Ibid., article 58, section 1.

36. Compare this with article 29 of the Nizam Majlis Oman; Sultan Qaboos bin Said, "Nizam Majlis Oman, marsum sultani 86/97," [Organization of the Majlis Oman, Sultani Decree 86/97], December 16, 1997, http://www.shura.om/ar/jurisdictnew.asp.

37. Sovereign ministers, by contrast, cannot be interpellated. Sultan Qaboos bin Said, "Marsum sultani raqm 99/2011," article 58, section 43; "Plea to Quiz Minister Later," *Oman Daily Observer*, June 24, 2012, http://main.omanobserver.om.

Majlis Oman) into the Basic Law.[38] There were, however, also modest additions; for example, the right to interpellate ministers was new.

Overall, Oman remains far behind Kuwait in the degree of power enjoyed by elected deputies. That said, the prospects for further change toward more participation appear to be better in Oman than in any of the other Gulf monarchies outside Kuwait, in no small part because the trajectory of change in Oman has been steadily, if slowly, in a more liberal direction.

Saudi Arabia

The Saudi ruling family drops even the pretense of holding national elections to its Consultative Council.[39] The Saudi Basic Law, issued by decree by the king in 1992, calls for a wholly appointive Consultative Council. This assembly, whose powers are determined by ordinary law rather than by the constitution (or Basic Law), has very modest legislative powers and no ability to remove confidence in ministers.[40]

In 2005, Saudi Arabia held elections to some seats in local municipal councils, although even these bodies have little power and only half of their members were elected. Municipal council elections were held again in 2011, two years after their originally scheduled date and without the participation of women, who were promised the right to vote in the elections of 2015.[41]

Bahrain

Bahrain has had more experience with parliamentary life than any other Gulf monarchy except Kuwait. Nonetheless, its serious sectarian conflict—and especially the fact that the ruling family is from the sectarian minority[42]—makes the prospect of a Kuwaiti-style ascendance of the parliament unlikely. Instead the political role of the parliament is determined by the sectarian balance of power. The

38. Sultan Qaboos bin Said, "Nizam Majlis Oman, marsum sultani 86/97."

39. Al-Fahad 2005, 376.

40. Ibid., 388; Kingdom of Saudi Arabia, "Nizam majlis ash-shura" [Law governing the Consultative Council], with subsequent amendments 1992, www.shura.gov.sa (accessed December 10, 2009).

41. Liam Stack, "Saudi Men Go to Polls; Women Wait," *New York Times*, September 30, 2011.

42. Shi'a make up around 60% of the citizen population (Gengler 2011). See also Justin J. Gengler, "Religion and Politics in Bahrain: Facts on the Ground: A Reliable Estimate of Bahrain's Sunni-Shi'i Balance, and Evidence of Demographic Engineering," Religion and Politics in Bahrain blog post, 2011, bahrainipolitics.blogspot.com/2011/04/facts-on-ground-reliable-estimate-of.html.

political history of Bahrain is essentially one of conquest by the Sunni Al Khalifa and the subjugation of the Shi'a.[43] Although the degree of sectarian tension has waxed and waned over the past decades, and although there are Bahrainis who argue that the politics of their country should not be seen through an exclusively sectarian lens, the events of 2011 crystalized the sectarian divide. In this context, the constitutional details do not matter much, as long as the dominant faction of the ruling family is not interested in any real sort of political participation by the majority of the population. The Shi'i majority, too, is unlikely to be impressed by the sort of incremental reforms found in the other monarchies of the region. This sort of incrementalism requires a reservoir of support—even soft, conditional support—for the monarchy in the political center. In Bahrain, there is no middle, only a Shi'i majority that wants real change and a Sunni minority that fears that such change will lead to its permanent eclipse. The constitutional problem of the relationship between the ruling family and the parliament, in this context, becomes a question not about the role of the ruling family but a question about which sectarian group rules. Monarchism offers some institutional flexibility in dealing with this problem, but only where the monarch makes a credible effort to stand above and astride the identity cleavage. In Bahrain, instead, the ruling family embodies Sunni hegemony.

That said, it is still worthwhile to compare Bahraini constitutional developments to 2011 with those of its neighbors. The initial 1973 Bahraini constitution was closely modeled on the Kuwaiti constitution, complete with provisions for a vote of confidence in ministers that required only a majority vote of the elected members of the assembly.[44] The assembly elected in 1973, however, endured less than two years before it was shut down, and it did not meet again. In 2000, a year after his accession to the throne following the death of his father, Hamad bin Isa appointed a committee to draft a National Action Charter. The charter—written, some said, mostly by an Egyptian—called for revisions to the 1973 constitution, including the creation of an upper house.[45] The voters approved the charter in a referendum, and the king then issued a revised constitution in 2002 without additional consultation. The new constitution, to the surprise of many Bahrainis, neutered the elected lower house. Both houses have the same number of members (forty), and legislation must pass both houses. In case of disagreement between the two houses, they are to meet together and vote as a single body. This makes it virtually impossible for elected deputies to push through legislation against the

43. Lorimer 1908a, 240, 248–49; Khuri 1980, 47–53.
44. Articles 67, 68, and 69 of the Constitution of Bahrain of 1973.
45. Niethammer 2006, 4–5; Wright 2008, 5.

wishes of the ruling family or to block legislation favored by the government. The new constitution also raises the threshold for a successful vote to remove confidence in a minister to a two-thirds vote of the elected lower house.[46] Given the sectarian divide, and the underrepresentation of Shi'a in the lower house, this is a very high bar.

In Bahrain, more than any other Gulf monarchy, the regime has engineered the electoral system to overrepresent one identity group at the expense of another. The elections of 2006 and 2010 both returned Sunni majorities by design.[47] The 2010 elections, in particular, were preceded by a crackdown on Shi'i political groups.[48] And the regime has embarked on a widespread campaign of naturalization of Sunni foreigners in an effort to change the electoral and demographic composition of Bahrain.[49]

★ ★ ★

Among the constitutions of the Gulf monarchies, the Kuwaiti constitution clearly stands out for its wide grant of political power (or potential political power) to Kuwaiti citizens. The National Assembly has the power to remove confidence in ministers or, in effect, the prime minister, and the assembly has used this power to exert an influence over both the composition of the government and the content of policies. In the next chapter, I ask how it is that Kuwait came to have a powerful National Assembly, when its neighbors did not.

46. International Crisis Group 2005, 5–6.

47. Wright 2008, 8; International Crisis Group 2011a, 8.

48. Ian Black, "Bahrain's Elections Overshadowed by Crackdown on Shia Protesters," *The Guardian*, October 22, 2010, http://www.guardian.co.uk/world/2010/oct/22/bahrain-elections-overshadowed-crackdown.

49. Gengler 2011, 61–67.

Chapter 3

Explaining Kuwaiti Exceptionalism

Why is it that Kuwait has a powerful parliament, but the other Gulf monarchies do not? The best explanation is exogenous to Kuwaiti politics—the threat of Iraqi irredentism impelled the Kuwaiti ruling family to embrace popular representation at key junctures in the 1960s and 1990s. It is important to understand why Kuwait has a strong parliament.[1] In later chapters I argue that the Kuwaiti National Assembly causes a set of political and economic outcomes in Kuwait. If the Kuwaiti National Assembly causes things, it is useful to know what caused the National Assembly itself. I find that the causal factor that triggered the creation of the National Assembly lies outside the borders of Kuwait and is thus largely exogenous to Kuwaiti politics. This makes for a reasonably clear causal chain (or as clear as one can hope for in comparative politics): an exogenous factor caused the rise of the Kuwaiti National Assembly, and the Kuwaiti National Assembly in turn caused a set of political and economic outcomes that differ from the outcomes of Gulf states without a strong parliament.[2]

Explanations

In this chapter, I first discuss existing explanations of Kuwaiti exceptionalism and then ask which explanations best fit the evidence. The larger literature on democratization explains the variation among widely dissimilar cases from a variety

1. Understanding Kuwaiti exceptionalism is also interesting because it has motivated some of the best comparative work on the Gulf, including pieces by Jill Crystal and Sean Yom.

2. If the National Assembly were primarily caused by factors endogenous to Kuwaiti politics, the causal argument would run the risk of becoming circular.

of world regions. This literature, understandably, has difficulty gaining traction in explaining the variation among the Gulf monarchies, largely because these countries resemble each other so much. This is broadly true of explanations that focus on institutions, culture, political economy, population size, and other variables. Kuwait does not stand out from the other five GCC monarchies on most of these variables: it is a dynastic monarchy; it has an Arab Sunni regime presiding over an Arab Sunni population; it is neither the largest nor the smallest in population size; its oil wealth is comparable to that of Qatar and the UAE, and more abundant that that of the other three GCC monarchies.[3] The existing literature on the Gulf, however, does offer several thoughtful explanations for Kuwaiti exceptionalism.

1. The pre-oil class structure (or, relatedly, the ruling coalition constructed by the ruling family) caused the ruling family to open a powerful parliament.
2. The Iraqi threat compelled the al-Sabah to set up the National Assembly.
3. Abdullah Salim (the Kuwaiti emir at independence) had a personal commitment to a strong National Assembly.

Many authors add to this list a fourth mechanism that amounts to a path-dependent argument:

4. Once the institution of the National Assembly was in place, it changed Kuwaiti politics in a way that made the National Assembly more likely to endure.

In this chapter, I focus on explaining the specific path of Kuwait toward greater political participation. This path, however, is not the only possible path that a Gulf state might follow to arrive at the same place (the emergence of a parliament is a phenomenon characterized by equifinality).[4] In the next chapter, I argue that the UAE in the 1970s might have followed a different path to a Kuwaiti-style constitution, although in the end it did not.

Pre-Oil Legacies

Several scholars trace Kuwaiti exceptionalism to the nature of the groups and classes in the pre-oil political economy and the character of ruling family's relations with these groups. In her landmark 1990 book, Jill Crystal compares pre-oil Kuwait and Qatar, arguing that in both countries "merchants renounced their historical claim to participate in decision-making" in exchange for "a sizable

3. Thus, as Sean Yom (2011, 217–18) observes, the rentier state theory offers very little by way of an explanation for Kuwaiti exceptionalism.

4. George and Bennett 2005, 161–62.

portion of oil revenues." But in Kuwait, the relative size, cohesion, and wealth of the merchant class ensured that it would be "bought off, by the state, as a class," and this buying off, even after oil, helped the merchants retain their class cohesion. In Qatar, by contrast, "because the merchant community was smaller and weaker, because it lacked experience in political organization, it did not fare so well" as did the Kuwaiti merchants. Thus, while in Kuwait the ruling family bought off the existing merchant class, in Qatar "the ruler had more scope in determining which nationals to favor." This account is not, itself, an explanation for Kuwaiti exceptionalism; it does, however, contribute to Crystal's explanation of the emergence of the National Assembly. She writes that the National Assembly performed a number of functions for the emir, including serving "as a vehicle for a balancing and, in part, replacing [the merchants] with new, more controllable allies."[5]

In a later article with Abdallah al-Shayeji, the Kuwaiti political scientist, Crystal extends her argument, writing that that the Kuwaiti merchants formed a "genuine class." This class, even deprived by oil of its historical economic power, could "nonetheless retain some negotiating strength, depending on factors rooted in society, not the economy."[6] Thus,

> In an effort to develop new allies to balance the merchants during the phase when the merchants were being pushed out of formal political power, the rulers appealed directly to the population for popular support. They did this in two ways: by offering economic benefits and also by offering political benefits in the form of an elected National Assembly. Political participation actually emerged as a by-product of the coalitional politics practiced by the rulers, as part of the effort to break the merchants' hold on the population.[7]

The merchants, Crystal and al-Shayeji implicitly argue, posed a serious enough threat to the al-Sabah, even in the 1950s and 1960s, that the ruling family found it expedient to open the National Assembly in an effort to bring to the fore political groups that could balance the merchants.

More recently, Sean Yom has engaged the issue of Kuwaiti exceptionalism in a thoughtful article in *Studies in Comparative International Development.* He argues

5. Crystal 1990, 9, 7, 8, 9, 85. The National Assembly also reinforced the distinct political status of the ruling family as an institution, drew a distinction between citizens and noncitizens, and "served at times as a foil for the amir when faced with difficult external problems—in the 1970s with the oil companies, in the 1980s with the Gulf Cooperation Council." (Pa85).

6. Crystal and al-Shayeji 1998, 109.

7. Ibid., 110. See also Crystal 1990, 85.

that the unusual degree of political participation in Kuwait (which he felicitously dubs "popular rentierism") originated in broad regime coalitions assembled in the era before oil, and that these coalitions persisted even after oil. He writes,

> the institutional preferences of rentier autocrats can stem from the legacies of pre-oil social conflict. When weak rulers are threatened by social opposition before oil wealth, they have strong incentives to bargain with those contentious actors in order to survive. These coalitional alliances persist during future hydrocarbon windfalls, because they require costly side payments and institutional investments that become difficult to reverse over time. Conversely, maintaining this wide social foundation precludes the growth of maximalist opposition: during crises, social actors endorse autocracy not out of apathy or fear, but because their own interests are married to the regime's perpetuity.[8]

Yom argues that the Kuwaiti ruling family—in contrast to those of Bahrain and Iran, his comparison cases—assembled a broad pre-oil coalition because (1) the ruling family was relatively weak in 1938 when it faced a major challenge from below and (2) the ruling family received little help from Britain, its great power patron of the time. The weakness of the ruling family—during this crucial period at least—is a trait that Kuwait shared with Bahrain and Iran. In those two cases, however, the regimes received more support from their great power patrons and thus were able to construct narrower regime coalitions.[9]

Rosemarie Said Zahlan suggests a third explanation in this vein, although she does not generalize it into a full theoretical contribution. The Al Khalifa of Bahrain, she observes, came to power through overt conquest, unlike the Kuwaiti ruling family. This contrast, Zahlan suggests, "may well provide an explanation of the difference between the government of Bahrain and that of, say, Kuwait, namely the absence of a traditional dialogue between the ruler and his people."[10] The process by which the ruling family founds its rule leaves a legacy that shapes later political arrangements.

The Iraqi Threat

Virtually all scholars who set out to explain Kuwaiti constitutional exceptionalism cite the Iraqi threat as an important factor.[11] Some scholars, especially Kuwaitis, argue that it is the foremost factor. Thus, Shafeeq Ghabra, a Kuwaiti political

8. Yom 2011, 218.
9. Ibid., 223.
10. Zahlan 1998, 61.
11. Yom 2011, 220.

scientist, writes that the Kuwaiti elite thought that a parliament would help make up for "the lack of population, the small area, and the limited military power" of Kuwait.[12] The title of a study by Abdallah al-Shayeji sums up the point: *Democratization in Kuwait: The National Assembly as a Strategy for Political Survival.*[13] He writes that the "inherent vulnerability, fragility, and quest for survival [of Kuwait] in an increasingly hostile . . . environment dominate and influence its decision making process." He goes on to say that "[t]here is no doubt that the Iraqi threat acted as a catalyst in convincing the ruling elites to facilitate the transition to a parliamentary system" in the early 1960s.[14] Salwa Jama'a, an Egyptian scholar, writes, "there is general agreement that the direct factor that made possible [the 1961 constitution] was the Kuwaiti-Iraqi crisis of 25 June 1961 resulting from the attempt by Abd al-Karim Qasim to annex Kuwait to Iraq."[15] Indeed, the notion that the Iraqi threat was among the most important factors leading to the creation to the National Assembly amounts to the conventional wisdom among Kuwaiti scholars.[16] Western scholars tend to be somewhat less enamored of this explanation, although it regularly appears as one among several explanations for the existence of the Kuwaiti National Assembly and is noted by both Yom and Crystal.[17]

The Kuwaiti emir himself vouchsafed to a Lebanese journalist that the Iraqi threat had a role in the writing of the constitution. The journalist asked if Qasim's threat had had a role in prompting the ruler to accelerate reforms; Abdullah Salim replied, "It is true to a degree if we take into account that adversity shows the true nature of people and rulers, and the truth is that the crisis that we went through made us accomplish in a year what would not [normally] be able to do in five years." He added, however, that "the constitution . . . is nothing more than a legal codification of existing practices in Kuwait, for rule in this country has always been based on consultation among its people."[18]

External threats clearly do not always impel authoritarian regimes to expand political participation. In fact, external threats more often than not have the opposite effect, enabling regimes to suppress dissent in the interest of maintaining

12. Ghabra 1998, 30–31.

13. Alshayeji 1988.

14. Ibid., 70, 69.

15. Jum'ah 1993, 167.

16. These scholars also mention other factors, especially pressure from below, but lead with the Iraqi threat. See for example, Al-Najjar 2000, 66; Baz 1981, 128–29; Al-Ebraheem 1975, 136; al-Ghazali 1985, 9; al-Nafisi 1978, 43–46. Al-Baghdadi (1985, 16–17) stresses the role of Abdullah Salim and pressure from below in addition to the threat from Iraq. See also Zahlan 1998, 48.

17. Crystal and al-Shayeji 1998, 111; Yom 2011, 229.

18. Quoted in Al-Sabah 2000, 495.

a solid front against the enemy. Why is Kuwait different? The explanation lies in the sheer defenselessness of Kuwait —the "lack of population, the small area, and the limited military power," noted by Shafeeq Ghabra.[19] No matter how determinedly Kuwaitis rally around their flag, Kuwait is not able to defend itself from Iraqi aggression without outside help. Kuwait has a small population, most of whom in any case are foreigners. Its territory is flat and poses no natural obstacles to an invading army. As a consequence, Kuwait relies for its protection on foreign powers.

A parliament helps to secure this protection in two ways. First, the outside powers that protect Kuwait have typically not been sympathetic to absolutist monarchies. (Saudi Arabia, of course, is itself an absolutist monarchy, but it is not capable of protecting Kuwait.) Visible signs of political participation lower the cost to these outside powers of protecting Kuwait. This is not to say that outside powers—such as Gamal Abdel Nasser's Egypt or the United States in 1990—have not had good reasons to protect Kuwait anyway. Nasser had no interest in giving up Kuwait to the Iraqis in 1961, and neither did the United States in 1990. The existence of the National Assembly, however, lowers the cost to these outside powers of protecting the Kuwaiti regime, making intervention easier to justify to their domestic constituencies. In 1991, this meant the al-Sabah's promising to restore the National Assembly; in 1961, it meant making concessions to the Arab nationalists that would make Nasser's defense of Kuwait less jarring in the context of his usual hostility toward monarchies.

Second, the National Assembly also gives the al-Sabah a powerful way to display, to the Iraqi regime and the world, the support of Kuwaiti citizens for both the independence of Kuwait and for the ruling family. Although Kuwait would not be hard to conquer, it would be easier to rule if the conquerors were welcomed by the citizens, and such a welcome would also make it much easier for a foreign power to justify its annexation to the world. The notion that some Kuwaitis might welcome an Iraqi invasion is not wholly fanciful; in 1938, following the suppression of the merchants' *majlis*, some Kuwaitis appealed to the Iraqi king to invade Kuwait.[20] And this history was hardly forgotten in 1961 and 1962—Abdullah Salim, the ruler, had played a central role in the events of 1938 and 1939.[21] Many Kuwaitis argue that the invasion of 1990 occurred, in part, precisely because the National Assembly was closed at the time. Neil Hicks and Ghanim al-Najjar write that "the absence of reliable indicators about the

19. Ghabra 1998, 30–31.
20. Crystal 1990, 50.
21. Al-Najjar 2000, 67.

popularity of the government and the ruling family among Kuwaitis citizens enabled Saddam Hussein to form the tragic misperception that an Iraqi takeover in Kuwait would be welcomed by its populace."[22] The National Assembly signals to foreign powers the support of Kuwaitis for their ruling family and for Kuwaiti sovereignty.

Leadership and the Role of Abdullah Salim

The third explanation for Kuwaiti exceptionalism is found in the role of Abdullah Salim, the Kuwaiti emir at independence. Kuwaiti contemporaries and historians tend to agree that he had a personal preference for expanding political participation.[23] Abdullah Salim's relative liberalism came in part from his personal history. He became crown prince before 1938 and had tense relations with the ruler, his cousin. When the merchants set up their assembly in 1938, he was appointed its president. This appointment reflected his favorable attitude toward the assembly, and he remained in good standing with the opposition until he became emir in 1950.[24] There are few other examples of really liberal rulers in the Gulf (and not so many elsewhere, although the ruler of Bhutan appears to be an exception). The father of the current emir of Qatar cultivated a reputation as a liberal after he overthrew his own father in 1995. This, however, did not last; "once the Amir was sufficiently secure in his hold on power, both internally and in relation to neighboring ruling families, promises of a parliament were conveniently forgotten."[25]

Path Dependence

A political institution, once in place, causes additional changes in political practices, institutions, and expectations. Sometimes these have the effect of reinforcing the existence of the institution and making it difficult to dispense with.[26] Yom and others employ path-dependent arguments of this kind to explain how constitutionalism has survived in Kuwait after the ebbing of the initial conditions that caused its emergence.[27] Ismail al-Shatti, a former elected deputy and minister in the Kuwaiti government, writes that the al-Sabah opened a parliament in the

22. Hicks and Al-Najjar 1995, 193.
23. Al-Baghdadi 1994.
24. Al-Najjar 2000, 68.
25. Kamrava 2009, 417; Ehteshami and Wright 2007, 931.
26. Pierson 2004, 20–22.
27. Yom 2011, 224, 239.

first place as a response to external threat but then found it difficult to undo these concessions. He closes an article on Kuwait,

> Kuwait is a treasure that still makes the mouths of the greedy water, and it cannot be protected except by mutual understandings both internally and externally. The rulers chose democracy to guarantee their understanding internally, but after they were able to solidify their external relations, they did not hesitate to retreat from democracy, but the elite had become broader, and the culture had spread to the masses, and retreat from democracy in Kuwait became costly.[28]

Once the National Assembly was in place, it shaped the political life of Kuwait in ways that constrained the ruling family's ability to return to absolutism.

Evidence

To evaluate the theories presented here, I trace the development of the Gulf monarchies through six periods:

- The period in which the ruling families came to power.
- The earliest years of the twentieth century, as a snapshot of the pre-oil political economy.
- The 1930s, which saw a burst of demands for parliaments and constitutions in several Gulf emirates.
- The pre-independence period, including the oil boom.
- Independence, including the writing of the 1962 Kuwaiti constitution.
- The post-independence period.

In each period I examine the evidence for the proposed explanations, asking whether the explanation fits the full set of cases, explains the timing of events in particular cases, and is supported by evidence of causal links between the explanation and the outcome.

The Founding of the Dynasties

Although documentary evidence is missing, there is wide agreement that the leading Kuwaiti families selected the al-Sabah to be the ruling family in the eighteenth century. Abd al-Aziz Al-Rushayd, the author of an early history of Kuwait, writes,

28. Al-Shatti 2003, 139.

"When Kuwait was first founded, governance had no importance, for the al-Sabah and their brothers [the other 'Utub families], owing to their small numbers at the time and owing to their forming one single family . . . did not see the necessity of organizing a government." He continues that this situation prevailed until foreigners moved to Kuwait and it was necessary to impose order on them. The leading families then selected Sabah as their ruler, sometime (it appears from other sources) in the middle of the eighteenth century.[29] Even then, the notion of Kuwait as a single tribe persevered. Midhat Pasha, the Ottoman governor of Baghdad from 1869 to 1872, said of Kuwait that "the incidence of complaints and disputes that would involve the government is rare, the inhabitants really all being like members of a family."[30]

This story of the origins of the ruling family has developed into a powerful political discourse (or creation myth) explaining Kuwaiti "democracy." The website of the Kuwaiti National Assembly retells this history:

> the spirit of democracy started in the year 1752 when the society agreed in this period on the appointment (*tansib*) of the al-Sabah as the rulers of Kuwait using a method known as consensus or consultation. The rule of the family came by way of a process close to what is known as elections (*intikhabat*), in that a majority of the people of Kuwait agreed on who would govern their small, simple society. . . . Those who have come to power in Kuwait have continued, over the course of time, to adhere to the style of dialogue and mutual understanding and consultation as a way of continuing the rule [of the family] and keeping it healthy. . . .[31]

The National Assembly website goes on to assert the existence of a social contract between the al-Sabah and their people. When the people of Kuwait came to give allegiance (the *bay'a*) to the first ruler they did so only "on the condition that he establish justice and equality among the Kuwaitis and consult them and avoid tyranny and that he conduct the affairs of the country according to established principles. . . ."[32] The intent of these retellings of Kuwaiti history is clear. The

29. Al-Rushayd 1978, 90. See also Slot 1998, 131, 155, 185; Abu-Hakima 1965, 54, 58.

30. Quoted in Anscombe 2009, 268. This is a notion of state formation that presages work by anthropologists on the emergence of states from tribal societies. As societies become more complex and kinship ties less comprehensive, a stronger—and usually autocratic—state emerges. On pre-oil Arabian states, see Lienhardt (1975); Rosenfeld (1965).

31. Kuwait National Assembly, "Masirat al-hayat al-dimuqratiyya fi al-kuwayt: Al-muqaddima" [The course of democratic life in Kuwait: Introduction], http://www.kna.kw/clt/run.asp?id = 150 (accessed October 4, 2012).

32. Kuwait National Assembly, "Masirat al-hayat al-dimuqratiyya fi al-kuwayt: mubaya'a ahl al-Kuwayt li-Al al-Sabah (1752)" [The course of democratic life in Kuwait: People of Kuwait give allegiance to the al-Sabah family (1752)], http://www.kna.kw/clt/run.asp?id = 152 (accessed October 4, 2012).

"election" of the ruling family defines the character of its rule even today as limited and consensual.[33]

Does this history provide a good explanation for Kuwaiti exceptionalism today? If so, we would expect to find that the Gulf ruling families, apart from Kuwait, came to power via conquest rather than consensus. And, indeed, this is the case for some of the ruling families. Bahrain offers a sharp contrast to Kuwait, as Zahlan observes. In the mid-eighteenth century Bahrain was a rich prize, with agricultural wealth from its date plantations, a thriving trade economy, and pearling.[34] Shi'i Arabs of no tribal affiliation, known as the Baharna, worked the date plantations. In 1783, the Sunni Al Khalifa family conquered Bahrain and virtually enserfed them.[35] This laid the foundations for the sectarian divide that dominates Bahraini politics today, leaving an unhappy legacy of conquest and repression rather than election and consensus.[36] The ruling families of Saudi Arabia and Oman also came to power via conquest, although neither ruling family is alienated from a majority group in its own population.[37] The Al Saud had historical support in the area around Riyadh, but other parts of the kingdom were conquered outright in the decades after Ibn Saud restored Al Saud rule.

The histories of Qatar, Abu Dhabi, and Dubai fit the theory far less well. Today these three emirates are highly autocratic, as they have been throughout their histories. Yet their ruling families came to power through a process in which one family emerged as the shaykhly family within a tribe or group of tribes—that is, through a process that resembles how the al-Sabah came to rule Kuwait. This was not followed by the conquest of additional territories (as was the case in Saudi Arabia). The first Al Thani ruler of Qatar, according to Crystal, was a pearl merchant with some (limited) influence in the hinterlands, whose power developed on the basis of tribal alliances and economic influence.[38] A more recent account of Qatari history, published in Doha, tells of the emergence of the Al Thani as the consequence of an effort by Qatari tribes to unite together—under the Al Thani—to throw off the influence of the Al Khalifa of Bahrain.[39]

33. See also Crystal 1990, 58; Tétreault 2000, 65.
34. Abu-Hakima 1965, 118.
35. Lorimer 1908a, 240, 248–49; Khuri 1980, 47–53.
36. For one aspect of the sectarian divide, see Holes 2005.
37. The current ruling family of Oman—the Al Bu Said—came to power in the mid-eighteenth century after its leader defeated the Ya'arib dynasty. He was then elected imam according to Ibadhi traditions, although the dynasty no longer claims that title (Allen 1987, 40; Wilkinson 1987, 13–17). The Al Saud have an historical base of support in the Nejd but conquered the Eastern Province, the northern Najdi emirate at Ha'il, the Hejaz, and parts of Yemen. This history left a legacy of provincial resentment (Al Rasheed 1992, 154).
38. Crystal 1990, 29–30.
39. Al-Abdallah 2003.

In Abu Dhabi, the precise events that led to the emergence of the Al Nahyan as the leading family in their tribe—the Bani Yas—in the early part of the eighteenth century are lost to history. It appears that the tribe itself expanded over time, adding to the tribe lineages present in the area of what became the emirate of Abu Dhabi and also developing close alliances with tribes in the shaykhdom that were not properly part of the Bani Yas.[40] This amounted to a process of assimilation rather than conquest, one symptom of which is that the Bani Yas formed a majority of the population of the shaykhdom for much of its existence. When Lorimer published his *Gazetteer* the Bani Yas alone made up nearly 8,000 of the 11,000 settled residents of the principality of Abu Dhabi.[41] In Dubai, the Al Maktoum came to power in 1833 when the family led a dissident faction of the Bani Yas from Abu Dhabi north to found a new shaykhdom along Dubai Creek.[42] The Al Maktoum family held a paramount position in the breakaway tribal section from the beginning.

The Qawasim ruling family—one branch of which now rules Sharjah and a second branch rules Ras al-Khaimah—once ruled an empire that straddled the lower Gulf, including Lingeh and other possessions on the northern shore.[43] Fauke Heard-Bey contrasts the empire with that of Abu Dhabi, which did not expand through conquest; of the Qawasim, she observes that "it could not have been an easy enterprise to bring under their domination the many tribes . . . living along both coasts of the Musandam Peninsula and the imposing mountains of the Hajar range," although—noting the lack of historical records—she also speculates that "most tribes were not subdued by force."[44] In any case, the empire shrank during the nineteenth and twentieth centuries to what is, today, Sharjah and Ras al-Khaimah. In Sharjah, the Qawasim ruling family wound up presiding over a citizen population in which the Qawasim are the largest tribe.[45] In Ras al-Khaimah, by contrast, the largest tribal group is the Shihuh, whom a British visitor in the mid-nineteenth century described as having "an implacable hatred of the Qawasim."[46] Hendrik Van der Meulen notes that this tension between the ruling family of Ras al-Khaimah and the bulk of its citizens continues to this day. As a consequence, "one notes [in Ras al-Khaimah] a much more self-contained and less 'representative' form of government."[47]

40. Davidson 2009, 4–7; Heard-Bey 2004, 42–47.
41. Lorimer 1908a, 408.
42. Heard-Bey 2004, 239.
43. Davies 1997, 56–60.
44. Heard-Bey 2004, 68.
45. Van der Meulen 1997, 208.
46. In Heard-Bey 2004, 80.
47. Van der Meulen 1997, 228, 431.

Overall, variation in the method by which ruling families came to power does little to explain Kuwaiti exceptionalism. The history of the accession to power of the al-Sabah family does not differ that much from that of the Al Maktoum of Dubai, the Al Nahyan of Abu Dhabi, or the Al Thani of Qatar.[48] In Kuwait, perhaps the "election" of the al-Sabah was more of a deliberate act than it was in the other emirates, although the details of the exact process were recorded only much later. In any case, the differences seem much too small to explain variation in the later development of the emirates.

Pre-Oil Political Economy in Lorimer's Gazetteer

The role of the merchant class in the pre-oil Gulf receives a good deal of attention in theories of Kuwaiti exceptionalism. In this section, I examine the strength of the merchant—and other—classes across the shaykhdoms of the Gulf to determine whether Crystal's thesis explains cases beyond Kuwait and Qatar, such as Bahrain, Abu Dhabi, and Dubai. I use data from Lorimer's *Gazetteer*, compiled by the British in the first years of the twentieth century. The *Gazetteer* provides an unequaled source of comparative data on the various shaykhdoms in the period not too long before the advent of oil. It thus provides an excellent baseline for understanding the pre-oil political economy. I examine each of the main sources of wealth in the pre-oil shaykhdoms—date plantations, pearling, and trade—and the classes arising from these; I then consider the comments in the *Gazetteer* concerning the nature of rule in the various principalities.

Date Plantations. In premodern societies, class structure was typically heavily influenced by the system of agrarian landholding, with the repression of agrarian labor often having long-term negative effects. In the Gulf, however, most shaykhdoms had little by way of agriculture. Of Kuwait, Lorimer writes that "neither Kuwait town nor its environs can boast of any agricultural resources. There are no date plantations, no fields, hardly even a kitchen garden."[49] Of Qatar, he writes, "Agriculture hardly exists."[50] So, too, the shaykhdoms of the Trucial Coast had little agriculture beyond the occasional date garden, and they were

48. The role of consensus in the history of any of the shaykhdoms should not be exaggerated. The pre-oil Gulf was not an egalitarian tribal democracy. The leading tribes exercised political, economic, and social domination over other groups: the Shi'a, those of no tribal origin, slaves, and subordinate tribes. See, for example, Sweet 1964, 269–70.

49. Lorimer 1908b, 1052. See also al-Jasim 1997, 194. Dickson (1956, esp. 61–65) documents a very modest agricultural economy in some of the outlying areas.

50. Lorimer 1908b, 1532, 1506.

TABLE 3.1.
Composition of state revenues around 1906

	Total revenue (INR)	Pearling (%)	Customs (%)	Dates (%)	Other (%)
Abu Dhabi	100,415	82		14	4
Ajman	4,600	Pearling, "inconsiderable" revenue from dates (Lorimer 1908a, 53)			
Bahrain	300,000	7	50	33	10
Dubai	68,362	"largely derived from the pearl fisheries" (Lorimer 1908a, 454)			
Kuwait	530,670	15	38	27	20
Oman	503,379		80	3	17
Qasimi realm (Sharjah & Ras al-Khaimah)	33,400	70	26		4
Umm al-Quwain	19,000+	Mostly pearling			

Sources: Lorimer (1908a, 53, 251, 409, 454; 1908b, 1076, 1421, 1760–61).

Notes: INR, Indian rupees. Revenue values not in Indian rupees were converted using the conversion suggested by Lorimer (1908b, 1414) for the value of Maria Theresa dollars to rupees (126 to 139) in Muscat in 1904. Kuwaiti agricultural revenues are from date plantations in Iraq. No data are given for Doha in the source.

net importers of dates.[51] But date plantations on a large scale did exist in what became the emirate of Abu Dhabi, in the Eastern Province of Saudi Arabia, and in Bahrain, where dates accounted for around one-third of the income of the ruler, according to the *Gazetteer* (see table 3.1). In the late nineteenth and early twentieth centuries, Oman also had a booming export industry in dates.

The cultivation of dates lent itself to a political economy based (at least potentially) on the repression of labor. Thus, we see the repression of the Baharna by the Al Khalifa and similar repression of the Arab Shi'a of the Eastern Province of Saudi Arabia by the local Sunni *bedu* (bedouin).[52] Slavery flourished in the Omani Batinah to supply the lucrative date industry with labor.[53] Yet where there was no sectarian divide between rulers and the ruled, repression of the agricultural work force was far less pronounced. The position of the Dhawahir of Buraimi illustrate the contrast. The *Gazetteer* says that the Dhawahir—the tribe of date cultivators in Buraimi—were "subservient to the shaykh of Abu Dhabi, to whom they even

51. Heard-Bey 2004, 115, 177.

52. Lorimer (1908b, 1536) writes of the settled population of Qatif that "in addition to the sedentary population some Bedouins . . . frequent the oasis and are held in fear by the timid Baharinah."

53. Hopper 2010.

pay tribute."[54] But the Dhawahir are Sunni; they raised camels and made up a fighting force whose allegiance could be useful. In some periods in the eighteenth century, the tribe had a prominent role in helping the Bani Yas establish control over the oasis.[55] Today, the Dhawahir occupy many key positions in the armed forces and are a privileged tribe in Abu Dhabi.[56]

Kuwaitis, including the ruler, owned date plantations along the Shatt al-Arab in Ottoman Iraq. Income from date plantations made up over a quarter of the ruler's revenues in the period covered in the *Gazetteer.* The ruling family owned these date plantations from sometime in the early nineteenth century through the end of World War II.[57] Thus, the political consequences of date plantations in Kuwait were limited to the extra income available to the ruler—but no class of subordinate date cultivators lived in Kuwait itself.

Pearling. Up to the 1920s, pearling provided the main source of income for the Gulf coastal shaykhdoms and was their principal tie to the world economy.[58] Pearling boats tended to be spread out among Gulf ports. Of the eight hundred or so boats in Qatar recorded in the *Gazetteer*, only about three hundred were in Doha, with the rest scattered among smaller towns. Bahrain had the largest pearling fleet, with 917 boats. The other major Gulf ports—Kuwait, Abu Dhabi, Dubai, Doha, and the Qasimi ports of Sharjah and Ras al-Khaimah (together)—had between three hundred and four hundred boats each (table 3.2).

Pearling tribes not infrequently lived in villages set somewhat apart from the seats of shaykhs and operated as potentially self-contained economic and social units.[59] This allowed them to migrate from one shaykhdom to another, and this in turn gave them some leverage against the shaykhs. According to James Onley and Sulayman Khalaf, "migration is a dominant theme in Gulf history."[60] Peter Lienhardt similarly notes that the threat of migration limited the power of shaykhs.[61]

54. Lorimer 1908a, 440. See also Heard-Bey 2004, 39, 120.
55. Heard-Bey 2004, 38, 47–50; Van der Meulen 1997, 157.
56. Van der Meulen 1997, 156–60, 379–83.
57. Slot 2005, 12, 65; Smith 1999, 47–48.
58. The exception is Oman, which exported dates. On pearling see Carter 2005.
59. Khuri 1980, 65–67.
60. Onley and Khalaf 2006, 197. Khuri 1980, 35–67.
61. Lienhardt 1975, 63. Even so, the threat of migration had declined in value even before oil. The British, over time, discouraged the founding of new shaykhdoms, discouraging the sort of migrations that led to the founding of Dubai and Zubarah. The migration of the Dawasir tribe from Bahrain to the mainland in the 1920s—in protest of being subjected to the same tax collection regime as the Baharna—ended in failure. Ibid., 72; Khuri 1980, 96–98.

TABLE 3.2.
Pearling fleets, population, and armed retainers in the Gulf shaykhdoms, circa 1906

	Pearling boats	Armed retainers	Settled population	Source
Abu Dhabi	410	n/a	11,000	Lorimer (1908a, 405–11)
Ajman	40	n/a	750	Lorimer (1908a, 52–53)
Bahrain	917	200 (plus 240 of brother and sons)	99,272 (including villages)	Lorimer (1908a, 238, 243, 252)
Doha	350 (817 in all of Qatar)	n/a (Ottoman garrison in Doha)	12,000 (27,000 in Qatar)	Lorimer (1908a, 487–91) Lorimer (1908b, 1532–33)
Dubai	335	100	"10,000 souls or rather more"	Lorimer (1908a, 454–56; 455 quote)
Kuwait	461	100	35,000 (plus 13,000 bedouin)	Lorimer (1908b, 1051, 1053, 1076)
Oman	None mentioned	1,050	471,650	Lorimer (1908b, 1411, 1423)
Sharjah Ras al-Khaimah	360	20 70	18,750 16,000	Lorimer (1908b, 1759, 1761)
Umm al-Quwain	70	n/a	5,000	Lorimer (1908b, 1475)

Notes: n/a, not available.

Although pearling was a constant in the shaykhdoms, some rulers depended on taxes from pearling to a far greater degree than did others, largely as a consequence of the availability of alternative sources of revenue from agriculture or trade. We might expect that these rulers would be less autocratic, given that their citizens were more mobile. Yet Kuwait—because it had a trading economy—relied on pearling *less* than some of the other shaykhdoms, especially Abu Dhabi, Dubai, and, very likely, Qatar (see table 3.1).

Trade. Although the pearling fleets of the Gulf were spread out among the shaykhdoms, trade was much more concentrated. One direct way of measuring the volume and importance of trade, at least during this period, was the frequency of visits from steamers, carefully recorded in Lorimer's *Gazetteer* (table 3.3).[62]

62. The importance of steamer visits was also apparent later on, after Ibn Saud established his control over Nejd and the Eastern Province. He attempted to convince the British to send steamers to the Gulf ports of the Eastern Province. Failing that and failing to negotiate collecting Saudi customs at the Kuwaiti port, he later imposed an embargo on trade with Kuwait (al-Jasim 1997, 59–60).

TABLE 3.3.
Visits by British flagged steamers to the Gulf shaykhdoms, 1905–1907

	Number of visits
Abu Dhabi	None
Ajman	None
Bahrain	65 visits in 1905
Doha	None
Dubai	34 visits in 1906–1907
Kuwait	50 visits in 1905–1906
Oman (Muscat)	302 visits in 1906–1907
Sharjah	None
Ras al-Khaimah	None
Umm al-Quwain	None

Sources: Lorimer (1908a, 246; 1908b, 1058, 1187, 1440).

Notes: In addition, Bushehr had 158 visits in 1905–1906, and Muhammerah, the port and capital of Arab shaykhdom of Arabistan (later subdued by Persia) had 143 during this period (Lorimer 1908a, 129, 356).

According to this measure, Bahrain was the most important port among the Gulf shaykhdoms, followed by Kuwait and Dubai (although we should keep in mind that the main ports in the Gulf were those in Basra and Bushire (Bushehr), which directly served Ottoman Iraq and Persia). Bahrain had long been an important pearling port (mentioned even in Roman times), and in Lorimer's time much of the Gulf trade in pearls was conducted there.[63] Dubai, at the time, was beginning its commercial ascent by attracting the trade that had begun to flee the port town of Lingeh, on the northern side of the Gulf. It also was the main port for the Trucial Coast emirates.[64] A great deal of trade also went on in Kuwait, which benefitted from its position outside the control of the Ottomans (whose rule otherwise stretched from Basra to Qatar).[65] This also meant that the mobility of merchants who relied on trade, rather than pearling, was limited: if they left Kuwait, they would lose the advantages of its privileged geographic position.

More steamers visited Muscat than any of the Gulf shaykhdoms, due to its flourishing trade in dates. Although this presumably produced a strong merchant

63. Carter 2005, 144; Wilson 1833, 284; Lorimer 1908a, 245.

64. Abdullah 1978, 104; Heard-Bey 2004, 189. According to Abdullah, steamers started visiting Dubai in 1903.

65. "Kuwait owes its mercantile, as distinguished from its political importance, to its pearling and coasting fleet, to trade—especially a lucrative smuggling trade—with Persia and Turkish Iraq, and to the fact that it is the only port served Najd which is not under Turkish control" Lorimer 1908b, 1055.

class, trade was almost wholly in the hands of foreign merchants, especially Indian Hindus and Khojas.[66] This made the merchants a less potent political force than otherwise might have been the case.

The shaykhdoms, then, fall generally into two groups: those with pearling and trade (Kuwait, Bahrain, and Dubai) and those that relied on pearling alone (Abu Dhabi and Qatar). Oman and, to a somewhat lesser degree, Bahrain also benefited from date farming. This provides a very useful understanding of the political economy of the pre-oil Gulf, but it does not explain later Kuwait exceptionalism. The pre-oil economy of Kuwait resembled that of Dubai and Bahrain, two emirates whose later history did not lead to sustained constitutionalism.

Lorimer's Comments on the Nature of Rule in the Shaykhdoms. In the *Gazetteer*, Lorimer also comments on the political structures of the Gulf emirates, comparing the degree of despotism across the shaykhdoms. Of Kuwait, he writes that it is "despotically and personally governed by the Shaikh. There is no delegation of authority. . . ." He continues,

> The present Shaikh's method of government is among the most remarkable peculiarities of the principality. Mubarak's rule is personal and absolute; and if in some respects it is mild and tolerant, in others it is exceedingly strict. On the whole, it may be said that in the town he exacts absolute submission and in the country is content with general loyalty and obedience; but this dictum implies a higher degree of control than might at first be supposed, inasmuch as in Kuwait the whole country depends for its wealth and prosperity on one town, and the political predominance of the capital is her greater than in almost any country.[67]

Bahrain, another trading port, was less strictly ruled: "The Government of Bahrain is of a loose and ill-organised character."[68] While Lorimer does not comment on the authority of the ruler of Dubai in the town, he does note that "Inland, the influence of the Shaikh of Dibai is doubtful."[69]

There is also variation among the principalities that relied mostly on pearling. Lorimer says of the ruler of Qatar that his authority "is not by any means absolute or despotic throughout [Qatar]."[70] But the ruler of Abu Dhabi had a stronger

66. Speece 1989, 503–7.
67. Lorimer 1908b, 1058, 1074–75.
68. Lorimer 1908a, 248.
69. Ibid., 454.
70. Lorimer 1908b, 1535.

position: "The present Shaikh . . . rules his principality absolutely within the limits to which his powers of coercion extend; and, though his control over the Bedouin portion of his subjects is incomplete, as is the case more or less in all Arab Shaikhdoms, his authority over them is unusually great."[71]

If Kuwait was exceptional in Lorimer's time, it was for the *greater* degree of its despotism. The *Gazetteer*, to be sure, paints a picture of Kuwait at a particular moment in its history. Mubarak the Great transformed the relationship between the ruler and the merchants after he murdered two of his own brothers and seized power in 1896.[72] Until then, the balance of power between the merchant aristocracy and the al-Sabah had favored the merchants. Abdalaziz al-Rushayd, in his 1926 *History of Kuwait*, writes that "Rule in Kuwait remained consultative from the days of [the first Sabah] to the days of Mubarak al-Sabah [who ruled from 1896]. The ruler consulted with the notables about issues, and how to protect the country from emergencies and protect it from attack. The ruler did not have the power of refusal or choice once the notables had made up their minds because the notables had the real power. . . ."[73]

Rulers before Mubarak had asked the merchants for money; Mubarak, by contrast, built a customs house and imposed taxes. Frederick Anscombe writes that he perfected "a market taxes regime" and became a rich man himself who, at least occasionally, lent money to others.[74] Thus, in at least one sense, the fiscal basis of Mubarak's despotism relied on the Kuwaiti trade economy; he could not have gotten away with this level of autocracy in a town that relied wholly on pearling. It is also possible that, compared to Dubai, the ruler of Kuwait could afford to be more autocratic because Kuwaiti trade benefitted from its privileged geographic position outside the tariff boundaries of the Ottoman Empire. Overall, however, it appears that a trade economy guaranteed neither merchant power nor shaykhly despotism.

The Majlis *Movements of 1938*

In 1938, the Kuwaiti merchants set up a legislative council (*majlis*) that both deeply challenged the authority of the ruler and introduced a number of innovations—and expansions—of state power. The Council is widely seen as a precursor to today's National Assembly, and thus this episode is often seen as an important

71. Lorimer 1908a, 409.
72. Slot 2005, 66–76, 123–24, 317–22.
73. Al-Rushayd 1978, 90.
74. Anscombe 1997, 114; Lorimer 1908b, 1076.

part of an explanation of Kuwaiti exceptionalism. But Kuwait was not the only emirate that experienced unrest in 1938; so, too, did Bahrain and Dubai, not coincidentally the other two Gulf shaykhdoms with a strong trade economy during this period and, thus, an influential merchant class.[75] All three of these cases resulted in the defeat of the merchants, although the winner varied across the three shaykhdoms. The Kuwaiti Council left a memory of merchant participation. In institutional terms, however, the events of 1938 and 1939 in Kuwait *strengthened* the hold of the ruling family as an institution over the state.

Kuwait. Why did the Council emerge in the late 1930s, and what do the circumstances of its emergence say about the later emergence of the National Assembly in the 1960s and about Kuwaiti exceptionalism generally? There is some agreement that new oil revenues had a major role in the emergence of the *majlis* movements in all three states. Crystal argues that the merchants challenged the ruler in the late 1930s "in part because of a dawning understanding that oil would deprive them of their critical role in providing revenue, and with that cost them their power."[76] In 1938, "the merchants demanded a say in the distribution of the new revenues; the rulers, realizing the merchants could no longer compel such input, refused. The merchants, however, fought back politically."[77] The emphasis here is on the Council as an outgrowth of the aspirations of the merchants, although Crystal also mentions two other factors: "economic dislocation of the preceding decade" and "divisions within the ruling family." Of these three factors, the first (merchant aspirations for a council) was reasonably constant throughout the 1930s—and, indeed, all the way back to the days of Mubarak the Great and forward to the writing of the constitution in the early 1960s. Economic problems, of course, also came and went. Although the economy was not good in the 1930s, Kuwait, Dubai, and Bahrain had trade to fall back on when the pearling industry collapsed. The factor that was different in the late 1930s was the struggle within the ruling family, prompted in part by new oil revenues.[78]

In the 1930s, the rulers of Kuwait, Dubai, and Bahrain were beginning to receive new sources of revenues from abroad in the form of actual oil revenues (Bahrain), oil concession agreements (Kuwait), and oil concessions and airfield landing rights (Dubai). Merchants, of course, wanted control of these revenues, but so did the rulers' relatives. The dynastic monarchies of later years had yet to emerge; few members of the ruling families held formal offices in the state, and

75. Zahlan 1980, 66.
76. Crystal 1990, 55.
77. Ibid., 57.
78. Zahlan 1980, 74.

few had direct access to the ruler's new revenues. In all three shaykhdoms, the merchants allied with dissident members of the ruling families to demand a council from the ruler. The result was an unusually isolated ruler, especially when, as in Kuwait, the British initially sided with the Council. On one side was the ruler and his closest allies; on the other were the other members of the ruling family (including, in Kuwait and Bahrain, the crown prince), the merchants, and sometimes the British.[79] This was not an equal match. To round out Ahmed's troubles, the Iraqi regime promoted the efforts of the Kuwaiti opposition, especially in Iraqi newspapers.[80] All this was more than the ruler could resist, and it is not surprising that in 1938 he acceded to the merchants' demands to hold elections to a *majlis*.

The merchant's *majlis*, however, could not survive after the dissident shaykhs and the British turned against it. The British turned against the Council because the British policy in the Gulf had been to maintain order by holding the ruling shaykhs accountable for what happened in their realms. The *majlis* in Kuwait threatened to upset this arrangement by interfering in the ruler's relations with the British.[81] For their part, the dissident shaykhs of the al-Sabah used the Council as a way to demand a share of the ruler's power and purse. When the ruler needed their help in 1939, the shaykhs of the ruling family came together to shut down the Council permanently. With the *majlis* out of the way, the shaykhs divided up control of the leading departments of the Kuwaiti state among themselves.[82] This fundamentally changed the nature of the political regime in Kuwait. Before the Legislative Council of 1938, the ruler had ruled largely alone. After the closing of the Council in 1939, the leading figures of the ruling family shared power with the ruler—and they shared his revenues.

The formation of a family regime—a dynastic monarchy—was imitated by the other Gulf ruling families over the subsequent decades. The regimes that were thus created were resilient enough to survive to the present day.[83]

The events of 1939 in Kuwait may have fed into the myth of consensual government in Kuwait, but the actual effect of the closing of the *majlis* was to make absolutism in Kuwait much more durable by giving the ruling family a much greater stake in its survival. Ahmad al-Khatib, in his memoirs, captures the nature of the change:

> None of the members of the al-Sabah, except rarely, received any [positions as heads of] government departments before the events that led to the dissolution of

79. Herb 1999, 72; Al-Sabah 2000, 129.
80. Crystal 1990, 53.
81. Al Rumaihi 1975, 38.
82. Herb 1999, 72–75; al-Khatib 2007, 259.
83. Herb 1999.

> the Legislative Council in 1939, and after these events Kuwait came to be ruled directly by the emir and some members of the ruling family in an absolutist style, and they began to behave according to a new mentality that did not differ from the mentality of princes of districts that arrive in power "by the sword."[84]

Dubai. The Dubai *majlis* movement of 1938 emerged after that of Kuwait and in response to it. It differed Kuwait on two main counts: (1) the composition of the merchant class differed and (2) the suppression of the Majlis did not lead to the formation of a dynastic regime.

In Dubai, the distinction between the ruling family and the merchants—which was quite clear in Kuwait—was blurred. The Council included merchants who in Kuwait would have been considered members of the ruling family; it also included merchants from the larger Al Bu Falasah section of the Bani Yas tribe, the section that had migrated from Abu Dhabi to Dubai to found the town. These were lineages distinct from that of the ruling family itself.[85] One result was that discussions about the Council tend to see it as an emanation of the ruling "family," which included what might better be called members of the tribal section of the ruling family.[86] This did not make it any less a council of merchants; as Zahlan points out, "the Ruling Family was made up essentially of merchants"[87] In Kuwait, by way of contrast, although it is the true that the aristocratic merchant families share a common Nejdi Arab descent with the al-Sabah and together made up the ' Utub tribal group, the 1938 *majlis* was an affair of the merchant aristocracy, and no one would confuse it with the ruling family. Dubai also had a larger non-Arab merchant class than did Kuwait.[88] The separation between the Bani Yas and other merchants had a geographic component. The Bani Yas Arab merchants lived mostly in Deira, on the north side of the creek that divides Dubai. The Persian merchants lived on the south side. The ruler, too, lived on the south side of the creek, in what often is seen as a residential indication of partiality.[89]

84. Al-Khatib 2007, 259.

85. For a discussion, see Van der Meulen 1997, 192–95. According to Rosemarie Said Zahlan, the members of the council suffered from an inability "to distinguish between themselves as part of a governing body and themselves as members of the Al-bu-Falasah, '*a'ilat al-hukuma*'" (Said [Zahlan] 1970, 260). Davidson (2008, 32), citing British documents, mentions several distinct families, apart from the ruling family, whose members led the *majlis* movement. Al-Rokn (1991, 126), who examined the names in the correspondence between the council and the ruler, says that "they were leading members of the ruling clan or tribe."

86. Al-Aqqad 1992, 282.

87. Said 1970, 249.

88. Crystal 1990, 39; Lorimer 1908a, 105); Slot 2005, 40, 336. Lorimer mentions Hindu merchants under British protection in Dubai and Bahrain, but not Kuwait.

89. Al-Sagri 1988, 164.

Two specific merchant complaints directly led directly to the 1938 Majlis: the ruler (under pressure from the British) sought to limit both slavery and the trade in firearms. The dissident merchants were heavily involved in both.[90] More generally, the double punch of the collapse of pearling and the depression of the 1930s harmed their interests to a greater degree than it did the interests of the substantial class of non-Arab merchants in Dubai. The Arab merchants, it is often noted, were more seriously hurt by the decline in pearling than were Dubai merchants of non-Arab origin, who were engaged in trade and were not directly involved in the pearling industry.[91] The ruler, meanwhile, enjoyed new revenues from oil concessions and airfield agreements with the British, and the dissident members of his family and the merchants of his tribe wanted him to share these funds more widely.[92]

For their part, the British were not enthusiastic about the Dubai *majlis* from the beginning, having had disputes with the dissident members of the ruling family over slavery, arms trading, and other issues in the past. But the British did not prevent the emergence of the Dubai *majlis*, and at a crucial point they advised the ruler to offer reforms.[93] Once the *majlis* was in place, the British opposed efforts by the Majlis to interfere in Dubai foreign relations and in relations with the oil company, which the British saw as a prerogative of the ruler alone.[94]

Despite the less propitious political environment, the Dubai Council nonetheless was formed in October of 1938, inspired by the Kuwaiti Council.[95] The *majlis* took over state income, giving the ruler an allowance of only one-eighth of the income; for a brief period before its end, the Council even took over the ruler's income from the oil concessions.[96] The *majlis*, like its Kuwaiti counterpart, set about to modernize the administration of Dubai, setting up schools, reforming the customs house, organizing a police force, and so forth.[97] As in Kuwait, the ruler eventually turned the tide and suppressed the Council, using the occasion of his son's marriage to a woman of the Abu Dhabi ruling family to invite bedouin into the town. The bedouin routed the dissident members of the ruling family and the merchants, bringing a permanent end to the *majlis*.

90. Said 1970, 254–55; Butti 1992, 219–21; Al-Sayegh 1998, 95.
91. Heard-Bey 2004, 253–54.
92. Al-Rokn 1991, 121; Said 1970, 256; Abdullah 1978, 128.
93. Said 1970, 257–59; Al Rumaihi 1975, 60.
94. Al Rumaihi 1975, 62–63; Al-Rokn 1991, 135.
95. Said 1970, 258; Abdullah 1978, 129; Al-Rokn 1991, 121.
96. Said 1970, 258, 261.
97. Al Rumaihi 1975, 61–62; Davidson 2008, 33, 36.

But when the ruler defeated the Council in Dubai, he also defeated the dissident branch of the ruling family. In Kuwait, by contrast, the dissident branch of the ruling family itself turned on the Council and helped the ruler suppress it. Thus, a dynastic monarchy emerged in Kuwait in 1939 but not in Dubai.[98] This is arguably the key distinction between the experiences of Dubai and Kuwait in the 1930s. It does not, however, offer us much in the way of an explanation for later Kuwaiti exceptionalism. Indeed, the Kuwaiti family regime created in 1939 was more durable and autocratic than the somewhat more personalized autocracy that emerged in Dubai.

Bahrain. The Bahraini *majlis* movement of 1938 did not result in the actual creation of a Council. Of the three *majlis* movements, the British displayed the greatest initial opposition to the idea of setting up a council in Bahrain, and this goes far in explaining its early failure. The initial and much stronger British hostility to the 1938 *majlis* movement in Bahrain can be explained by the much greater level of British involvement in the administration of Bahrain. In the early 1920s, the British resident (the senior British official in Bahrain) deposed the Bahraini ruler in favor of the ruler's son; the British resident then imposed a series of reforms on Bahrain that were intended, in large part, to force the ruling family to tax, and otherwise rule, the Shi'a on the same basis as the Sunnis.[99] One consequence of the imposition of these reforms in the 1920s was the emergence of the British adviser as, in many ways, the effective ruler of Bahrain. Bahraini reform movements thus focused as much on the British resident as on the ruler himself, a development that did not occur in Kuwait or Dubai, and that did not endear the reform movement to the British.[100]

The movement emerged in the summer of 1938, inspired by the movements in Kuwait and Dubai. Like the movements in those two shaykhdoms, in Bahrain the *majlis* movement was led—at least initially—by, in Khuri's words, "merchant nationalists."[101] Initially, the merchants had the support of the crown prince, who was concerned that his uncle would make a bid for power in the event of the death of his father, the ruler. He did not, however, seem to have much of

98. Herb 1999, 141.

99. Up to that point, the Al Khalifa had not levied much in the way of taxes on Sunnis. "The plan for levying equal taxes, such as land-revenues, on all inhabitants without distinction, though egalitarian in spirit, would, in effect, have amounted to imposing taxation for the first time upon the dominant groups" (Al-Tajir 1987, 37, see also 52). Sunnis protested the reforms vigorously. The Dawasir tribe went so far as to emigrate to Saudi Arabia, although they soon relented and returned (Khuri 1980, 94–99).

100. Musa 1987, 32; Khuri 1980, 110.

101. Khuri 1980, 197; Al Rumaihi 1975, 43–44.

a subsequent role.[102] A younger leadership also emerged, drawn from students, oil company workers, and the like; they were unhappy that foreigners—mostly Indians—were receiving jobs in the new oil industry. This younger group led strikes and demonstrations in early November. The regime—which is to say the British adviser—suppressed the movement by placating the Shi'a and arresting Sunni leaders.[103] The result was the expeditious defeat of the reform movement.

Qatar, Abu Dhabi and the Other Shaykhdoms. In the shaykhdoms without a large merchant class, there were no reform movements in the 1930s. Instead, the era was marked by a precipitous economic decline as a result of the collapse of the pearling industry.[104] Crystal writes that the population of Qatar declined from 27,000 in Lorimer's time to 16,000 at the end of the Second World War; oil exports revived the economy after 1949.[105] Abu Dhabi flourished in the latter part of the nineteenth century but stagnated in the first half of the twentieth, even before pearling collapsed. The population of Sharjah fell from 15,000 in 1909 to 5,000 in 1939.[106]

The absence of a *majlis* movement in Oman was not due to the absence of a merchant class. For two centuries, until the mid-nineteenth century, Oman was "the major Asian power in the western Indian Ocean" with trading networks ranging from the Gulf to India to East Africa and beyond.[107] Decline set in thereafter, but Muscat nonetheless had a very substantial trade by the standards of the Gulf shaykhdoms. The political quiescence of the merchant class seems to be best explained by the fact that the merchant class of Muscat and Matrah was composed almost wholly of Indians. As a foreign minority, the merchants had little to gain through political agitation to expand political participation.[108] Recall that in Kuwait and Dubai, it was the Arab merchants—not the foreign merchants—who led the reform movements of 1938.

The Postwar Period

After the defeat of the *majlis* movements in Kuwait, Dubai, and Bahrain, the Gulf as a whole saw fewer organized protest movements in the 1940s and into the 1950s. When protest and reform movements emerged again in the 1950s and

102. Al-Tajir 1987, 239; Al Rumaihi 1975, 43.
103. Al Rumaihi 1975, 48, 49; Musa 1987, 34.
104. Zahlan 1978, 8–13.
105. Crystal 1990, 117–18.
106. Zahlan 1980, 66.
107. Allen 1987, 35.
108. Speece 1989, 503–4; Allen 1981.

1960s, the merchants were joined by workers, students, and other newly educated groups, many of them inspired by Arab nationalist ideology.[109] In the 1930s, the pattern of unrest was clear—it occurred in the trading ports. In the 1950s, the most serious unrest was in Qatar, following its oil boom.

Qatar. Qatari politics were turbulent in the 1950s and 1960s—an adjective not associated with politics in Qatar in recent decades. Many of the protests were limited to oil workers, outside Doha, but in 1956 and 1963, protests also occurred in the capital. After that, unrest faded, and Qatari politics took on their current, somnolent mien.

Oil workers led the protests of the first half of the 1950s and directed their ire at the British-run oil company rather than at the ruler. Saleh, in an excellent study of labor in the Gulf in this period, makes it very clear that the problem lay with the management of the oil company, which favored foreign workers over Qataris. In the labor camps, the Qataris lived in huts while foreign labor lived in better quarters; a Qatari worker complained of hunger from inadequate rations at his camp.[110] This led, not surprisingly, to serious protests, whose political impact was blunted only by the fact that the oil camps were hard to access from the capital. The ruler acted as an intermediary between the oil company and the workers, although without much effect until a change in company attitude in 1955.[111] Once the oil company came around and began offering more privileges (and better conditions) to Qatari workers, the ruler took a harder line against strikers, and the protests eventually receded.[112]

Later, in 1956, protests broadened and appeared in Doha. Dissident shaykhs allied with Arab nationalists (of whom there were a few in Qatar) and unhappy oil workers (of whom there were more) agitated against the ruler and the British, culminating in a protest in which some 2,000 participated. The ruler responded not with concessions but by reforming and strengthening his police force, a step he had previously resisted.[113]

Protests resumed in 1963 when dissident second-tier shaykhs, members of well-known Qatari families, Arab nationalists, and oil workers demanded reforms following an incident in which the authorities opened fire on a demonstration.

109. This was true even in the late 1930s in Bahrain, and by the 1950s, education (and oil company hiring) had spread to much of the rest of the Gulf. On the emergence of the new middle class generally, see Halpern 1963.

110. Saleh 1991, 186–87.

111. Ibid., 206.

112. Ibid., 206–7, 268–69; Crystal 1990, 139–45.

113. Crystal 1990, 123, 126–27.

The ruler responded to the protests (and an accompanying petition) with arrests and expulsions; those targeted included members of prominent families. According to Ali Khalifa Al-Kuwari, the residents of several towns, along with a tribal clan, fled to Kuwait. The ruler also announced reforms in response to the protests, including expanding state services and the election of a municipal council in Doha.[114] This combination of repression and concessions quieted the opposition.

Nonetheless, the episode remains one of the more serious bouts of protest in the pre-independence period in the Gulf emirates. The best explanation for it seems to lie in the tardiness of the Al Thani in building a strong state and in distributing oil revenues. The delay not only stoked unhappiness among citizens but also led to a late institutionalization of a family regime by the notoriously factious Al Thani ruling family.

Bahrain. If the sheer volume of dissent determined the level of political liberalization in Gulf monarchies, there is little doubt that Bahrain would be the most liberal of the Gulf monarchies, not Kuwait. As in other periods, Bahrainis protested with frequency and spirit against their rulers in the 1950s and 1960s. In part this was because the oil industry started production in Bahrain early, producing a restive working class that was not quickly made into a labor aristocracy of the sort seen, eventually, in Kuwait, Qatar, and the UAE.[115] A surprisingly wide group led the opposition in the 1950s, including Sunni and Shi'a, workers and merchants.[116] In the end, however, the protests achieved little in the way of substantive reform. From 1956, the British and the regime cracked down, imprisoning some opposition leaders and forcing others into exile.

More unrest occurred in the mid-1960s when the oil company set off an "intifada" by dismissing several hundred Bahraini employees as part of a program to create efficiencies.[117] Merchants did not seem to have much of a role in these protests, which had a distinctly leftist tone.[118] The 1965 protests were, too, met with repression rather than conciliation, which is a general theme in the reaction of the Bahraini regime to demands for greater participation. It was not until after independence, in 1973, that the ruling family allowed the formation of an elected assembly, and then only briefly.

114. Ibid., 153–155; Ali Khalifa Al-Kuwari,"Rahim allah Nasir al-Misnid al-rajl al-ramz" [God bless Nasir al-Misnid, the man, the icon], *Al-Taleea* (Kuwait), April 11, 2007; Al-Tabtabai 1985, 122–23.

115. Khalaf 1985.

116. Khuri 1980, 199–217. Nakhleh (1976, 78) emphasizes the importance of labor in the 1950s opposition.

117. Musa 1987, 84–85; Nakhleh 1976, 79–80.

118. Musa 1987, 76, 83–97.

Abu Dhabi and the Smaller Shaykhdoms of the Trucial Coast. Alone among the major Gulf shaykhdoms, Abu Dhabi escaped political protests in the 1950s and 1960s. For the most part, this seems to have been a result of an economic decline in Abu Dhabi. An observer in the 1950s wrote that in Abu Dhabi "[t]here is little trade and customs revenue is insignificant."[119] Mohammed Al-Fahim, an Abu Dhabi citizen who lived through the period, says that the population of Abu Dhabi (of the town, not the entire territory) had declined by the 1950s to a few thousand.[120] Oil operations developed later in Abu Dhabi than in Kuwait, Qatar, or Bahrain, and it appears that the oil company successfully maintained peace with labor at its operations. In Abu Dhabi town, there were grumblings about the miserliness of Shakhbut bin Sultan Al Nahyan, who ruled from 1928 to 1966, but this did not take form in any sort of opposition movement.[121] Instead, Shakhbut's brother Zayed overthrew him in 1966 and transformed the emirate virtually overnight, spending oil money freely and winning a great deal of popular support among Abu Dhabi citizens.

The smaller emirates had neither oil nor robust trading economies, and thus they had few of the protests seen elsewhere. One author says that, except for Dubai, the Trucial Coast economies in the 1950s were "at a low ebb."[122] Another observer says that the three poorest emirates "lived in a state of almost complete isolation from the outside world, because of their poverty, and because some of their rulers . . . had a policy of imposing isolation upon their emirates."[123] These were not fertile grounds for the emergence of merchant-led or labor-led opposition movements.

Dubai. In the 1950s and 1960s, labor had a much smaller role in dissent in Dubai, in part because Dubai had not yet developed an oil industry. It was, however, a thriving port city, and it had a fractious ruling family. Dissent in the pre-independence period came from merchants and members of the family, sometimes in alliance. In contrast to Kuwait, the ruling family had not yet formed a ruling institution. In the 1950s, dissident members of the family again challenged the ruler, in alliance with Bani Yas merchant families. The result, however, was similar to that in 1938, although less bloody, and the ruler had the British send the dissident shaykhs, along with a member of the Futtaim merchant family, into exile.[124] Before he was exiled, however, the leading dissident shaykh supported

119. Hay 1959, 118.
120. Al-Fahim 1995, 53, 78.
121. Rabi 2006; Al-Fahim 1995.
122. Hay 1959, 117.
123. Al-Tabtabai 1978, 393.
124. Davidson 2007a; Herb 1999, 141–44.

the formation of a Dubai National Front, an organization that espoused Arab nationalism and opposed the influence of non-Arab merchants in Dubai. The front enjoyed the support of prominent Dubai merchant families, including some from the ruling family's Bani Yas tribe, and favored Arab over Persian merchants.[125] The ruler responded to this agitation with a council of merchants (which later became the Chamber of Commerce) and a Municipal Council in 1957.[126] The council of merchants, at least initially, excluded Persian merchants.[127] As was the case in the 1930s, the Arab merchants were in part responding to the commercial successes of non-Arab merchants.

In the 1960s, nationalist agitation against the Al Maktoum faded away, and the Dubai merchants did not again mobilize against the Dubai ruling family. Christopher Davidson's explanation for this bears comparison with Crystal's account of Qatar and Kuwait. Crystal argues that Kuwaiti merchants were bought off as a class while in Qatar the traditional merchant class was so weak it did not require buying off. Davidson says of Dubai,

> as oil revenues finally began to flow (some 20 years later than the first Kuwaiti oil exports), a new form of rentierism began, providing the ruling family with far greater sources of wealth . . . : the population was freed of taxation and able to import goods on an unprecedented scale. Consequently, the previously belligerent merchant families that had formerly backed the National Front lost much of their power base: local young men had money in their pockets and businesses to run, and busied themselves with keeping pace with the region's oil boom rather than concentrating on political reform. Moreover, the powerful notables were themselves handsomely placated as they received exclusive import and construction licences from the ruler. Many of these licences are still in place today, and grant certain families the sole right to operate certain franchises (including Rolex imports, Mercedes distribution, European supermarket chains, etc.). Indeed, it is no coincidence that some of the biggest and wealthiest of Dubai's family trading empires today were the recipients of these licences in the 1960s, and most tellingly featured prominently among the described proponents of the National Front in the 1950s.[128]

That is, if the merchants of Kuwait were "bought off, by the state, as a class"[129] then the fate of the Dubai merchants was similar. Moreover, in both cases, the

125. Davidson 2007a; Al-Sagri 1988, 168–72.
126. Abu-Baker 1995, 140–41.
127. Ibid., 139.
128. Davidson 2007a, 890.
129. Crystal 1990, 7.

process was not nearly the bargain that *buying off* implies. Oil created opportunities for the merchants that, being merchants, they pursued in the absence of any real prospect of gaining traction with their political demands. The differences between the two shaykhdoms become prominent only in the 1960s, when the Iraqi threat induced the al-Sabah to grant a liberal constitution.

Kuwait. During this period, Kuwait experienced little of the labor unrest seen in Bahrain and Qatar. Hassan Saleh attributes this to relatively better conditions for workers, ruling shaykhs who intervened on behalf of workers, a more enlightened oil company, and merchants too busy making money to ally with workers.[130] Opposition to the al-Sabah thus came not from oil workers but, instead, from merchants and (as we have seen in the other shaykhdoms) Arab nationalists, some of whom were the sons of merchant families and others of whom came from more modest backgrounds. Ahmad al-Khatib, the first Kuwaiti medical doctor and a long-time leader of the Arab nationalist opposition, is a preeminent example of the new sort of opposition leader who came from a less privileged background and who gained respect and prestige based on his education.

Major protests in the 1950s included a 1956 demonstration that drew 4,000 onto the streets during the Suez Crisis (and in response to Nasser's call for a strike) and a 1959 rally in which another Arab nationalist leader, Jasim al-Qatami, made a fiery speech. Jasim al-Qatami was the first Kuwaiti graduate of a police academy and had been head of the police force until his resignation in 1956.[131] None of this opposition activity, however, threatened the basic stability of the regime. Indeed, Crystal writes that "in general . . . , especially by regional standards, the opposition was contained," and she documents the increasing authoritarianism of the al-Sabah throughout the 1950s.[132]

Note that the pressure from below that did emerge in Kuwait in the 1950s is a necessary but commonly present condition for the drafting of a liberal constitution. That is, without pressure from below it is hard to imagine a liberal constitution emerging in a Gulf shaykhdom. Nevertheless, pressure from below has been present during several periods in most of the shaykhdoms, and only one adopted a liberal constitution.[133]

130. Saleh 1991, 171–84.
131. Crystal 1990, 81–83; Hamza Olayan, "Jasim al-Qatami: 'Ata'at fi sabil al-kuwayt wa huquq al-'insan wa al-'uruba" [Jasim al-Qatami: Contributions to Kuwait, human rights, and Arabism], *al-Qabas*, July 1, 2012.
132. Crystal 1990, 83.
133. Mahoney, Kimball, and Koivu 2009, 119.

From the closing of the Council in 1939 to the elections in late 1961, the al-Sabah ruled Kuwait in the style of Gulf absolutists. The municipal council continued to meet through the 1940s and into the 1950s; it is not clear whether those elected in August 1938 continued to serve through this period.[134] Elections to advisory councils for several of the government departments (religious foundations, education, and the municipality) were held in 1954. Elected members of these councils sent a delegation to the ruler asking him to form an advisory council for the government as a whole; the ruler refused, and the elected councils resigned. They were replaced by appointed councils.[135] In 1958, an election to an advisory council was held, but it never met as a result of a dispute over government demands that three elected members resign.[136]

Throughout this period, and especially after Abdullah Salim became ruler in 1950, Kuwaiti merchants continued to demand representation on elected councils (and the members of these various councils whose names are available in the sources were mostly merchants). Yet overall, the opposition accomplished little through the 1950s. No elected councils wielded any significant authority, with the possible exception of members of the municipal council, who may have served through the crackdown in 1939 and into the 1940s. The merchants posed no greater threat to the al-Sabah than they had in the 1940s and noticeably less than in the 1930s or earlier. Thus, it seems unlikely that the al-Sabah would set up a National Assembly at independence to "break the merchants' hold on the population."[137] The al-Sabah had captured the state in 1938. Despite the long history of merchant participation in Kuwaiti politics, there is little evidence that the al-Sabah found it difficult to maintain their autocracy. The writing of a constitution and the opening of a new National Assembly hardly seem reasonable responses to the residual threat to the al-Sabah posed by the merchants, whose ability to really threaten the power of the ruler had came to an end in 1939 when the dissident shaykhs of the ruling family formed a dynastic monarchy.

134. Al-Jasim 1980, 40, 43.

135. Al-Najjar (2000, 50, 52–54) also mentions elections to four advisory councils (health was the fourth) in 1951; these, again, were stymied by conflicts with the shaykhs. Al-Jasim does not mention 1951 elections to the municipal council. On this period, see also Al-Sabah 2000, 433–34.

136. Al-Khatib 2007, 198–200.

137. Crystal and al-Shayeji 1998, 110.

Independence

In 1962, following an extended period of absolutist rule, Kuwait adopted a liberal constitution—the most liberal in the Gulf at the time and still the most liberal today. Why in 1962, and why in Kuwait? In this section, I trace the process that led to the writing of the 1962 constitution and introduce evidence that two factors had a role: the Iraqi threat and the liberal leanings of Abdullah Salim. I then consider the role of similar threats to the UAE and Bahrain.

Kuwait and the Iraqi Threat. Kuwait achieved its independence on the June, 19, 1961. A few days later, Abd al-Karim Qasim, the Iraqi prime minister, demanded the annexation of Kuwait by Iraq. By the end of the year, Kuwait had held elections to a Constitutional Convention, and by the end of the next year, the constitution had been issued. Elections were held shortly thereafter. This sequence of events, set out in table 3.4, strongly suggests a causal relationship between the 1962 constitution and the Iraqi threat. No other explanation for Kuwaiti exceptionalism has such a close temporal relationship between the proposed cause and the actual writing of the 1962 constitution.

Iraq posed a diplomatic as well as a military threat. When Kuwait became independent in 1961 its claim to be a fully sovereign member of the international state system was not, on its face, an entirely strong one. The Iraqi historical argument was specious; Kuwait had never in any real sense been part of Iraq. Nevertheless, the other inconvenient facts remained: Kuwait was very small in both population and size, it had a large noncitizen population, it was identified with a single family that ruled it autocratically, it had an (unjustified) reputation as the arbitrary creation of British imperialism, it provoked envy rather than sympathy, and its oil wealth generated the (in fact, well-placed) suspicion that Western powers would have had little interest in making Kuwait a sovereign state if it had not been for its oil. As the Iraqi representative to the UN Security Council put it, Kuwait "was in fact a small town, not to be compared in status with the other States which were United Nations Members." Moreover, oil "was the real motive behind British policy, and the enormous profits of the oil companies coupled with the Sheikh's billion-dollar investments in the United Kingdom were the basis for an unholy alliance between feudalism and colonialism."[138] The Iraqi foreign ministry criticized the Kuwaiti autocracy, saying that the Kuwaiti people had no voice in the government.[139] Even the British ambassador saw problems, writing that "Kuwait

138. This is a summary of the representative's views as presented in the UN *Yearbook of the United Nations 1961* (United Nations 1963, 169).

139. Al-Najjar 2000, 66.

TABLE 3.4.
Time line of the 1962 Kuwaiti constitution

Date	Event
19 June 1961	Independence
22 June 1961	Kuwait applies for membership in the Arab League
25 June 1961	Qasim claims Kuwait for Iraq
30 June 1961	Kuwait requests admission to the United Nations
1 July 1961	British troops land in Kuwait
4 July 1961	Arab League debates whether the admission of new states (such as Kuwait) requires unanimity of member states or a simple majority
7 July 1961	Soviet Union vetoes a British Security Council resolution to "respect" Kuwaiti independence
10-26 July 1961	A delegation of prominent Kuwaitis visits Egypt; Nasser agrees to assemble an Arab force to replace British troops The delegation also visits Saudi Arabia, Sudan, Libya, Tunisia, Morocco, Jordan, and Lebanon
20 July 1961	Kuwait admitted to the Arab League The Iraqi delegation walks out of the meeting in protest The following day the Arab League makes preparations to send Arab troops to Kuwait
26 August 1961	Kuwaiti emir appoints a committee to write a law on elections to the Constitutional Convention
6 September 1961	Law on elections issued
10 September 1961	Arab forces begin to arrive in Kuwait under the auspices of the Arab League; forces are from Saudi Arabia, the UAR, Jordan, Sudan, and Tunisia
10 October 1961	British forces complete withdrawal from Kuwait
30 November 1961	Kuwait applies again for United Nations membership, and the Soviet Union vetoes the application again
30 December 1961	Elections held to the Constitutional Convention
20 January 1962	Opening session of the Constitutional Convention
27 March 1962	Jasim al-Qatami, a prominent Arab nationalist, appointed deputy minister of foreign affairs
11 November 1962	1962 constitution issued
23 January 1963	Elections held to the first National Assembly
9 February 1963	Qasim overthrown and killed
14 May 1963	Kuwait admitted to the United Nations
4 October 1963	Iraqi government formally recognizes Kuwait
12 October 1963	Kuwait provides a loan of 30 million British pounds to the Iraqi government

Sources: Middle East Journal 1961, 423, 433-35; 1962, 71; and sources cited in the text.

faced the task of proving that she was something more than a collection of oil wells sheltering under a new form of British Imperialism."[140]

This sort of sentiment, not limited to Iraqi officialdom, made international recognition of Kuwaiti independence an important thing indeed for Kuwaitis in 1961. And Iraq blocked this recognition in its most important form, which was admission to the United Nations as a full member. Kuwait applied for admission to the United Nations within days of its independence. The Soviet Union vetoed a subsequent British resolution to "respect the independence and territorial integrity of Kuwait."[141]

A few days after the Soviet veto of the Kuwaiti bid for United Nations membership, the ruler sent a delegation of Kuwaitis to visit Arab capitals to seek support for Kuwaiti independence.[142] The delegation included Jaber al-Ahmad, later the emir; two other members of the delegation were from very prominent merchant families (as were the two secretaries and the lawyer who accompanied the mission), and two were associated with the Arab nationalist movement in Kuwait.[143] One prominent member of the delegation, Abdulaziz Hamad al-Saqr, was later elected president of the first National Assembly in 1963, refused his seat in the National Assembly following the electoral fraud of 1967, and headed the Kuwaiti Chamber of Commerce from 1959 to 1996.[144]

Nasser's first question on receiving the delegation was whether it was a delegation of the ruling family or of the Kuwaiti people. Abdulaziz al-Saqr—because of his position and that of his family—was able to answer that it was a delegation of the Kuwaiti people; Shaykh Jaber was there, he said, in his capacity as head of the finance department, and thus was responsible for writing the checks that reinforced the Kuwaiti case.[145] The merchant members of the delegation did most of the talking, reinforcing that the people of Kuwait were united behind their ruler's position.[146] At the end of the meeting with Nasser, he said he would put together an Arab force to replace the British force protecting Kuwait from Iraq.[147]

140. In Smith 1999, 124.

141. Note that this was not, in fact, a motion to admit Kuwait to the United Nations. The United Arab Republic (i.e., Egypt and Syria) abstained from the vote on the UK resolution. "Letter Dated 30 June 1961 from the State Secretary of Kuwait to the Secretary-General," Document S/4852 (United Nations Security Council, June 30, 1961), www.un.org; "United Kingdom of Great Britain and Northern Ireland: Draft Resolution," Document S/4855 (United Nations Security Council, July 6, 1961), www.un.org; "Summary Statement by the Secretary-General on Matters of Which the Security Council Is Seized and on the Stage Reached in Their Consideration," Document S/4858 (United Nations Security Council, July 10, 1961), www.un.org.

142. Al-Najjar 2000, 67–68.

143. Khalifa c2002, 186.

144. Haydar 1997, 24–25.

145. Khalifa c2002, 187–88; Smith 1999, 108.

146. Khalifa c2002, 196.

147. Ibid., 188.

The delegation wrote a report on its return, noting that there was a general sense in the Arab capitals that the system of government in Kuwait was backward and did not reflect the wishes of the Kuwaiti people, and that this should be remedied. The report went on,

> One of the impressions we received on our trip [to the Arab capitals] was that the internal situation of Kuwait has an influence on the image of Arab countries about the Kuwaiti entity. So long as the internal situation in Kuwait is sound and in accordance with modern systems and ways of governing, then the appreciation for Kuwait is greater. It is unfortunate that the prevailing idea among many is that our system of government does not accord with, and is not based on, the opinion of the [Kuwaiti] people.
>
> Despite the consensus of the Kuwait people in the current circumstances, and despite the ties that bind all Kuwaitis by virtue of being a single family bound by fraternal feeling, the demands of the modern age and our participation on the international scene . . . make it impossible for others to imagine the possibility of basing a sound regime except on the basis of a democracy which requires that the people participate, in some form, in taking on the responsibility for rule. And indeed by creating the possibility for this participation we take away a weapon that is often used against us, and which no doubt will be exploited more broadly if we do not take the initiative to create an appropriate system. . . .[148]

Thus, the message of the report was that support from Arab capitals—particularly Cairo—was threatened by the perception that Kuwait was a small, retrograde despotism ruled by a family with little popular support. Changing that perception would make it more likely that the al-Sabah could find support for Kuwaiti sovereignty among the other Arab countries.

From the perspective of decades later, it seems odd that a delegation of Kuwaitis might visit republican Egypt—a regime that eventually produced the thirty-year rule of Hosni Mubarak—and feel that Kuwaiti despotism compared badly. This was, however, 1961, when the intellectual and political bankruptcy of the president-for-life republics were still well in the future and when the republican regimes—and Nasser himself, personally—enjoyed wide popular support. Ghanim al-Najjar points out that Iraqi propaganda in the early 1960s criticized the autocracy of the al-Sabah,[149] a criticism that made more sense in the context of an age when Arab monarchies were viewed by Arab public

148. Ibid., 264–65.
149. Al-Najjar 2000, 66.

opinion as backward and the new republican presidents as leaders of progressive change.

Given utter inability of Kuwait to defend itself without help from larger powers, its need to muster support from the Arab capitals was pressing. The approach to Nasser paid immediate dividends; Nasser agreed to put together a force of Arab troops to defend Kuwait. Even though the troops did not arrive until September 1961, Kuwait was admitted to the Arab League on the July 20; the Iraqi delegation walked out of the meeting in protest.[150]

The British were the first to come to the aid of Kuwait, sending troops that arrived less than a week after Qasim's threat—and the British, too, sent a letter to the emir (according to Ahmad al-Khatib) advising him to broaden political participation.[151] Simon Smith observes that the British "supported the al-Sabah's attempts to broaden the political basis of the regime," even though they were not so enthusiastic about the embrace of Nasser and Arab nationalism.[152]

Nasser, of course, had his own reasons for opposing the Iraqi claim to Kuwait, as did the British during this period (and also, in 1990, the George H. W. Bush administration). In all cases, however, the foreign powers that had an interest in defending Kuwait also found the Kuwaiti autocracy awkward. For Nasser, the problem was that Kuwait was a monarchy dependent on British support that he was defending against Iraq, an Arab nationalist republic. Nasser had built his own popularity on his hostility to the British and his claim to lead a new era in Arab politics built on the support of the people. Political participation in Kuwait would lessen the distance between his proclaimed ideals and the exigencies of power politics that dictated Egyptian support for Kuwait against Iraqi claims.

On August 26, the emir appointed a committee to write a law on elections to a constitutional convention. The commission worked with blinding speed, and the law was issued two weeks later, on the September 6, scarcely two and half months after Qasim issued his threat. The committee included two men who had been members of the second elected council of 1938 along with its secretary, who had fled into exile following the closure of the council.[153] In December 1961, the elections were held. In the meantime, the Arab troops promised by Nasser had arrived in September of 1961,[154] and in November 1961 the United Arab

150. Middle East Journal 1961, 434.

151. Ahmad al-Khatib 2007, "19 June," 7. Al-Najjar (2000, 70) mentions articles in the British press during the period encouraging Kuwait to broaden political participation "in order to preserve its independence."

152. Smith 1999, 124.

153. Al-Ghazali 1985, 9–10; al-Adsani (n.d., "Introduction").

154. Middle East Journal 1961, 435.

Republic (UAR) asked the UN Security Council to take up again the Kuwaiti application for membership in the United Nations; the Soviet Union again vetoed the request.[155]

During this period, the emir continued his rapprochement with prominent Arab nationalists in Kuwait. He appointed two of them, Yacoub al-Humaydi and Jasim al-Qatami, to positions in the emiri *diwan* (the office of the ruler).[156] Yacoub al-Humaydi was from a prominent merchant family and served on the five-man committee that drafted the 1962 constitution; he later resigned from his seat in the National Assembly in 1965 in protest over what he (and other nationalists) saw as anti-democratic laws.[157] Jasim al-Qatami, as noted previously, was the first Kuwaiti to attend a police academy; he was appointed director of the Kuwaiti police force, a position from which he resigned, refusing to participate in a crackdown against Arab nationalist demonstrations.[158] From there, he became the manager of a cinema, but following a fiery speech he made in 1959, the company that owned the cinema was forced to dismiss him.[159] Abdullah Salim rehabilitated him by appointing him to a position in the *diwan al-emiri*; then, in March 1962, he appointed al-Qatami deputy secretary of the Foreign Ministry, "tasked with setting up the ministry of foreign affairs." Al-Qatami hired the nucleus of the Kuwait diplomatic corps from Kuwaitis with Arab nationalist leanings and was thus able to lay the basis "for the clear Arab nationalist leaning of Kuwaiti foreign policy."[160] Of course, Abdullah Salim got something from this as well. The Arab nationalists in the Foreign Ministry represented the face of Kuwait to the Arab world, and their adherence to the Arab nationalist cause defused accusations that Kuwait was a reactionary opponent of Arab nationalism. Ghanim al-Najjar writes that the agreement of prominent Arab nationalists to serve in the government "gave Abdullah Salim's government Arab political cover, and won the high ground in seeking the support of Arab countries and political movements of an Arab nationalist orientation."[161] It helped, in particular, to win support for Kuwait in Egypt.[162] This was of particular importance given Nasser's standing in the Arab world at the time—and it was hard to achieve given the Kuwaitis dependence on Britain to defend it

155. United Nations 1963, 168–69.

156. Al-Khatib 2007, 214.

157. Michael Herb, "Yacoub Yusuf al-Humaydi," Kuwait Politics Database, http://www2.gsu.edu/~polmfh/database/DataPage1668.htm (accessed October 12, 2012).

158. Al-Zayd 1981, 6; Olayan, "Jasim al-Qatami," *al-Qabas*, July 1, 2012.

159. Al-Khatib 2007, 204.

160. Ibid., 214; Al-Najjar 2000, 69–70.

161. Al-Najjar 2000, 69.

162. Ibid., 70.

from Iraq. The Kuwaiti Arab nationalists had a crucial role in squaring this circle, and what they wanted from the ruling family in return was a liberal constitution and an elected assembly.

In January 1962, with the UN membership of Kuwait still blocked, but now with Arab League troops in the country, the Constitutional Convention held its first meeting, and by November of the same year, the emir issued the new constitution. In January 1963, the first elections were held to the National Assembly.[163]

Then, in February 1963, Qasim was overthrown and executed. Relations between Kuwait and Iraq immediately improved, and the Iraqi foreign minister said that Qasim's policy toward Kuwait had been "erroneous."[164] In May 1963, Kuwait finally joined the United Nations after the Soviet Union dropped its objections.[165] On October 4, Iraq formally recognized Kuwait and a few days later, Kuwait made a long-term, interest-free loan of 30 million British pounds to the Iraqi government.[166]

By this time, Kuwait had a new constitution and a newly elected National Assembly with some real constitutional authority. Less than two years earlier, Kuwait had been an absolute monarchy as thorough as any in the Gulf today and had been so since the closing of the Legislative Council in 1939. The timing of the 1962 constitution provides strong evidence of the causal importance of the Iraqi threat in the emergence of a strong parliament in Kuwait.

Kuwait and the Role of Abdullah Salim. Any shaykh of the al-Sabah who had been ruler of Kuwait in 1961 would have felt powerful pressure to broaden political participation and very likely would have opened a parliament. That said, Abdullah Salim seems to have embraced the idea, not grudgingly but out of conviction. Had a different member of his family been ruler in 1961, the ruling family might very well have been much stingier in its grant of real powers to the National Assembly. Ghanim al-Najjar writes that "there were among the members of the ruling family those who believed that the existence of a parliamentary system meant a form of retreat in their political and social standing, and as a consequence they opposed the idea in principle." Some shaykhs, al-Najjar points out, left their ministerial posts in the first years of rule under the 1962 constitution.[167] The government of January 1962 had eleven shaykhs, whereas the government of January 1965 had only five shaykhs.

163. Haydar 1997, 103, 139.
164. Middle East Journal 1963, 116; Marr 1985, 185.
165. United Nations 1965, 91–92.
166. Smith 1999, 129.
167. Al-Najjar 2000, 77, 70.

After the immediate threat of Iraqi invasion had passed, some members of the family wanted to return expeditiously to absolutism. Ahmad al-Khatib writes that shaykhs of the ruling family went to Abdullah Salim following the admission of Kuwait to the United Nations (spring 1963) and asked him to close down the National Assembly:

> they complained about parliamentary life and how men who had been their servants had begun demanding from them in the National Assembly what they could not bear, and if admittance to the United Nations was dependent on parliamentary life, this goal has now been achieved. So why are we continuing in this unacceptable situation? There is the Kingdom of Saudi Arabia and it is a member in the United Nations and there is no National Assembly in it.[168]

Abdullah Salim told them, "Do you not have tongues with which to respond [to the deputies]? Those who do not want to do that should resign from the government."

Al-Khatib writes that Abdullah Salim had the constitution written in the interests of "protecting the future of the [family], but the family did not understand this, very unfortunately, and this made them hurry to destroy all of what Abdullah Salim achieved, in the way of a balance for the family, immediately on his death."[169] More generally, one of the underlying themes in al-Khatib's memoirs of this period is the tension between the shaykhs of the al-Sabah and the ruler, Abdullah Salim, caused by the ruler's efforts to change the despotic mind-set of some members of his family, an endeavor in which, al-Khatib writes, he was not successful.[170]

There is evidence of Abdullah Salim's liberal inclinations during the drafting of the 1962 constitution. The constitution was not—like most Gulf constitutions—a grant by the ruler to his people. Instead, elections were held to a Constitutional Convention, which then elected a committee to draft the constitution. This was then voted on by the full convention—although only the elected members—and issued by the emir.[171] In fact, the draft written by this committee, with very few changes, became the 1962 constitution.

The committee had only five members: one shaykh (the emir's son Sa'd Abdullah al-Sabah) and four members of merchant families.[172] One of the four

168. Al-Khatib 2007, 268–69.
169. Ibid., 264.
170. Ibid., 259.
171. Al-Dayeen 1999, 8.
172. Al-Tabtabai 1999, 450; Al-Najjar 2000, 73.

merchants tended to be more conservative and often sided with shaykh Sa'd. The other three merchants favored a more liberal constitution. These three, Ahmad al-Khatib writes in his memoirs, met with other members of the Constitutional Convention to coordinate their positions on issues in the committee.[173]

Sa'd Abdullah al-Sabah consistently advanced a more restrictive view of parliamentary powers. At a key point in the deliberations Sa'd read out a list of nine proposed changes, saying that he had serious problems with key provisions in the draft constitution. Among these, Sa'd wanted to increase the requirement for removing confidence in a minister from a vote of one-half the members of the National Assembly to two-thirds.[174] This would have crucially weakened the powers of the National Assembly. The meeting adjourned, and at the next meeting of the committee the head of the convention reported that he had sought the help of the emir in overcoming the differences between Sa'd and the majority on the committee. It appears that the emir told Sa'd to back down because, in the end, Sa'd conceded on most of the nine points, and on all the really crucial ones.[175] Of this incident, Ahmad al-Khatib writes that "Abdullah Salim [the emir] always had a positive role in reducing the difficulties faced by the committee."[176]

Following the approval of a draft by the committee on the constitution, the draft went to the full Constitutional Convention, which voted on each article separately. A number of shaykhs had seats in the convention by virtue of holding cabinet posts, even though the emir earlier had decreed that ministers would not vote on the constitution. In debates in the convention over the constitutional draft, the shaykhs clearly favored a more restrictive text but were constrained by the emir's support for the draft written by the committee on the constitution. Thus, when changes were proposed from the floor that would further weaken the power of the ruling family, the shaykhs responded with some ferocity. At one point, shaykh Jabir al-Ali said that a proposal by Ahmad al-Khatib "incites our feelings too much to bear" and implied that the shaykhs had "other methods" if it were approved.[177] When the debate moved to the crucial issue of the number of deputies required to remove confidence in a minister, three shaykhs spoke in favor of raising the requirement to a two-thirds vote. (This provision is the key source of parliamentary power.) The most liberal member of the committee on the constitution began the discussion, however, by observing that "his highness

173. Al-Khatib 2007, 235.
174. Al-Tabtabai 1999, 283–87.
175. Al-Dayeen 1999, 15–16; Al-Najjar 2000, 75.
176. Al-Khatib 2007, 234.
177. Al-Dayeen 1999, 29; Al-Tabtabai 1999, 629.

the emir does not want there to be any debate in the Convention that will harm the reputation or traditions of Kuwait."[178] The three shaykhs did not press the point, and the convention approved the committee draft.[179]

The Iraqi threat is a sufficient explanation for the emergence of an elected parliament in Kuwait at independence. The Iraqi threat, however, did not wholly determine the content of the constitution, and there is good evidence—in the form of the clearly more liberal stance of Abdullah Salim compared to his relatives—that Kuwait adopted a more liberal constitution in 1962 than would have been the case had another man been emir.

Irredentist Threats to the United Arab Emirates and Bahrain. Did the other Gulf states experienced threats from abroad that comparable to the Iraqi threat to Kuwait and that, thus, should have induced a move toward greater political participation? In Oman and Qatar (as well as the much larger Saudi Arabia), there were no threats of a similar magnitude and risk. The UAE and Bahrain did (and to some extent still do) face irredentist threats, but, on the whole, these were not nearly as serious.

Immediately before the UAE declared its independence in late 1971, Iran occupied three islands also claimed by Sharjah and Ras al-Khaimah. This issue continues to poison relations between Iran and the UAE to this day. But the Iranian claim is much more limited than was the Iraqi claim to Kuwait—Iran asserts its sovereignty over the islands but not over other UAE territory. Hendrik Van der Meulen, who served as the political officer at the U.S. Embassy in Abu Dhabi, explicitly contrasts the Iranian threat to the UAE with the Iraqi threat to Kuwait and finds the Iranian threat to be much more modest.[180] Iran and that UAE are separated by a body of water. This makes it vastly more difficult for Iran to launch an occupation of mainland UAE territory and makes it much easier for the UAE and its allies—especially the United States—to defend UAE territory. Overall, the UAE does not face the same level of threat as faced by Kuwait.

Abu Dhabi and Saudi Arabia have long disputed the Buraimi oasis, and Saudi Arabia delayed its recognition of the UAE until 1974 over the issue.[181] But in the very extensive coverage of the negotiations among the various rulers leading up to independence in 1971, the issue of Buraimi hardly appears. It was not an existential threat.

178. Al-Tabtabai 1999, 669.
179. Ibid., 668–75.
180. Van der Meulen 1997, 279.
181. Ibid., 23.

Bahrain presents a more comparable case. Like Kuwait, Bahrain adopted a liberal constitution at independence. And, like Kuwait, Bahrain also faced an irredentist threat—but, again, one that was not nearly as pressing as that faced by Kuwait at independence. The Iranian claim to Bahrain formed the backdrop to discussions about Bahraini independence.[182] In the negotiations that led up to Bahraini independence, the British initially sought to broker the creation of a nine-member federation that would have included Bahrain, Qatar, and all seven emirates that now form the UAE. One of several obstacles to this federation was the Iranian threat to Bahrain because the other emirates worried about becoming entangled in a conflict with Iran.[183] This also influenced Bahraini attitudes toward the proposed federation—the Bahrainis found the idea of a federation substantially more attractive in the earlier negotiations, when the Iranian threat was more pressing.[184]

The shah, however, softened his stance toward Bahrain in 1969, and by 1970, it had become "abundantly clear" that Iran would drop its claim to Bahrain.[185] In 1970, the issue was resolved with an informal UN plebiscite, in which only a few Bahrainis declared their desire to unite with Iran.[186] Iran then dropped its claim, and Bahrain gained its independence in August 1971 without any of the difficulties faced by Kuwait, joining the United Nations in September 1971 without opposition and without a parliament.[187]

In December 1971, a few months after independence, the emir announced his intention to draft a constitution. He appointed a committee, which was advised by the same Egyptian constitutional adviser who helped to draft 1962 Constitution of Kuwait.[188] In June 1972, the emir announced elections to a Constitutional Assembly; the election were held in December. A year later, after the emir issued the new constitution—which closely resembled that of Kuwait in its form and content—elections were held to the new parliament.[189]

Why did the Al Khalifa ruling family decide to put into place a liberal constitution in 1973? The Iranian threat is not much discussed in accounts of Bahraini politics during this period, although it was before independence and has emerged again in more recent years. Pressure from below was (and is) more pronounced in

182. Bahrain was ruled as a Persian dependency by an Arab ruler when the Al Khalifa conquered it in the early 1780s; Iran revived its claim to Bahrain in the 1930s (Al-Tajir 1987, 6–7, 219–25; Abu-Hakima 1965, 111, 116).

183. Al-Tabtabai 1978, 55–61.

184. Taryam 1987, 128; S. Smith 2004, 98–100.

185. Taryam 1987, 143.

186. Ibid., 145.

187. United Nations 1974, 219–20.

188. Hamzah 2002, 24.

189. Nakhleh 1980, 166–67.

Bahrain than in any of the other Gulf monarchies—and although this rarely results in genuine liberal openings in Bahrain, it has some causal power in explaining why the Al Khalifa occasionally experimented in that direction.[190] Emile Nakhleh, who gives a good account of Bahraini politics in 1972, writes that there were those in the ruling family who thought that "the Khalifa family would ultimately have to give up part of its power to popularly elected bodies; therefore, it was more advisable that the family promulgated a constitution voluntarily before it was forced to do so."[191] In any case, the urge to liberalize among the Al Khalifa was transitory. By August 1975, the emir had dissolved the parliament and abandoned the 1973 constitution for good. The revival of parliamentary life in 2002 came with a unilateral rewriting of the Bahraini constitution that deprived the elected lower house of its authority.[192]

In recent years, the Iranian threat (or the threat as perceived by the Al Khalifa) has again had a central role in Bahraini politics. This threat, however, has had very different consequences in Bahrain than the Iraqi threat did in Kuwait. The Bahraini regime has used the specter of Iran to win the support of Saudi Arabia and to distract Western powers from its mistreatment of the Shi'i majority.[193] Note that Iran has not revived its formal claim to Bahrain, even though occasionally Iranian officials let loose with bellicose rhetoric.[194] The real problem that the Al Khalifa face is their increasingly complete alienation of the Shi'i majority.

After Independence

Since independence Kuwait has seen a series of political openings and closings, usually signaled by elections, in the case of political openings, or the unconstitutional suspension of the National Assembly, when the ruling family wants to close off political participation. These openings and closings are only partly correlated with the threat from Iraq. In 1965, Abdullah Salim died, thus removing the second force pushing the ruling family to take a liberal attitude toward the National Assembly. In 1967, the ruling family rigged the elections to the National Assembly in some districts, with the effect of excluding some Arab nationalist opposition figures. Other deputies resigned in protest, and the result was a National Assembly that had very little opposition. This did not seem to suit at least

190. Khalaf 1985, 25.
191. Nakhleh 1976, 135.
192. Niethammer 2006, 5.
193. International Crisis Group 2011b, 22–23.
194. "Iran Claim Rapped by Councillors," *Gulf Daily News* (Bahrain), February 17, 2009, http://www.gulf-daily-news.com/NewsDetails.aspx?storyid=243252.

some members of the ruling family, and the elections of 1971 were fair, as have been subsequent elections to the National Assembly. In 1976 the ruling family dissolved the National Assembly, in violation of the constitution, only to reopen it in 1981.

These events do not correlate with threats from Iraq, and indeed there is no particularly compelling single explanation for the timing of these events. The closing in 1976 is often attributed to the baleful example of the Lebanese civil war, with the lesson seeming to have been that the war illustrated the dangers of a more open political environment.[195] The decisions to hold elections in 1971 and 1981 are harder to explain, apart from a general sense among the al-Sabah that Kuwait is hard to rule without a National Assembly. The election of 1981, it is true, was preceded by a serious attempt by the ruling family to amend the constitution, and it appears that the ruling family still thought that the National Assembly could be relegated to a largely consultative role and viewed the 1981 opening as a tactic to accomplish a more permanent curbing of parliamentary power. The ploy failed, and the ruling family put up with the National Assembly for only a few more years before closing it more definitively in 1986.

Although the National Assembly on occasion caused difficulties and embarrassment, it did not fundamentally challenge the preeminence of the al-Sabah in the political system until elections returned an opposition majority in 1985. In that year, the National Assembly first used the threat of a vote of no confidence to force a minister to resign. Opposition deputies continued to press the ruling family, announcing their intent to interpellate several ministers in June 1986; on July 3, the emir dissolved the National Assembly and suspended key provisions of the constitution.[196]

After the 1986 closing, the family became much more serious about undoing the liberalism of the 1962 constitution. In 1990, the emir (Jaber al-Ahmad) issued a decree that created a new representative institution, the Majlis al-Watani, which effectively replaced the National Assembly; its powers, set out in the emir's decree, made it a shadow of the National Assembly.[197] The ruling family had used force to suppress demands for a resumption of parliamentary life in the spring of 1990. Most political organizations boycotted the elections to the Majlis al-Watani; it met only once or twice before the Iraqi invasion later in the summer of 1990.[198] Thus, on the eve of the Iraqi invasion, the Kuwaiti ruling family had reverted to the Gulf

195. Al-Najjar 2000, 99–100.
196. Kuwait News Agency (KUNA) 1999, 123.
197. Ibid., 127–132.
198. Al-Qamis and al-Jatili 2009.

absolutist norm, despite the strong political tradition in Kuwait favoring broad political participation.

The Iraqi invasion of 1990 forced the al-Sabah to restore the constitution. The causal relationship between invasion and the constitutional restoration is clear. As had been the case at independence, the invasion forced the ruling family to demonstrate to the powers that protected it, and to international public opinion, that it enjoyed the support of Kuwaiti citizens and that the citizens fully supported the survival of Kuwait as a sovereign state. This was accomplished at a meeting in exile in Jedda during the occupation, attended by representatives of all important Kuwaiti political groups. The assembled groups expressed their support for the al-Sabah, the price for which was a promise by the senior members of the family to restore the 1962 constitution. This the al-Sabah duly promised, and after liberation, they eventually made good on the promise.[199]

The senior leadership of the al-Sabah did not restore the National Assembly with any enthusiasm, but the ruling family's position in the wake of the invasion was weak. Many Kuwaitis blamed the ruling family (or various shaykhs of the ruling family) for the disaster, and the family itself had very little presence in Kuwait during the occupation.[200] The surprising thing is not that the family grudgingly agreed to a restoration of the constitution but that the family was able to reconstruct the Kuwaiti political system after the complete destruction of the regime. The restoration of the 1962 constitution was a crucial step toward rebuilding the regime.

In the period since the 1992 restoration, the ruling family has abided by the letter, if not always the spirit, of the 1962 constitution. In recent years, the National Assembly has mounted increasingly determined challenges to the political primacy of the ruling family, culminating in an episode in late 2011 when the National Assembly forced the resignation of the prime minister—who was also a senior shaykh in a central branch of the ruling family.

The senior leadership of the ruling family has consistently—although not usually successfully—sought to deflect and frustrate the demands of the parliamentary opposition for a greater voice in governance. The family, however, has not unconstitutionally suspended the National Assembly (as it did in 1976 and 1986), and its failure to do so is something of a puzzle. One obvious explanation is that an unconstitutional suspension would create problems in the relationship between Kuwait and the United States, the main source of protection for

199. Tétreault 2000, 85.
200. Boghardt 2006, 150.

Kuwait from regional threats. Again, the United States has reasons to protect Kuwait regardless of the degree of absolutism of its ruling family; it is easier to do so, however, when the al-Sabah live under the 1962 constitution. Official U.S. statements on its relationship with Kuwait make it clear that the Kuwaiti tradition of relative political freedom is applauded in Washington and that deviations from liberal norms—especially those having to do with free speech—are not welcome.[201]

The relationship with the United States, however, is not the only reason that the National Assembly has survived. The National Assembly is one of the two most influential political institutions in Kuwait (with the ruling family), and its continued presence since 1993 has shaped the nature of Kuwaiti politics in important ways that make it more difficult for the ruling family to return to the absolutist practices of the other GCC dynasties. The Kuwaiti political elite today is a political elite generated via elections, and virtually all Kuwaiti political groups, ideological tendencies, and identity groups have participated in electoral politics. The political leadership largely consists of those who are successful in electoral politics. The persistence of the National Assembly has affected the view of Kuwaiti citizens—and thus the state bureaucracy and the security forces—on the legitimate role of the ruling family in Kuwaiti politics and on the value of the 1962 constitution. Indeed, the National Assembly has become closely associated with Kuwaiti national identity. What distinguishes Kuwait from its neighbors—in the view of a great many Kuwaitis—is precisely the National Assembly and the 1962 constitution. In a real sense, an assault on the 1962 constitution is, for many, a threat to Kuwaiti identity. The persistence of the National Assembly over time and its effect on the political expectations of Kuwaiti citizens bear very directly on the sort of opposition that the al-Sabah would face were they to attempt to impose an unvarnished autocracy on Kuwait and on the degree to which the individual Kuwaitis who occupy positions of power in the state apparatus would support the ruling family in such an effort. The senior leadership of the ruling family worries that Kuwait would be ungovernable without a National Assembly.

My argument here is path-dependent. The restoration of the 1962 constitution following liberation from the Iraqi occupation set Kuwait on a political trajectory that is different from that of the GCC absolutisms. Once on that path, institutional and ideational changes occurred in Kuwait that make it quite difficult for the ruling family to move off that path and toward the Gulf norm of absolutism. Other scholars who study Kuwaiti exceptionalism have also made

201. Herb 2013.

path-dependent arguments. Sean Yom, for example, cites path dependency when explaining how the regime coalitions established in the late 1930s continue to influence Kuwaiti politics today.[202] Crystal's argument also has a path-dependent aspect to it, at least implicitly; the pre-oil strength of the Kuwaiti merchant class shaped its politics even after oil undermined the initial economic basis of merchant power.

My argument differs from those made by Crystal and Yom in the nature of the event that put Kuwait on its distinctive path. I place particular emphasis on two events: the Iraqi irredentist claim at independence and the Iraqi invasion of 1990. This fits the historical record better than arguments that locate the crucial event earlier in Kuwaiti history. There is little to suggest that in the 1950s Kuwait was on a path that differed from the other Gulf shaykhdoms. But by the end of the 1990s, it was much more apparent that Kuwaiti politics had begun to differ in systematic ways from those of the other extreme rentiers, the UAE and Qatar. These differences were reflected in Kuwaiti political institutions, in the structure of the political elite, and in the discourse among Kuwaitis regarding their political identity.

★ ★ ★

Explanations of Kuwaiti exceptionalism tend to fall into one of two categories: (1) differences in pre-oil political and economic structures and (2) the influence of the Iraqi threat (along with the role of the Kuwaiti emir at independence). In this chapter, I have argued for the second, comparing Kuwait with the other smaller Gulf shaykhdoms, from its founding through the present, to identify the crucial episodes when Kuwait began to diverge from its neighbors. Through the late 1950s, Kuwait was not exceptional among the Gulf shaykhdoms in its level of political participation; it was an undiluted family autocracy. Nor, in the pre-oil period, was Kuwait all that remarkable for the strength of its merchant class; although the Qatari merchant class was weak compared to that of Kuwait, the other shaykhdoms had more robust merchant classes. Kuwaiti exceptionalism emerged in 1961 as a result of the confluence of two factors: a liberal emir and a serious threat from Iraq. Abdullah Salim's role in Kuwaiti exceptionalism may have been necessary (the 1962 constitution would not have been as liberal in his absence), but it was not sufficient. Abdullah Salim had ruled for over a decade without any appreciable development in Kuwaiti democratic institutions; he pushed through a liberal constitution only in the context of the Iraqi threat. When he died, the constitution lost its most powerful defender among the shaykhs of the al-Sabah, and Kuwait moved toward the Gulf norm of absolutism over the following years,

202. Yom 2011, 224, 239.

culminating in the Majlis al-Watani of 1990. It took an Iraqi invasion to save the 1962 constitution. The constitutional restoration after liberation set Kuwait on a different path, making it more difficult over time for the ruling family to revert to absolutism.

In the next chapter, on the UAE, I bring together the two themes of the first half of the book: (1) distorted labor markets in the extreme rentiers, and (2) variation in the level of political participation among the Gulf states. In the UAE, these produce a very specific political economy. In chapter 5, I then show the political consequences of participation in Kuwait in the context of extreme rentierism.

Chapter 4

The Consequences of Absolutism

What happens when absolutism is combined with extreme rentierism? The answer, in short, is that ruling families adopt policies that suit their own economic interests, interests defined by their status as the leading capitalists in their societies. In this chapter, I advance the following arguments:

- In the absence of a strong parliament in the UAE, the ruling families become, at least potentially, the dominant local capitalists in their emirates. Ruling-family control of undeveloped land is a major source of wealth.
- The ruling family of Dubai, as a result of its position within the federation and ownership of land, had a particularly strong incentive to pursue economic growth.
- The success of Dubai was later imitated by the ruling families of other UAE emirates.
- Citizens of extreme rentiers benefit less than their rulers from unrestrained economic growth and bear more of its costs. As a consequence, it is unlikely that the Dubai model of growth is compatible with citizen democracy.

In the first part of this chapter, I consider Dubai and the story of its growth; I then consider the responses from Emirati citizens to the Dubai model of growth. In the final part of the chapter, I draw some brief comparisons with the other Gulf absolutisms.

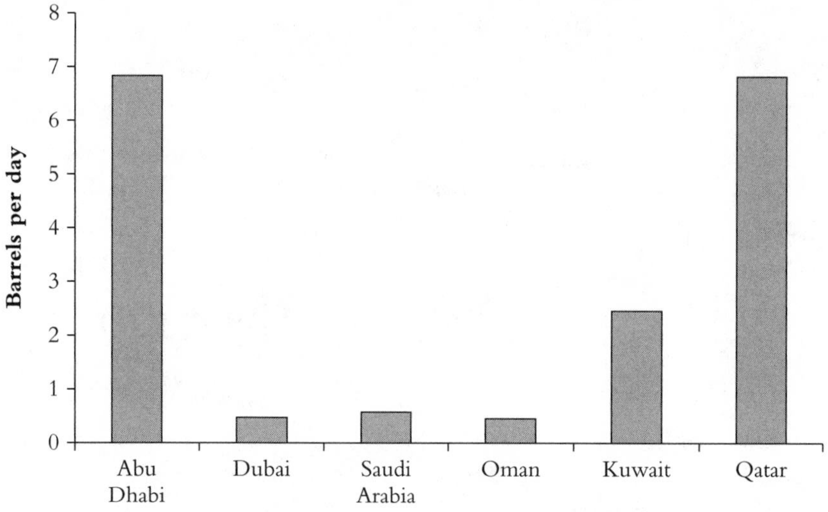

Fig. 4.1 Per citizen oil production, 2011. Production data for 2011 from U.S. Energy Information Administration, "Countries," http://www.eia.gov/countries/; population estimates: Abu Dhabi Government 2012, 123 (includes citizens of other UAE emirates living in Abu Dhabi); United Arab Emirates 2011, 10 (2010 figures for Dubai); Kingdom of Saudi Arabia, Central Department of Statistics and Information, "Estimates Of Population By Sex And Nationality (Saudi / Non Saudi) In The Kingdom For The Years (2004 To 2012)." http://www.cdsi.gov.sa/socandpub/resd (accessed June 21, 2013); Sultanate of Oman 2011, table 2.1 (2010 data); State of Kuwait 2012a, 42; State of Qatar 2010a, chap. 3, fig. 37; 2010b, fig. 24 (2010 data).

Dubai

If oil revenues alone determined the status of the UAE ruling families, the Al Maktoum of Dubai would be distinctly second-class, bush league in a federation dominated by the Al Nahyan of Abu Dhabi. The UAE is composed of seven separate emirates, each with its own ruling family. Each emirate in the UAE owns the oil found in its territory. The UAE as a whole produces about 3 million barrels of oil daily, and almost all of it comes from Abu Dhabi.[1] Production in Dubai peaked at 420,000 barrels per day in 1991 and has since declined to under 100,000 barrels per day.[2] The remaining emirates produce even less, and the poorest emirates (along with the federal government) rely on benefices from the richer emirates.

Figure 4.1 compares the per citizen oil income of Abu Dhabi and Dubai; it also compares them to the oil incomes of other Gulf states. We can see that

1. U.S. Energy Information Administration, *Country Analysis Briefs: United Arab Emirates*, October 17, 2012, www.eia.gov/countries/cab.cfm?fips=TC.

2. Himendra Mohan Kumar, "Offshore Oil Find Expected to Be a Shot in the Arm for GDP," *Gulf News*, February 5, 2010, http://gulfnews.com/business/oil-gas/offshore-oil-find-expected-to-be-a-shot-in-the-arm-for-gdp-1.578622; Davidson 2008, 101.

Dubai per capita income is comparable to that of Oman; that is, Dubai on its own is a middling rentier, not an extreme rentier. Of course, Dubai is but one emirate in a confederation of seven, and the confederation—by virtue of Abu Dhabi's oil riches—is an extreme rentier, as evidenced by the degree to which labor markets across the UAE resemble those of Qatar and Kuwait (see chapter 1).

To avoid becoming vassals of the Al Nahyan, the Al Maktoum of Dubai have sought to develop alternative sources of distinction, prestige, and wealth. The ruling family's strategy (which, in fact, predates oil) has been to make Dubai a friendly and profitable place to do business. At the end of the nineteenth century, the Iranian government imposed heavy customs duties on the port cities on the northern coast of the Gulf. The Al Maktoum seized this opportunity and encouraged unhappy merchants to move their operations to Dubai.[3] Lorimer, in his *Gazetteer* published at the turn of the century, applauded the Dubai commercial spirit: "the trade of Dibai [Dubai] is considerable and is rapidly expanding, chiefly in consequence of the enlightened policy of the late Shaikh, Maktum-bin-Hashar, and the stringency of the Imperial Persian Customs on the opposite coast."[4] Over the following decades the Al Maktoum's strategy succeeded to the degree that by the 1950s—on the eve of the oil era—Dubai was the most prosperous and important emirate on the Trucial Coast. When oil production came online, the rulers of Dubai invested in infrastructure to encourage further growth.[5] Mohammed bin Rashid's attitude toward outside investors is clear in his 2006 book, *My Vision:*

> When a manager of a company that had moved to Dubai asked me if there was anything I wanted from his company. I answered: I want your success only. Development is beneficial and so is national participation but what concerns the investor, in the end, is return on investment. If an investor comes to Dubai and starts and enterprise and makes a million, he will invest two million, and if he makes two million he will invest four.[6]

By the eve of the 2008 financial crisis, the ruling family's strategy had produced spectacular results, especially in tourism and logistics. In 2010, Dubai had the world's ninth busiest container port, the thirteenth busiest passenger airport, and the eighth busiest cargo airport.[7] Dubai has built a brand known worldwide.

3. Davidson 2008, 72–73. On entrepreneurialism in Dubai, see also Hvidt 2009; Sampler and Eigner 2008.

4. Lorimer 1908a, 455–56.

5. Hvidt 2009, 400.

6. Al Maktoum 2006, 145.

7. American Association of Port Authorities, "World Port Rankings—2010," http://www.aapa-ports.org; Airports Council International, "Passenger Traffic 2010. Final" and "Cargo Traffic 2010 Final," August 1, 2011, http://www.aci.aero.

In the early 1990s, few people around the world had heard of Dubai; by the economic crisis of 2008, few had not. When *Foreign Policy* magazine developed its list of major world cities in 2008, Dubai ranked twenty-seventh among all cities in the world, ahead of every other city in the Middle East; it remained in the top thirty in 2010 and 2012.[8]

The Al Maktoum, in short, succeeded in bringing wealth and prestige to their realm through the determined pursuit of development. Dubai became an influential model in the Gulf, and in some circles, a cautionary story of what to avoid, but in any case, it formed the standard against which other Gulf states were measured. Mohammed bin Rashid himself became, for a time, one of the most admired of Gulf rulers precisely because he was viewed as a man who built something through hard work and determination—traits not often associated with Gulf ruling families. The crisis of the late 2000s damaged the Dubai brand and weakened it politically. It was the classic crisis of the real estate developer: too much money had been invested in projects that had not yet sold. When real estate prices fell, the developer became insolvent. But the role of Dubai as an entrepôt—a trading hub and logistics center for a sizable portion of the Eastern Hemisphere—survived the real estate crash. The world rank of Dubai in terms of traffic at its airport and container port held steady through 2011. Passenger traffic at the airport, for example, went from 34 million in 2007 to 51 million in 2011.[9]

The Al Maktoum as Real Estate Developers

Dubai is famously referred to as "Dubai Inc.," suggesting that the emirate is run as a private business corporation (or, as John Duke Anthony puts it, a "vast holding company").[10] The chief executive officer is Mohammed bin Rashid. The blurred line between the assets of the ruling family and the assets of the state suggests that, in practice, the corporation is owned by the ruling family more than by the citizens as a whole. The Dubai chief of police—a man of importance in Dubai—once tried to explain the system in a television interview. He started by asserting that "what the ruler has, we have, meaning that the money as a whole is our money, and his money." When the interviewer asked if, in fact, the budget of the state was separate from the budget of the ruling family, and the police chief replied, "our ruler, he is the state, and the state is the ruler, we do not have

8. *Foreign Policy* 2008; Hales and Pena 2012. The other Middle Eastern cities on the list were Istanbul, Tel Aviv, and Cairo.

9. Airports Council International, "Passenger Traffic 2011 Final," July 8, 2013, http://www.aci.aero.

10. Anthony 1975, 154.

a separation between the two funds, as citizens we put our hands in the personal funds of the ruler to a degree that makes us well-off." The interviewer then asked him if the ruler put his hand in the state money, and the chief of police replied that "on the contrary, what is the state's is the state's, and what is the ruler's is shared among the people . . . believe it or not."[11] The vision here is of the state as a family that owns a business but has responsibility for the welfare of its family members—the citizens of Dubai. A less generous interpretation would observe that the ruling family in the end controls exactly who gets what and is accountable to no one at all.

Although it is not possible to determine with any precision the sources of income of Dubai Inc. as a whole, clearly real estate has a central role in the enterprise.[12] Oil, to be sure, still matters, and the IMF points out that oil and gas revenues come first to ruler's court and then are sent to the Dubai Finance Department.[13] The ruler, mostly via Dubai Holding, also owns a number of businesses, including a share in one of the national wireless companies, various financial companies, part of the stock exchange, the Wild Wadi water park, and hotels. (The state owns, mostly outright, Emirates airlines, the port, the airport, dry docks, an aluminum company, and many other businesses.[14]) The most lucrative source of Al Maktoum income, however, appears to be real estate. It is here that the blurring of lines between the government and the ruler are most profitable for the ruler. A tradition in Dubai (found also throughout the Gulf) holds that the ruler is the default owner of undeveloped land in the emirate. As Heard-Bey said of Dubai in 1982, "the accepted pattern is based on the principle that land outside the built-up areas, and reclaimed land, belongs to the Ruler. Certain areas in the town have also traditionally belonged to the Ruler and his family, and the rest of the built-up land is owned by individuals who either obtained it as a gift from the Ruler or bought it. . . . Much of the land which is owned by the Ruler is managed as an asset of the State. . . ."[15] Land in Dubai, Heard-Bey says, "was in the past . . . common tribal grazing land . . . for which the current generation has no use any more." It is "being turned into a source of instant wealth in the form of marketable real estate."[16] The ruler's ownership of undeveloped land extended—and still

11. Zayd Binyamin, "Khalfan: Hal min al-haqq an nabqa aqalliyya bi-biladna?" [Khafan: Is it right that we remain a minority in our own country?], *Elaph*, March 4, 2009, www.elaph.com (no longer available on the website).

12. Hvidt 2009, 409.

13. IMF 2003, 27.

14. For a particularly good overview of Dubai Inc., see IMF 2011b, 5.

15. Heard-Bey 2004, 262.

16. Heard-Bey 2005, 358.

extends—also to reclaimed land. Thus, the dredging of the Dubai creek, to allow larger ships to dock, also generated fill that could be used to create new land along the creek. "[N]o amount of dredging work seemed too large when the cost of that work was already debited against the expected commercial value of the new building sites. The Ruler personally became the owner of such reclaimed land."[17] More recently, the various islands and "palms" built off the coast of Dubai are, in the end, "a huge revenue-raising exercise" for the ruler and for Dubai Inc.[18] To be clear, it is not that there is no distinction at all, today, between land owned by the ruler and land owned by the state; it is, however, the case that both types of land are under the direct control of the ruler and can be transferred by him from one category to the other at will. One of the dominant real estate companies in Dubai—Dubai Holding—is personally owned by the ruler of Dubai and, as the ratings agency Moody's puts it, Dubai Holding "benefits from the unique provision of free land by the government."[19] The annual report for the main Dubai Holding subsidiary in 2009 made the point explicitly, noting that in 2009 "the Group was granted land by the Government of Dubai."[20] The word *grant* is used here in its usual sense—no payment was made for the land.

In short, there is much to be said for viewing Mohammed bin Rashid as one of the world's most prominent real estate developers (before the crash of recent years, he was a contender for the title of the world's most *successful* real estate developer). His interests, and those of his family, lie in the further economic growth of Dubai; this goes far in explaining the incessant boosterism of the Dubai government.

This marriage of interests between land owners and political elites is not unique to Dubai; it has been noted in other cities, in other parts of the world, and a substantial literature has emerged inspired by Harvey Molotch's 1976 "The City as a Growth Machine."[21] In that article, and in works that followed, Molotch explains civic boosterism as the product of local rentiers who owned land and stood to benefit from economic growth in the local economic region. He also observes that the interests of others who lived in the city did not always lie in the same direction as the interest of the property rentiers, although the voices of those promoting growth tended to predominate in the local press, government, chambers

17. Heard-Bey 2004, 261.

18. Hvidt 2009, 409.

19. Haseeb Haider, "Dubai Holding to Remain Dominated by Real Estate Activities: Moody's," *Khaleej Times*, January 12, 2007, http://www.khaleejtimes.com; Standard and Poor's, "Gulf Cooperation Council Credit Survey," April 2007, 105.

20. Dubai Holdings Commercial Operations Group, "Consolidated Financial Statements," December 31, 2009, 39, 27.

21. Molotch 1976. See also Logan and Molotch 1987; Jonas and Wilson 1999.

of commerce, and other elite circles.[22] Dubai is perhaps the world's most extreme case. The boosterism of the Dubai government is, if not unprecedented, certainly quite remarkable. This grows out of one family effectively owning a great deal of real estate and that family controlling the local government, which—as we will see—has maintained its autonomy from the federal government.

In his 1976 article, Molotch spends some effort arguing against the notion that growth benefits everyone by creating jobs; "perhaps the key ideological prop of the growth machine, especially in terms of sustaining support from the working-class majority," he writes, "is the claim that growth 'makes jobs.'"[23] In highly productive non-oil societies, growth does in fact create jobs and does give citizens a stake in the success of the "growth machine" (even university professors). In the extreme rentiers of the Gulf, however, the urban growth machine generates jobs for foreigners, not citizens. These countries are thus the best extant examples of the tension identified by Molotch between the interests of those who benefit from the growth of the city and the interests of its less privileged citizens. The interests of foreign residents, by contrast, are more closely aligned with those of the Al Maktoum, at least in terms of the benefits of growth.

The deep involvement of the Dubai ruling family in real estate development gives the family very strong incentives to promote population growth. The natural growth of the citizen population is entirely insufficient to fill the many flats, office towers, and other real estate developments of the family—only massive immigration from abroad can make the Al Maktoum's real estate projects successful. The current ruler's father, once questioned about the number of illegal residents in Dubai, replied, "What is the problem, so long as they are paying rent in Dubai?"[24]

Some numbers may help illustrate the point—and the demographic vulnerability felt by UAE citizens. The total population of the UAE—all seven emirates, citizens and expatriates—on the eve of independence was about 180,000 souls, most of whom were citizens. By 2010, the total population was well over 8 million, of whom approximately 11% were citizens. That is, the total population of the UAE increased *forty-six times* from 1968 to 2010 (figure 4.2).[25] Indeed,

22. Molotch 1976, 314–18.

23. Ibid., 320.

24. Davidson 2008, 91.

25. Abdulla 1984, 103; United Arab Emirates 2011. The 2010 figures were substantially higher than previous figures released by the National Bureau of Statistics and were greeted with a measure of skepticism in some quarters. Others, however, thought the figures to be reasonable. Gulf states are not known for overstating the demographic imbalances. Martin Croucher, "Door-to-Door Census in UAE Is Scrapped," *The National* (Abu Dhabi), April 6, 2011, http://www.thenational.ae/news/uae-news/door-to-door-census-in-uae-is-scrapped.

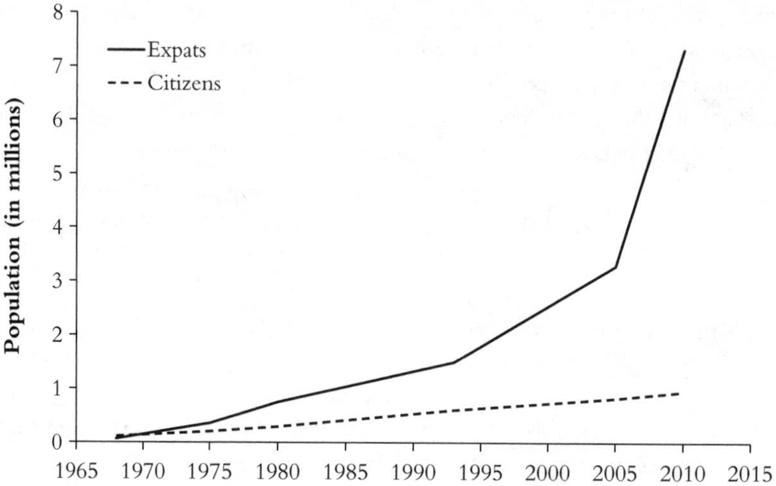

Fig. 4.2 Population growth in the UAE, 1968–2010. Abdulla 1984, 103; United Arab Emirates, 2006, 11; United Arab Emirates 2011; Ghobash 1996, 102.

according to many reports, UAE citizens are not—and have not been for a long time—even a plurality in their own country. As early as 1984, there were more citizens of both India (and perhaps Pakistan) in the UAE than there were citizens of the UAE, a situation that continues today.[26] For many years, more foreigners than citizens were born in the UAE.[27] It is not for nothing that Emirati citizens feel that they are being overwhelmed by a tidal wave of immigration (figure 4.3).

In the years immediately preceding the 2008 crisis, the rulers of the UAE had ambitions for yet more immigration. Government agencies in Dubai planned for a city of 5 million (up from 1.4 million in 2008) by 2020.[28] In 2006, Mohammed bin Rashid told the head of a state-owned real estate company that he had achieved only 10% of his ambitions in Dubai. That, said the executive, "scares the hell out of me."[29] In 2008 a state-owned real estate company announced plans to build an artificial island—Palm Deira—that would have a population of 1.3 million people.[30] The entire citizen population of the UAE (i.e., all seven emirates, not just Dubai) would fit onto this "palm" with room to spare. The real estate

26. Abu-Baker 1995, 173; Janardhan 2011, 96; Kapiszewski 2001, 65.
27. United Arab Emirates 2009, 26, 27.
28. Foreman 2008.
29. Anthony Shadid, "The Towering Dream of Dubai," *Washington Post*, April 30, 2006.
30. Eugene Harnan, "Palm Deira Blueprint Unveiled," *The National (Abu Dhabi)*, October 7, 2008, http://www.thenational.ae/news/uae-news/palm-deira-blueprint-unveiled.

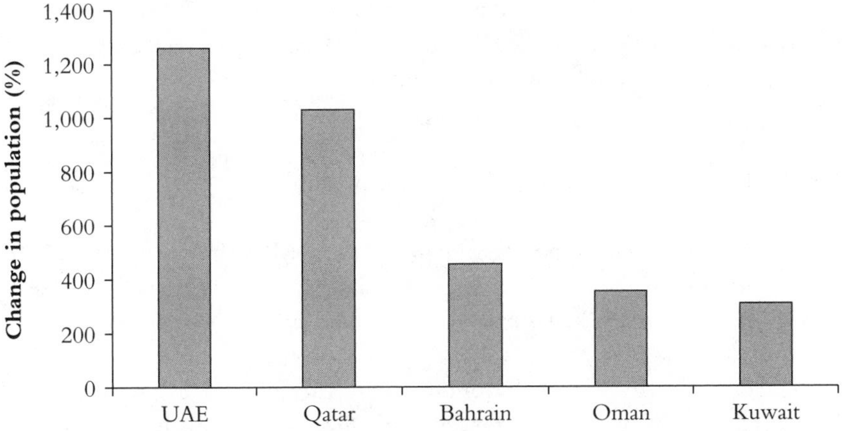

Fig. 4.3 Change in total population in five Gulf monarchies, 1975–2010. Population figures for Saudi Arabia are particularly unreliable, so they are excluded from the chart (Winckler 2008); data for 1975, Kapiszewski 2001, 37; for 2010, Central Bank of Bahrain, "Economic Indicators," June 2012, 3, available at http://www.cbb.gov.bh/page-p-economic_indicators.htm; State of Kuwait 2013b, 5 (2011 data); Sultanate of Oman 2011, table 1.2; Qatar 2010b, table 1; United Arab Emirates 2011, 10.

crisis, of course, kept many of these plans firmly on the drawing board. Nevertheless, the ambitions of the rulers are clear.[31]

The overwhelming demographic dominance of foreigners in Dubai has led to the geographic marginalization of its citizens. Not so long ago, in the mid-twentieth century, citizens lived in the heart of Dubai. Over time they have migrated outward from the city center and today live in suburbs such as Mizhar and farther out.[32] Few citizens live in vast swaths of the city. Muhammad Rokn, an Emirati citizen, describes the geographical marginalization of citizens as "internal exile."[33] Geographic marginalization has been accompanied by cultural marginalization. The need to "strengthen [Emirati] national identity" is a matter of common discussion; one response was the creation, at the direction of Mohammed bin Rashid, of a well-funded institute to do just that. It adopted the fingerprint as its logo, to emphasize the connection with *huwiya* (identity).[34] The institute runs summer camps that "strengthen the understanding of national identity and confirm

31. For a book-length exposition of this theme, see Al-Shehabi 2012.

32. Dresch 2006, 205–206.

33. Shadid, "The Towering Dream of Dubai," *Washington Post*, April 30, 2006. Also see "Dubai Natives Protect Identity in Fast-changing Land," *Agence France Presse* (via Lexis Nexis), May 31, 2006.

34. Watani Program, "Su'al wa jawab" [Questions and answers], 2010, http://www.watani.ae/ (accessed August 19, 2010).

belonging to the nation."[35] The effort is reminiscent of the programs employed by religious and ethnic communities in the United States to connect their children to their ancestry—but Emiratis live in their home country.

The Other Emirates of the United Arab Emirates

The ruling families of the poorer emirates of the UAE—Sharjah, Ajman, Umm al-Quwain, Ras al-Khaimah, and Fujairah—share many of the same incentives initially faced by the Al Maktoum of Dubai. They have little or no oil, and they have followed the example of Dubai by becoming real estate developers.[36] The ruling families, of course, benefit from this quite directly as the major landholders in their emirates, as the owners of businesses, and from their role in SOEs. Nor is it difficult, for some of these emirates at least, to ride on the coattails of the growth in Dubai. Dubai, Sharjah, and Ajman are essentially one metropolitan agglomeration, a city that will some day envelop Umm al-Quwain and eventually Ras al-Khaimah. A Kuwaiti newspaper published an advertisement paid for by Umm al-Quwain that consisted largely of a satellite map showing just how close Umm al-Quwain was to Dubai, with the goal of attracting Kuwaiti investment into Umm al-Quwain. In 2006, the government of Umm al-Quwain commissioned a plan to accommodate a tenfold increase in the population of the emirate over twenty years.[37] The mixture of the interests of the ruling family and the emirate of Ras al-Khaimah clearly resemble that found in Dubai. Real estate companies in the emirate are owned by the ruler personally (Al Hamra Real Estate), by the emirate government (RAK Investment Authority), by shareholders (RAK Properties), or some combination of these.[38] Rakeen, which at one point was said on its website to be the "the land master-planned and developer to be responsible for RAK's property development" is owned in part by the ruler (via Al Hamra Real Estate) and is "one of the largest developers in the Gulf region in terms of land-bank value."[39] RAK Properties also receives land grants from the government.[40]

35. Watani Program, "600 tifl yuqadhun 'utlathum al-sayfiyya fi ajwa' mukhayyam sayf watani lil-atfal 2009" [600 children spend their summer vacations in the atmosphere of the national summer camps for children 2009], June 28, 2009, http://www.watani.ae/ (accessed August 19, 2010).

36. Davidson 2008, 133.

37. Thomas 2008.

38. Zawya, "RAK Investment Authority," January 16, 2006, http://www.zawya.com (accessed December 20, 2007); Zawya, "Al Hamra Real Estate Development Company," June 5, 2007, http://www.zawya.com (accessed December 20, 2007).

39. Rakeen, "About Rakeen," 2007, www.rakeen.com/about_rakeen.html (accessed December 20, 2007); Rakeen, "Sales FAQ," http://www.rakeen.com/en/faq.aspx (accessed October 30, 2012).

40. RAK Properties, "Directors Report for the Three Month Period Ended 31 March 2011," April 23, 2011.

In contrast, the incentives facing the ruling family of Abu Dhabi differ from those facing the ruling families of the poorer emirates. The oil wealth of their emirate ensures the ruling family's political and economic predominance in the UAE and its status among the Gulf ruling families. That said, the Dubai model does exercise a strong attraction over the shaykhs of the Al Nahyan, for reasons of both profit and vanity. There is money to be made (and, more recently, losses to be avoided)—and there is little reason to suppose that the shaykhs of the Al Nahyan are indifferent to the size to their fortunes. Going into business is an especially attractive proposition for those members of the family who have relatively less direct claim on the oil wealth of the emirate. Business income thus acts as a way to raise their social, political, and economic influence.

Vanity also has a role. The success of the Al Maktoum in branding Dubai made it possible for the rulers of Abu Dhabi (and Qatar, also) to envisage prominent roles for themselves and their emirate on the world stage. Instead of backing away from the Dubai model, they have embraced it, or at least some parts of it. The success of Dubai set off competition among the richer ruling families to promote the achievements of their respective realms. And in this competition, the ruling families of Abu Dhabi and Qatar have the advantage of not lacking for capital.

As in Dubai, the ruling family of Abu Dhabi controls real estate, and benefits from development. After Sheikh Zayed died in 2004, the Abu Dhabi government lifted restrictions on the private ownership of land, and, Davidson writes, "a select few firms" began building mega-projects. Land, however, was still available only to some, and mega-projects were "only really a possibility for powerful businessmen who are either part of, or closely linked to the ruling family. . . ."[41] By 2008, the Abu Dhabi ruling family, its SWFs, and many of its leading citizens had come to have a direct stake in the pell-mell economic growth that Dubai had pioneered in Dubai itself and throughout the rest of the UAE. Many members of the ruling family, and those close to the ruling family, became deeply involved in business ventures in Abu Dhabi and have a stake in the continued growth of the emirate.[42] Many shaykhs of the Al Nahyan, for that matter, also invested in the Dubai and were hurt by the end of the boom there.

Some of the projects undertaken by the Al Nahyan seem to be driven as much by vanity as profit.[43] At the height of the boom, Abu Dhabi announced plans to build a complex of museums on an island off Abu Dhabi, including branches of the Guggenheim and Louvre, with the goal of laying the foundation for a high-end tourist economy.[44] The world economic crisis prompted a reconsideration

41. Davidson 2007b, 41; "Sitting Pretty: Abu Dhabi," *The Economist*, June 10, 2006; Gorvett 2005, 41.
42. Davidson 2009, 89–90.
43. On the strategy, see Government of Abu Dhabi, "The Abu Dhabi Economic Vision 2030," https://www.abudhabi.ae/.
44. Tomlinson 2009.

and led to delays in projects throughout Abu Dhabi as the government assessed the size of the debt problem among the various government and government-related enterprises.[45] By 2012, however, the government affirmed its commitment to building the museums.[46]

Another high-profile project—the construction of a branch campus of New York University (NYU)—has even more tenuous link to the needs of Emirati citizens. The new campus benefits from the support of senior members of the Al Nahyan, and the Abu Dhabi government pays all its costs.[47] The university recruited highly qualified students from around the world and offered them full scholarships. It was, in its first year, more selective than the NYU New York City campus.[48] Citizens of the United States made up the largest group of students, followed by the UAE, China, Hungary, and Russia.[49] Some Emirati academics wondered why the funds lavished on NYU Abu Dhabi, which mostly benefited foreign students, were not instead spent on education at state institutions such as the United Arab Emirates University, which has a student body consisting largely of citizens.[50]

From one point of view, all this spending on culture and education served the higher purpose of diversifying the Abu Dhabi economy. A (much more) cynical interpretation was that the spending on the museums stroked the vanity of the Al Nahyan and encouraged a tourism boom that would benefit, first and foremost, those in Abu Dhabi with the connections necessary to build the hotels, malls, and other tourist development projects.

Emirati Citizens and the Dubai Model

The differences between Kuwait and the UAE are a product, in the largest part, of the fact that Kuwait has a powerful parliament. Kuwaiti citizens have the opportunity to shape policy in a way that reflects their preferences, while Emirati

45. Roscoe 2011; Foreman 2011.

46. Samia Badih, "Revival of Saadiyat Museums 'Energises Abu Dhabi Tourism,'" *Gulf News*, January 26, 2012, http://gulfnews.com/business/property/uae/revival-of-saadiyat-museums-energises-abu-dhabi-tourism-39-1.971317.

47. Ursula Lindsey, "NYU-Abu Dhabi Behaves like Careful Guest in Foreign Land," *Chronicle of Higher Education*, June 8, 2012, A15–A17; New York University Abu Dhabi, "Frequently Asked Questions," http://nyuad.nyu.edu/about/faqs.html (accessed November 2, 2012).

48. Chiranti Sengupta, "World's Best in Abu Dhabi," *Gulf News*, April 14, 2011, gulfnews.com/gn-focus/getex/world-s-best-in-abu-dhabi-1.790846.

49. Lisa W. Foderaro, "N.Y.U. Abu Dhabi Scours Globe for Top Students," *New York Times*, June 20, 2010.

50. Lindsey, "NYU-Abu Dhabi Behaves like Careful Guest in Foreign Land," *Chronicle of Higher Education*, June 8, 2012, A15–A17; United Arab Emirates University, "Statistical Year Book 2010–2011," http://www.uaeu.ac.ae.

citizens do not. This presumes, however, that the preferences of Kuwaiti and Emirati citizens are largely similar. Measuring preferences in Kuwait is not difficult; candidates for seats in the National Assembly adopt positions designed to win support from voters. Measuring citizen preferences in the UAE is much more difficult; elections are so constrained they hardly deserve the name, and public opinion surveys conducted in the UAE avoid sensitive domestic political issues—as Ahmad al-Astal makes very clear in his book on survey research in the UAE.[51] In the discussion here, I thus present two sorts of evidence showing that many (although not all) Emiratis have deep reservations about the Dubai model of development: (1) unavoidably anecdotal evidence from Emirati intellectuals and others, and (2) the debates over the constitution in the 1970s, a time when Emiratis enjoyed the opportunity to express their opinions on the Dubai model in public and had little good to say about it.

Citizens' Views on the Demographic Imbalance

Emirati citizens have repeatedly and for a long time expressed concern—sometimes bordering on panic—about the demographic imbalance in their country. In an interview in *Gulf News* in 2007, Jamal Al Suwaidi, head of the Emirates Center for Strategic Studies and Research and adviser to the crown prince of Abu Dhabi, said that, when he had visited a major mall in Dubai, "I felt awkward as everybody there was staring at me as if I were from another planet. It was because I wore a kandoura [the traditional robe worn by male Emiratis]. . . . I was in the middle of a sea of expatriates, many of whom might not have seen something like that before." He continued, saying that it was "too late" to solve the demographic imbalance and that "the best we can do is to search for ways to best co-exist as nationals with the expatriate majority. . . ."[52] An even more well-connected Emirati—the chief of the Dubai police force—said at a Conference on National Identity held in Abu Dhabi in 2008, "I fear that we are building buildings but losing the emirates" (this is alliterative in Arabic: *nabni 'amarat wa nufqid al-imarat*). He continued, wondering whether "an Indian named Kuti" would someday be the president of the UAE.[53] Abdulkhaleq Abdulla, in an editorial responding to the Al Suwaydi interview, wrote that "there is a limit to how much one can

51. Al-Astal 2008.

52. In Mohammed Al Mezel, "Who Are We, That's the Question," *Gulf News*, March 21, 2007, http://gulfnews.com/news/gulf/uae/general/who-are-we-that-s-the-question-1.167534. See also Kanna 2011, 121–22.

53. In *Al-Jazeera*, "Tahthirat imaratiyya min tada'iyat khalal al-tarkiba al-sukaniyya" [Emirati warnings about the dangers of the demographic imbalance], April 15, 2008, http://www.aljazeera.net/news/archive/archive?ArchiveId=1088314 (accessed August 26, 2010).

conceal the deadly demographic imbalance in the UAE. The numbers alone, which have reached critical levels, are frightening."[54] In a separate interview, he said that, even though the progress of Dubai was a source of some pride among Emirati nationals, there is "fear that we may lose everything that we have built. This feeling comes from the fact that we are a small minority in a city that's full of foreigners. We are very scared."[55] Ibtisam al-Ketbi, an Emirati political scientist, told one interviewer that "Many people oppose this hyper-development and wonder who are we building all these projects for. . . . You feel this is not your country anymore. There is a great feeling of alienation among Emiratis."[56]

Other Emirati intellectuals are even less hopeful. Hussein Ghobash in 1999 wrote, "The UAE, with its current population structure, does not have a future"; what is needed is "the return of balance to the population structure before all else, in that it is necessary that the native people of the country are the largest single group in their country."[57] According to Ghobash, to redress the demographic imbalance it is necessary to reduce the Asian population by at least half, "no matter what the cost."[58] He ends his discussion of the demographic imbalance by suggesting that the UAE needs a new constitution and a stronger FNC.[59] Abdullah Taryam, who served as a minister in the federal government for eight years in the 1970s, writes that the population imbalance is a problem "which gives constant worry to the citizens since it causes the proportion of nationals to shrink every year and threatens their very survival."[60] Yousif Al-Yousif, an Emirati professor of economics at the national university, writes that the "existence [of the UAE] as a state is threatened because its population is a mixture, with nothing uniting it, neither language nor religion nor heritage, so that its Arab-Islamic heritage is almost erased."[61] Citizens, in these discussions, often express a specific preference for Arab and Islamic culture, and sometimes a hostility toward foreigners. Their concerns, however, should not be dismissed as mere expressions of xenophobia. Citizens are concerned about the possibility of what amounts to national dispossession. Thus, for example, Omar Al-Shehabi takes pains to say that he does not

54. Abdulkhaleq Abdulla, "UAE's Demographic Imbalance," *Gulf News,* April 14, 2007, http://gulfnews.com/.

55. In Hamza Hendawi, "A Gulf State Grapples for Identity in Sea of Foreigners," Associated Press, May 1, 2008.

56. In "Dubai Natives Protect Identity in Fast-Changing Land," *Agence France Presse* (via Lexis Nexis), May 31, 2006 (accessed December 31, 2007).

57. Ghubash 1999, 14.

58. Ibid., 18–19.

59. Ibid., 33.

60. Taryam 1987, 261.

61. Al-Yousif 2008, 85.

blame immigrants for the demographic imbalance; they come to the Gulf out of the understandable desire to build a better life for themselves and their families.[62]

Who do these intellectuals blame for their predicament? Yousif al-Yousif clearly blames the ruling families; his article, published in 2008 in the journal *Al-Mustaqbal Al-Arabi,* is entitled "When Power Becomes Booty" and condemns how the ruling families have exploited their control of political power.[63] Al-Shehabi blames the capitalists and ruling elite, pointing out that they are often one and the same. "What we have found . . . is the absence of a role for the basic element in the society—that is to say, the citizens. Their voice is marginal in determining the policies or projects that we have discussed, whether that be real estate projects, labor policies, or other policies of vital importance. Instead, we find the hegemony of decision-makers and capitalists over all crucial decisions. . . ."[64] Others are not quite so blunt, but it is still clear that the ruling family of Dubai, along with the other ruling families, receive the lion's share of the blame. Often this is clear from the focus on policies that have long been associated with the ruling family of Dubai. Taryam says that the failure of constitutional reform led to "haphazard development, coupled with unhealthy competition between emirates" (both long attributed to Dubai), which in turn "led to unprecedented influxes of foreign workers who eventually outnumbered the local population and caused grave social, cultural and economic problems. All these challenges were ignored, and the tentative endeavours aimed at dealing with them were stopped."[65] Abdulkhaleq Abdulla writes, "The few rather practical ideas put through to tackle the growing demographic problem received scant attention. The authorities relentlessly pursue a policy of double digit economic growth that only perpetuates the chronic demographic imbalance."[66]

In contrast, Mohammed bin Rashid, the ruler of Dubai, thinks little of his critics. In a 2006 interview he said that critics of growth are "short-sighted or just speaking their minds or suffering from inferiority complexes, which are hard to cure."[67]

There are, to be sure, those who are less concerned by the demographic imbalance and the current trajectory of the UAE. The recent rapid development of the UAE and the rise of the Dubai brand to international prominence have

62. Al-Shehabi 2012, 27; Kanna 2011, 49–50.
63. Al-Yousif 2008.
64. Al-Shehabi 2012, 28, 21.
65. Taryam 1987, 247.
66. Abdulla, "UAE's Demographic Imbalance," *Gulf News,* April 14, 2007, http://gulfnews.com/.
67. In Sheikh Mohammed bin Rashid Al Maktoum, "Al Ittihad Interviews Sheikh Mohammed," December 4, 2006, http://www.sheikhmohammed.co.ae (accessed April 14, 2007).

produced a sense of pride among many Emiratis, as we might expect. Mishaal Al Gergawi writes of the "romantic perception . . . that this is the only place where Arabs have attempted to build modern institutions and not failed since Andalusia." Although receptive to the advantages of UAE development, he dwells on the "melancholy" that Emiratis feel for the "loss of their identity . . . or their incapacity to incubate a contemporary interpretation of their own identity under the avalanche" of migration.[68] Al Gergawi, at least, suggests that there is some possibility of forging a new Emirati identity that adapts to demographic realities. In a similar vein, Ahmed Kanna describes a group he calls "flexible citizens" of Dubai, who have embraced, to some degree, Dubai cosmopolitanism. Anecdotal evidence suggests that these "flexible citizens" are more prominent in Dubai than elsewhere in the UAE. Their embrace of the Dubai model is born of a pride in Dubai (and its brand) alongside, often, a discomfort with the "traditional" social mores of Emirati society. This is accompanied by strong support for Mohammed bin Rashid. Kanna does not make any claims for the demographic weight of these "flexible citizens" among the Dubai population (or in the UAE as a whole), and many of these "flexible citizens" come from Dubai citizen families that have, as he puts it, less "pedigree" in the traditional hierarchy of Emirati society.[69]

The financial crisis that struck in 2008 slowed down the growth in the expatriate population, at least for a while, and was initially welcomed by many citizens. Abdulkhaleq Abdulla told a reporter from the *New York Times,* "This is a blessing, we needed it. . . . The city needs to slow down and relax. It's good for the identity of our country."[70] Yet the incentives for the ruling families to encourage growth and immigration have not lessened—the crisis made it all the more imperative to attract foreigners who could fill the empty buildings—and in 2010 the UAE National Bureau of Statistics released population estimates (after announcing the cancellation of the census) that revealed that citizens had fallen to 11% of the total population.[71]

In Kuwait the public debate over the demographic imbalance differs starkly from the UAE. While Emiratis see immigration as a threat to their identity and to their future, Kuwaitis see immigration in far less apocalyptic terms—the basically Kuwaiti nature of Kuwait is not in doubt. Part of the explanation for the difference in rhetoric surrounding the number of foreigners has to do with the role

68. Mishaal Al Gergawi, "A Forty-Year-Old Minority in the UAE," *Gulf News*, December 2, 2011, http://gulfnews.com/opinions/columnists/a-forty-year-old-minority-in-the-uae-1.939898.

69. Kanna 2011, 143–46.

70. In Michael Slackman, "Emirates See Fiscal Crisis as Chance to Save Culture," *New York Times*, November 12, 2008.

71. Croucher, "Door-to-Door Census in UAE Is Scrapped," *The National (Abu Dhabi)*, April 6, 2011.

of expatriates in the Kuwaiti economy. Foreigners take jobs that Kuwaitis do not want, and almost all these jobs provide services, broadly conceived, to citizens. In the UAE, by contrast, large parts of the economy operate largely independently of citizens (the tourist economy, for example, consists of foreigners offering services to other foreigners). In Kuwait, the jobs performed by foreigners are typically much more closely connected to a need—or perceived need—of citizens; the demographic imbalance is not imposed from above but is a failure of society as a whole.

This difference has a direct impact on the political salience of the demographic issue. In the emirates, the issue of the population structure is a point of contention between the citizens and the rulers; talking about the issue of the population structure thus has the sense of airing opposition to the regime.[72] In Kuwait, by contrast, the population structure is seen more as a collective failure of Kuwaitis as a whole to resist the temptation to hire a maid (or two, or three, or four). The parliament could do something about it if it wanted to, but it does not want to much, and the issue has a low profile in parliamentary politics. It certainly is not a point of contention between the ruling family and the National Assembly.

Failed Efforts to Constrain Dubai in the 1970s

While the consequences of the Dubai growth model on the demographic structure of the UAE have consistently worried Emirati intellectuals, the struggles over the UAE constitution in the 1970s provide even stronger evidence of citizen disquiet with the Dubai model. From 1976 to 1979, a space opened in Emirati politics as a result of the dispute between Abu Dhabi and Dubai over the powers of the federation. Citizens used this political space to press for reforms that would create a UAE with a stronger federal government, a more equitable division of oil wealth among the emirates, and a political system that would give citizens a stronger voice. In short, they wanted the UAE to be more like Kuwait.

For all of this, reformers won the support of the ruler of Abu Dhabi and the vociferous opposition of the ruler of Dubai. One consequence of the failure of the 1970s reforms is that the constitutional structure of the UAE is built around the Dubai economic model. Even more significantly, in recent years the Al Nahyan ruling family of Abu Dhabi seems to have adopted elements of the Dubai

72. The FNC has raised the issue repeatedly since independence, and Davidson (2005, 196–97) gives this as an example of input from the FNC that the rulers did not much welcome. In a 1978 meeting of the FNC, a deputy feared that citizens had become a minority "melting" into the mass of humanity in the UAE. United Arab Emirates Federal National Council, "Minutes of the Fifteenth Meeting of the Second Session of the 3rd Term of the FNC," April 25, 1978, 5.

model, reversing the stance held by Zayed in the 1970s. The story of how his came to be is crucial in understanding the political economy of the UAE and how it differs from that of Kuwait.

The constitution under which the UAE gained its independence in 1971 was meant to be temporary; indeed, the word "temporary" (*mu'aqqat)* was in the title of the constitution. Moreover, it had an expiration date, 1976.[73] Sheikh Zayed—the ruler of Abu Dhabi and the president of the UAE—wanted a stronger federation and wanted to use the process of writing a permanent constitution as a way to achieve it. In 1975, Zayed issued a decree appointing the members of a commission to write a permanent constitution. An Egyptian member of the commission, it appears, wrote the draft that formed the basis of the commission discussions.[74] The overall effect of the draft permanent constitution was to strengthen the power of the federation and federal institutions: Abu Dhabi and Dubai would lose their vetoes in the Council of Rulers, individual emirates would surrender 75% of their wealth to the federal government, and the president would gain additional powers.

The draft constitution strengthened the FNC along with the presidency, and its new powers were clearly modeled after those of the Kuwaiti National Assembly, albeit somewhat diluted. The reformed FNC could vote to remove confidence in ministers but would need to do it twice to force the minister to resign. As in Kuwait, ministers served in the assembly but did not have the right to vote on motions of confidence. Unlike Kuwait, there was no provision that amounted to removing confidence in the prime minister.[75] The draft constitution called for elections to select "some or all" members of the FNC, but it did not specify a deadline for them to be held, and in the meantime, rulers would select an electorate of at least five times the number of the available seats, which would then select the members of the FNC.[76] Overall, the Emirati reformers of the 1970s clearly were inspired by the Kuwaiti model and sought to reshape the political structure of the UAE along Kuwaiti lines.

Why did Zayed support these changes to the constitution, some of which diluted the authority of the ruling families and his emirate? The revised constitution shifted Zayed's power from the emirate level (Abu Dhabi) to the federal level. The proposed constitution would have made the UAE less a confederation of independent emirates, each led by its own ruling family, and more a single state led

73. Article 144 specified that the temporary constitution of 1971 would be in force for five years.

74. Taryam 1987, 234–35; Al-Tabtabai 1978, 446; al-Shahin 1997, 496–98.

75. Articles 93 and 94. The text of the draft constitution can be found in al-Tabtabai 1978, 537–74. Al-Tabtabai (1978, 450–51) discusses the powers of the FNC.

76. Al-Tabtabai 1985, 362.

by a group of families, first among whom would be the Al Nahyan. An historical parallel (albeit imprecise) would be the once-independent monarchs of the German states that were absorbed into the German Empire (under the Hohenzollern dynasty) in the nineteenth century; they retained their titles but little of their former power or glory. Thus, the expansion of federal power threatened the Al Maktoum of Dubai much more than the Al Nahyan—it threatened to make the Al Maktoum second fiddle to the Al Nahyan in the federation, a status that did not at all suit the ambitions of the Al Maktoum.

At least initially, Zayed could have counted on the support of a strengthened FNC. He enjoyed a real popularity among Emiratis. Heard-Bey writes that Zayed's

> generosity and largess in committing Abu Dhabi's fast increasing wealth knew no bounds. He traveled all over the UAE . . . to take charge of projects in distant parts of the country, to witness the progress, and to get feed-back from the population. In consequence, the population—in particular in the five poorer and more remote northern and eastern emirates—was beginning to see Abu Dhabi and the "Union" as their best hope for a better life. The local ruling families of these emirates had reason to worry, lest their tribal population eventually transfer their allegiance to a more distant benefactor with much more power to satisfy their expectations.[77]

In short, the popularity of Zayed meant that he was likely to have allies in an elected FNC, at least initially, and the promise of an elected FNC helped to cement Zayed's support among the Emirati citizenry. There were good reasons then—growing out of the confederal nature of the UAE—for Zayed to support, at least in the short run, a more liberal constitution.

Zayed's support for the new draft constitution, however, was not strong enough to overcome the opposition of Dubai, supported by Ras al-Khaimah.[78] To break the deadlock, and to put pressure on Dubai and Ras al-Khaimah to concede to a stronger federation, Zayed threatened to refuse to serve as president for a second term.[79] Dubai still did not budge, and the Council of Rulers, in 1976, decided to extend the term of the temporary constitution for an additional five years.[80]

The extension of the constitution did not resolve the issue, and in 1979, the FNC and the federal cabinet (i.e., two of the three principal political institutions of the federation) wrote a joint memorandum to the Council of Rulers demanding

77. Heard-Bey 2005, 363.
78. Taryam 1987, 234–35.
79. Al-Tabtabai 1978, 447.
80. Al-Shahin 1997, 284–85. On this period, see also Heard-Bey 1999.

reforms.[81] These reforms had the support not only of the government and the FNC but also of the wealthiest emirate, Abu Dhabi, and the most popular figure in the country, Sheikh Zayed. The memorandum can be read as a plea for a unified federation and a repudiation of the Dubai model of development, and it won support from Emirati intellectuals via the journal *Al-Azmina Al-Arabiya*.[82] The memorandum contains several specific recommendations designed to increase the power of the federation, including a demand that oil revenue be combined into a single federal budget that would be used to "achieve a complete and equal renaissance among all of the emirates. . . ." The memorandum continued, "It is not acceptable that the state relies, in organizing its finances, on what one emirate might give it, and what another emirate does not."[83] The memorandum also demanded that the police, military, and judiciary be unified at the federal level. Several demands in the memorandum directly engaged Dubai's economic policies and implicitly criticized the failure of Dubai to follow laws passed by the Council of Rulers and its obstruction of reforms in the council. The memorandum demanded the end of illegal immigration and demanded that the federal Ministry of the Interior carry out its duties "according to the laws and decisions agreed to by the Supreme Council."[84] Implicitly, this was a criticism of the flouting by Dubai of the federal ministry. The authors of the memorandum criticized duplication in development projects, seeking an end to the waste that resulted from a lack of planning, especially the duplication and random distribution of facilities.[85] Several additional demands criticized the paralysis in federal institutions brought on by disputes among the ruling families of the emirates; in practice, this was also criticism of Dubai, which had blocked new laws and obstructed the implementation of laws already approved by the Council of Rulers.

Finally, the authors of the memorandum (the appointed members of the FNC and the appointed members of the federal cabinet of ministers) recommended an expansion of political participation, writing that "developing citizens politically deepens the links between the base and the summit [i.e., the rulers and the ruled] and strengthens the bonds of national unity and develops feeling of allegiance to the nation." Furthermore, the memorandum continued, "Experience has shown the necessity of broadening the basis of the FNC's membership . . . and enabling

81. Taryam 1987, 238–39. Taryam mentions two memoranda, one in 1978 and one in 1979. The second is the one that is more frequently mentioned; see also Taryam (note 55). The text of the memorandum can be found in al-Shahin 1997, 484–95.

82. Some articles from the journal can be found in Ghabbash 1990.

83. In al-Shahin 1997, 489.

84. Ibid., 488.

85. Ibid., 492.

deputies to undertake their charge to effectively practice real democracy, by giving the membership complete legislative authority to become the real legislative authority and not just a consultative council, the role of which is limited to providing mere advice."[86]

The memorandum prompted a meeting of the seven rulers, and on the occasion of the meeting, demonstrators took to the streets across the UAE in support of the demands made in the memorandum. Heard-Bey writes that citizens and students "converged on the venue of the seven Rulers in Abu Dhabi," demanding a stronger federation. This continued over the following days, accompanied by "a surge in enthusiastic expressions of support for the President, Shaikh Zayed, who was seen as the proponent of speedier unification."[87] Abdullah Taryam—who served in the cabinet for most of the 1970s—writes that

> Thousands of citizens from various walks of life, students, government officials and tribesmen, assembled in procession from the various emirates and marched towards the place where the meeting was in progress. There they shouted slogans, calling upon the rulers to collaborate, demanding consolidation of the union, more powers for the federal institutions, support for the President of the state, and approval of the memorandum.[88]

Zayed addressed the crowd, acknowledged their demands, and "asked them to return to their work and leave their demands in his good care."[89] He then returned to the meeting, where the rulers agreed to the request by Dubai to postpone a decision on the memorandum.[90] Over the next week, citizens mobilized to put pressure on the rulers—or, specifically, on the rulers of Dubai and Ras al-Khaimah. Taryam writes, "Processions and demonstration were staged in all towns in the emirates, and even women participated. All demanded the preservation and consolidation of the union, and even called for complete unity."[91] The meeting of the rulers, however, proved anticlimactic. The rulers of Dubai and Ras al-Khaimah did not show up; the ruler of Dubai thought that the demonstrations had been "pre-engineered . . . to pressure him into agreement."[92]

86. Ibid., 492, 494. Heard-Bey (2004, 408–9) argues that the memorandum did not explicitly demand democracy because it did not explicitly call for elections to the FNC. The text of the memorandum, however, leaves little doubt that its authors favored much greater political participation.
87. Heard-Bey 2004, 409.
88. Taryam 1987, 242–43.
89. Ibid., 243.
90. Al-Shahin 1997, 286.
91. Taryam 1987, 243.
92. Al-Shahin 1997, 2860; Taryam 1987, 244.

Following the failure of the rulers to arrive at a decision, Abu Dhabi issued a statement pointing out the opposition of Dubai to strengthening the federation. In response, the rulers of Dubai and Ras al-Khaimah engaged Abu Dhabi in a "war of statements."[93] The ruler of Dubai argued that the proposed constitution "was not the product of a serious study by the representatives of the emirates as much as it was an academic exercise by some of the experts, and it does not emanate, in its foundations and origins, from our true religion." To remedy this, the ruler called for a new committee to be formed that would "study the issue of the permanent constitution on two principles, our glorious Islamic religion and our inherited traditions, in order to arrive at a constitution emanating from our religion and in accordance with the traditions of our society."[94] The ruler of Dubai then told a newspaper that he thought that the other emirates were supporting the demonstrators on the streets and added that a unified state "means holding elections and we do not know who would win them, and would mean all the money and income and decisions of the state would be in the hands of a unified central government alone."[95]

In the end, the reformers' efforts came to nothing. The intransigence of Dubai defeated Sheikh Zayed's effort to build a stronger federation. Sheikh Rashid, the ruler of Dubai, was made the prime minister of the federation in the hope that this would, perhaps, give him an investment in the federal institutions. Some leading proponents of a stronger federation left their ministerial posts. Taryam observes that "mediation was a success only in so far as it helped to meet the desires of those who were in favour of no change. . . ."[96] Taryam suggests that Sheikh Zayed gave up his quest to strengthen the federation because he "became convinced of what he had been told by the Kuwaiti minister [Sabah al-Ahmad, who mediated between the rulers], who had particularly warned of popular extremism, pointing out what was then happening in Iran. Sheikh Zayed was also told that certain persons, aspiring to influence and rule, were endeavoring to create divisions among the rulers. Thus he was persuaded to withhold his demand for a stronger union. . . ."[97] Zayed did not put his weight behind the issue again, and any serious effort to change the nature of the federation ended in 1979. The issue of constitutional reform came up with less and less frequency after 1979. The government shut down the journal *Al-Azmina Al-Arabiya* in 1981.[98] In 1991, a commission was formed to study the issue of a permanent constitution, but a member of the Al Maktoum was

93. Taryam 1987, 244.
94. In al-Shahin 1997, 286–87.
95. Ibid., 287.
96. Taryam 1987, 244–47
97. Ibid., 245–46.
98. Abdulla 1984, 285.

appointed to lead it. In 1996, the Council of Rulers put to rest the problem of the temporary nature of the constitution with the straightforward expedient of removing the word "temporary" from its title, leaving the rest of the text virtually unchanged.[99] This marked—or further confirmed—the triumph of the status quo and the failure of the idea of a different sort of UAE with much stronger federal institutions. The idea of constitutional reform has not been forgotten, but the issue has faded into the past, and today the idea of constitutional reform is rarely broached in the UAE by those who have the influence to make it happen.

Consequences of the Failure to Constrain Dubai

The failure to revise the constitution in the 1970s set the UAE down a very different path than Kuwait, one defined in no small part by the commercial and real estate interests of the Al Maktoum. The consequences of the failure include the solidification of the structure of political privilege in the UAE, the perpetuation of the demographic imbalance, and the exacerbation of inequality among the various emirates of the UAE.

The ruling families of Dubai and Abu Dhabi made up their differences after 1979, and this made it possible for the federation to operate more effectively within the constraints of the original 1971 constitution. On some specific issues, Dubai made compromises that brought its position closer to the demands made in the memorandum: the Council of Rulers met on a reasonably regular basis, the individual emirates no longer maintained their own armed forces (although today the federal armed forces are, in practice, the armed forces of Abu Dhabi), naturalization slowed to a trickle, and border disputes among the emirates no longer led to armed conflict. The experience of the several decades since 1979 suggests that the federation has been made into a reasonably effective form of government for the UAE, one that delivers, at least, internal and external security. The UAE does well on the World Bank governance indicators.[100] This state, however, is not the one that the writers of the memorandum sought. Those authors sought to build a state that would be something more than the creature of the seven ruling families. The word *dawla* recurs repeatedly in the document—the state viewed as an institution, or set of institutions, separate from the families, to which loyalty is owed and that serves the interests of the citizens as the nation. The failure of the reform movement of the 1970s meant that UAE institutions, rather than taking on the form of a

99. Al-Shahin 1997, 289. The only other change was to make Abu Dhabi the permanent capital.

100. World Bank, "Worldwide Governance Indicators," http://info.worldbank.org/governance/wgi/index.asp (accessed December 20, 2012). The exception, of course, is the indicator that measures political accountability.

more standard state (such as that found in Kuwait), instead were molded around the interests of the ruling families, hence the term *Dubai Inc.* remains quite descriptive, capturing a truth about the political institutions of Dubai. Today a UAE state exists, in the sense that the UAE is a well-governed territory, but that state, compared especially to the Kuwaiti state, is the creature of the ruling families, molded around their arrangements for sharing power, presiding over a population consisting mostly by foreigners, and oriented toward the interests of the ruling families.

A debate in the FNC in 2003 gives us a flavor of the problem. The FNC—which at that time was entirely appointive—questioned the federal minister of planning about the activities of his ministry. One deputy questioned the direction of development in the UAE, especially its effect on the demographic imbalance. The minister replied that he could not address the issue because a committee, headed by the ruler of Dubai, was examining the problem. Another FNC deputy—to judge by his name, from the poorer emirate of Fujairah—said that many excuses had been offered for the failings of the Ministry of Planning, but that

> I believe that the issue is very simple. The intention—as I see it—has never been present to energize and create a real role for this ministry in this country, and this is the problem in all simplicity. The National Council for Planning is frozen, funds and personnel are absent, and the local offices in most of the emirates and especially the influential emirates in the union perform the functions of the federal ministry of planning. . . . This is the case in most of the federal ministries—the ascendance of the role of local authorities over the role of the federal ministries. . . . I say that from the beginning of this discussion until now no clear replies have come from the minister, and in all simplicity I say that there is no need to be blind from the truth, and that is that the ministry is a dead body, and the main cause of this is the triumph of the local departments over the ministry. There is no true intention to revive the role of the ministry, and in the end the ministry is helpless. [101]

The failure to change the constitutional structure of the UAE in the late 1970s left in place the political and social structure of power in the emirates. Hendrik Van der Meulen, writing in the mid-1990s, paints a picture of a profoundly stratified citizen society with the ruling lineages of the ruling families at the apex, followed by other lineages of the ruling family, and then by prominent merchants, tribal lineages, and families traditionally associated with the ruling family.[102] Technocrats

101. United Arab Emirates Federal National Council, "Minutes of the Second Meeting of the First Session of the 13th Term of the FNC," March 11, 2003, 71.

102. Van der Meulen 1997, 87–88.

also do well in the UAE, but citizens with less education, from the poorer emirates, and without ties to traditionally prominent families have little voice. This is in sharp contrast to Kuwait, which had a similarly stratified society before independence. Citizens who are relatively less privileged in Kuwait—in terms of both class and the traditional stratification of Gulf society—can make themselves heard in the parliament; similarly situated citizens in the UAE and Qatar have no similar institution.

The reformers of the 1970s sought to even out the disparities in wealth among the emirates. This was to be accomplished by making the wealth of Abu Dhabi the wealth of the federation itself, thus giving the citizens of the poorer emirates a more direct claim on the Abu Dhabi oil income. Moreover, as the Kuwaiti experience also makes clear, a stronger FNC would have given Emirati citizens from the poorer emirates a sturdier platform from which to demand a more equitable distribution of wealth. The failure of the constitutional reform movement solidified the distinctions among the citizens of the emirates and made them more permanent.[103] The ruling family of Abu Dhabi has long handed out plots of lands to citizens, along with loans to build small apartment buildings.[104] The intent was to distribute wealth to citizens, and this policy accomplished a great deal in helping to enrich at least some of the citizens of Abu Dhabi, although not the citizens of the other emirates of the UAE. In the poorer emirates, citizens more commonly work for the federal government rather than for the government of their emirate, and competition for positions is noticeably more intense than in the richer emirates. Van der Meulen notes that "virtually all" female schoolteachers in Ras al-Khaimah are citizens, while in the richer emirates they are expatriate Arabs.[105] Unemployment is higher in the poorer, more distant emirates of Ras al-Khaimah and Fujairah than in Dubai or Abu Dhabi.[106] Although citizens from the poorer emirates can often find state positions, in many cases this requires commuting (or moving) to Abu Dhabi or Dubai. Even then, the "place of issue" line in UAE passports typically indicates Emiratis' home emirates, and government agencies in the richer emirates sometimes discriminate against those from other emirates.[107]

103. IMF 2007, 6.

104. Abu-Baker 1995, 170; "The President," United Arab Emirates, 2006, Government.ae, www.government.ae/gov/en/gov/federal/president.jsp (accessed December 18, 2007); Samir Salama, "Residents Sore over Raffle System for Flat Leasing," *Gulf News*. The committee started operations in 1981.

105. Van der Meulen 1997, 226.

106. United Arab Emirates 2009, chap. 3, table 49; IMF 1998, 26, 28.

107. Those whose tribes span multiple emirates can sometimes change the "place of issue" in their passports, but those whose tribes are specific to one emirate face more difficulties. Sultan Al Qassemi, "The UAE Is One Nation . . . It's Time Our Passports Said So," *The National* (Abu Dhabi), October 11, 2009. Abdulrahim al-Shahin, who comes from Ras al-Khaimah, calls for an equalization in pay and benefits between jobs (for citizens) in the federal government and those in emirate-level governments so that local government becomes more attractive and citizens do not need to move to find work (al-Shahin, 1997, 396).

Yet these disparities, perhaps surprisingly, have not prevented the emergence of a strong sense of Emirati national identity. When Davidson asked 250 Emiratis what they considered their identity to be, almost 80% said Emirati.[108] In some sense, Emirati citizens are a nation in search of a state; the UAE state is a creature of the ruling families who treat the citizens as but one constituency among the many groups who live in their realms. UAE citizens feel a stronger sense of community as a single nation than is warranted by the political structures under which they live.

The 2008 world financial crisis provided the clearest opportunity in several decades for the UAE to revisit the debates of the 1970s. The crisis pushed Dubai Inc. into effective bankruptcy, requiring a bailout from Abu Dhabi.[109] Given the long history of tensions over the consequences of the Dubai economic model in the UAE, we might expect that the bankruptcy of Dubai would have opened the way for far-reaching changes in economic policy in Dubai and in the UAE as a whole. But the desire for deep changes, which emerged so forcefully in the 1970s, had disappeared in the institution that emerged as dominant after the functional bankruptcy of Dubai—and that is the ruling family of Abu Dhabi. In the 1970s, Zayed fought to strengthen the federation, equalize opportunity across the various emirates, and give citizens a voice in how they were governed. In the 2010s, the ruling family of Abu Dhabi invested billions in Dubai and became real estate developers in their own right. The Dubai model appears to have triumphed, despite the Dubai bankruptcy.

The Other Gulf Absolutisms

Qatar

The development of Qatar over the past few years has resembled that of Abu Dhabi more than any other Gulf emirate. Like Abu Dhabi, Qatar is rich in petroleum, and it is just as authoritarian. Qatar has borrowed a page from Dubai in becoming a logistics hub with a state-owned airline and increasing numbers of passengers coming through its airport, and a remarkable increase in air-freight shipments (now more than in Saudi Arabia, although well behind Dubai; see figures 5.4 and 5.5 in the next chapter). Land in Qatar is largely owned by the state and distributed by the ruler. Mehran Kamrava observes that citizens, when they want a free plot of land on which to build a house—with an interest-free loan—must apply to the Emiri Diwan: "the underlying assumption—that all unclaimed land technically belongs to the Amir—is also not lost on Qataris."[110] The Emiri Diwan managed

108. Davidson 2005, 84.
109. IMF 2010b, 38–48.
110. Kamrava 2009, 406.

the early reclamation of the West Bay district, a major area of Doha north of the old center of Doha across the bay. One advantage of reclamation, according to a Qatari official involved in the project, was that "the state" wound up in possession of "large parcels of serviced residential and commercial land which could be granted or leased to political allies."[111] A more recent development built on reclaimed land—the Pearl—is owned by a publicly listed company with a shaykh on the board of directors; another large real estate company—Barwa—is also publicly listed and receives grants of land from the government, but its ties with the ruling family are less clear.[112] Al-Waab city, a development to the south of the old city core, was developed by a company led by members of the ruling family.[113] Ali Khalifa al-Kuwari criticizes the land policies of the regime:

> Many of these lands and properties have passed into private hands either for token, non-competitive prices, or as gifts and bequests. Privately owned hotels, commercial and residential projects and towns are built. The upshot is projects like Souk Waqif, Al-Jasra, Mushairib, Kahraba Street, the fifteen million square meter Education City, the Katara cultural village and the various institutes and projects of the Aspire Zone. The market value of these public properties is in the hundreds of billions.[114]

As in the UAE, foreigners are allowed to buy land freeholds in some developments, notably the Pearl megaproject built on reclaimed land off the coast at Doha. The government, however, has been more solicitous of citizen mores than has been the government of Dubai—in late 2011, the Qatari government precipitously banned the sale of alcohol in restaurants in the Pearl, prompting the closure of several.

The demographic transformation of Qatar resembles that of the UAE, with a tidal wave of immigrants swamping the citizen population.[115] The prominent Qatari intellectual Ali Khalifa al-Kuwari has criticized the demographic imbalance throughout his career. In a 2008 opinion piece published in a number of Gulf newspapers, he wrote, "the demographic imbalance is a violation of the rights of citizens . . . for it is among the rights of citizens that they have a role in their country, and that they be the leading group in their society. . . ." Al-Kuwari writes that "as for the main reason for the deepening of the problem of the current demographic imbalance . . . it goes back, for the largest part, to decisions that

111. Nagy 1997, 133–35.

112. Barwa Real Estate Company, "Annual Report 2011," n.d., 49, 54, http://www.barwa.com.qa; United Development Company (UDC), "UDC 2011 Annual Report," n.d., http://www.udcqatar.com.

113. Al-Wa'ab City, "Sheikh Nawaf Nasser Bin Khalid Al Thani—Chairman of Al Wa'ab City," 2012, http://www.alwaabcity.com/chairmanenglish.html (accessed December 27, 2012).

114. Al-Kuwari 2012, 13.

115. Kamrava 2013, 162.

were taken and policies put in place to execute these decisions." He criticizes in particular the land policies of Qatar and the other Gulf states, particularly the sale of land to foreigners. Lusail City in Qatar, he observes, is "designed to house 200 thousand people, most of them—if not all of them—non-Qataris."[116]

The emir of Qatar (now the former emir, having abdicated in favor of his son in 2013), like the rulers of Abu Dhabi, has indulged in vanity projects designed to bolster the international reputation of Qatar—indeed, his vanity projects are substantially more impressive. He won the rights (some would say he purchased the rights) to host the World Cup tournament in 2022. In doing so, Qatar promised to build a series of soccer stadiums that would achieve the stunning feat of being both open to the air and also air conditioned, so that players and spectators alike would not perish in the heat of the Gulf summer.[117] Less widely noticed, the twelve stadiums would comfortably seat the entire citizen population of Qatar. Twice.[118] The ruling family's activist foreign policy is also on a much greater scale than that required for the narrow security interests of Qatar; moreover, it has the air of an effort growing more out of the personal ambitions of the ruling elite than any sort of necessity.

The trajectory of Qatar thus resembles that of the UAE in key respects: the state has pursued policies largely oriented toward furthering the interests of capitalists, in no small part because the ruling family is heavily involved in business ventures. The private sector employs exceedingly few citizens, and the population policies pursued by the regime have left citizens as a small minority of the population as a whole. The ruling family has a strongly outward-oriented vision for the future of its realm, one that goes far, far beyond the capacities of the roughly 250,000 citizens of the country. The ruling family's ambitions have outgrown the citizens, and its solution—like that of the ruling families of the UAE—is to build a society in which citizens are but one, relatively small, and increasingly less central part.

The Middling Rentiers

In the middling rentiers of the Gulf—Oman, Bahrain, and Saudi Arabia—the ruling families are an important, and leading, part of the capitalist class, and public

116. Ali Khalifa Al-Kuwari, "Al-khalal al-sukani i'tada' 'la huquq al-muwatan" [The demographic imbalance is a violation of the rights of the citizen], *Al-Arab* (Doha), April 10, 2008. See also Al-Shehabi 2012.

117. On top of that, it was also promised that the stadiums would be environmentally friendly. Fédération Internationale de Football Association (FIFA), "2022 FIFA World Cup Bid Evaluation Report: Qatar," 11, 14, http://www.fifa.com/worldcup/qatar2022/bidders/qatar.html.

118. The citizen population is a bit under 250,000. The FIFA evaluation of Qatar's World Cup bid lists twelve stadiums with 540,884 seats (ibid., 12–13). State of Qatar 2010a, chap. 3, fig. 37; 2010b, fig. 24.

policy reflects their economic interests. The rulers of the middling rentiers, however, do not have enough oil wealth to hire almost all citizen graduates into public-sector jobs. Thus a substantial fraction of the citizen labor force must find positions in the private sector or remain unemployed (Saudi Arabia is something of an exception, at least for males). Private-sector employers, as in the extreme rentiers, prefer to hire expatriates rather than citizens. And in all of the Gulf's middling rentiers, expatriates dominate private-sector employment. The labor market imbalances are not quite as severe as in the extreme rentiers, but in the long run, all three of the middling rentiers must decide what sort of societies they want to become: poor imitations of the UAE, with cheap labor and high citizen unemployment, or more normal economies built on the labor of citizens but with correspondingly smaller economies. Put differently, the ruling families of the middling rentiers—unlike the ruling families of the extreme rentiers—must balance the interests of business owners against the political imperative of making jobs available to citizens. The politics of these countries are shaped, in a decisive way, by the degree to which the ruling families adjust their policies to suit employers or citizens.

Oman. Oman has less oil, and more citizens than the other small Gulf monarchies. Its economy thus looks much more like the economy of a nonrentier country in a better-off part of the developing world. This is apparent to visitors traveling from the UAE or other extreme rentiers in the Gulf, who immediately notice that Omani citizens occupy a fairly large number of service positions in the private sector (although they are handily outnumbered by expatriates across the private sector).

As in the rest of the Gulf, the Omani economy is dominated by a small group of families (including the ruling family) and access to state resources helps to determine business success and failure. A U.S. State Department cable reported, "Oman's business landscape remains dominated by a handful of local families who work either in tandem with, or in the shadow of, government-run enterprises," continuing that "Oman's private sector is best described as an oligopoly."[119] The sultan's cousin partnered in developing—or attempting to develop—one of the largest Omani mega-projects, Blue City. He, it appears, arranged the initial purchase of the land from the Omani government—34 square kilometers of beachfront property not far from Muscat—paying something like 10% of its market

119. U.S. Department of State, "Oman, Inc.: Business Oligarchs and Government in Oman's Economy," Wikileaks, August 16, 2009, wikileaks.org.

value.[120] The project failed spectacularly, partly as a result of the real estate crash and partly because of infighting among the owners. Another real estate project, Bar Al Jissa, was a joint venture between a well-established business family and the government, with the government probably providing the land.[121] That said, the best-known mega-project in Oman—The Waves, west of Muscat along the coast—apparently has an ownership structure that features less overt profiteering by (Omani, at least) private parties; it appears to be owned in the largest part by the government and a variety of Omani pension funds, along with a UAE developer.[122] Land distribution on a smaller scale has also been controversial. The government gives out free plots of land to citizens for the construction of houses, and one of the early demands of Omani protesters during the Arab Spring in March 2011 was an independent commission to investigate why some received land "in prime areas and others got land in remote areas. . . ."[123]

The Omani labor market resembles that of Bahrain much more than of, say, the UAE, in that Omanis dominate the public sector but many Omanis also work for a wage in the private sector. Specific percentages are difficult to come by. The government does not report figures for employment in the military, and some other numbers clearly are not reliable—the number of expatriates who were reported to hold jobs in the private sector in 2010 was greater than the total number of expatriates in the country reported in the census of the same year.[124] Keeping in mind these problems with the data, it does appear that the role of expatriates in the workforce grew noticeably in the decade up to 2011. The number of foreigners in the country as a whole increased from 535,000 in 1993 to 559,000 in 2003 and then jumped sharply to 816,000 in 2010, rising from 23.9% of the population in 2003 to 29.4% in 2010.[125]

Not surprisingly, citizen resentment toward foreign labor had a role in the Omani protests during the Arab Spring. James Worrall, the author of one of the best accounts of the protests in Oman, writes that "[w]orking-class Omanis feel increasingly at a disadvantage, from the sheer numbers of South Asians employed

120. Some of the details are set out in Muscat Confidential, an unsigned, but clearly knowledgeable, blog. "Oman's Blue City's Future in the Balance as Debates Continue," *Arabian Business*, May 25, 2010, www.arabianbusiness.com/oman-s-blue-city-s-future-in-balance-as-debates-continue-271088.html#.Ua0dRkDbMvo; "An Independent Assessment of Blue City: Broker Analysis," blog post, Muscat Confidential, May 13, 2010, http://muscatconfidential.blogspot.com/2010/05/independent-assessment-of-blue-city.html; "Blue City Part 2: The Money and the Big Gamble for Wealth," blog post, Muscat Confidential, April 7, 2011, http://muscatconfidential.blogspot.com/2011/04/blue-city-part-2-money-and-big-gamble.html.

121. U.S. Department of State, "Oman, Inc.," 2009.

122. The Wave Muscat, "Shareholders," 2013, http://www.thewavemuscat.com/en/article/about-the-wave-muscat/shareholders.html (accessed June 3, 2013). At The Waves, it is possible to buy freehold property and with it the right to apply for residency in Oman. http://www.thewavemuscat.com/en/section/media-center/faqs (accessed March 29, 2014).

123. Saleh al Shaibany, "Omani Protesters Call for Body to Look into Land Distribution by Ministry," *Times of Oman* (via LexisNexis), March 15, 2011 (accessed March 29, 2011).

124. Sultanate of Oman 2011. Compare tables 2.1 and 5.6.

125. These are all census years. Ibid., fig. 2.1.

in menial jobs, to those increasingly hired in more skilled occupations and the Indian business elite at the top. . . ."[126] These resentments had a particularly important role in the protests in the city of Sohar, along the coast west of the capital. Sohar has emerged as an industrial center in recent years, and the labor force in the area is made up of both expatriates and citizens. As in the rest of the Gulf, capitalists prefer to hire expatriates rather than citizens for most positions, citing the usual concerns about the quality and cost of citizen labor.[127]

In the aftermath of the Arab Spring, the regime hired more citizens in the public sector and stepped up pressure on the private sector to hire citizens. This produced the usual concerns in business circles; as noted in a U.S. State Department publication, Omanization policies are "of particular concern for many international firms in Oman," and international and Omani firms alike find the quotas "difficult to satisfy."[128] The issue, however, is crucial to the future of Oman. Economic growth built largely on foreign labor will take Oman down the path pioneered by the UAE but without the oil wealth of the UAE. The Omani regime's response to the Arab Spring, however, suggests that it may take a more conventional path toward economic development, building an economy in which citizen labor has a major role, even in the private sector.

Bahrain. The ruling family of Bahrain had much to gain from the Gulf real estate boom of the 2000s because the ruling family had spent the preceding decades expropriating much of the available land in Bahrain. Not content with this, the ruling family has also set about reclaiming land off the coast of Bahrain, in many cases cutting off existing villages from access to the sea.[129] The transformation of the shoreline is clearly visible on satellite imagery, and the regime went so far as to block access to Google Earth in 2006 to prevent Bahrainis from viewing satellite images of the ruling family's expropriation of land (along with the construction of many large palaces).[130] When perusing Bahrain on Google Earth, one can see

126. Worrall 2012, 100.

127. Valeri 2009, 201–13.

128. U.S. Commercial Service and the U.S. Department of State, "Doing Business in Oman: 2012 Country Commercial Guide for U.S. Companies," 2012, http://export.gov/oman/build/groups/public/@eg_om/documents/webcontent/eg_om_055867.pdf.

129. William Wallis, "Bahraini Royals under Fire over Development of Offshore Reefs," *Financial Times* (London), May 8, 2006; see also Gengler 2011, 134–41; Justin J. Gengler, "What Happens in the Villages Doesn't Stay in the Villages," Religion and Politics in Bahrain blog post, December 31, 2012, http://bahrainipolitics.blogspot.com/2012/12/when-what-happens-in-villages-doesnt.html; Al-Shehabi 2012, 24.

130. Faiza Saleh Ambah, "In Bahrain, Democracy Activists Regret Easing of U.S. Pressure," *Washington Post*, November 27, 2006, http://www.washingtonpost.com/wp-dyn/content/article/2006/11/26/AR2006112601135_pf.html; Gus Lubin and Michael Kelley, "New Satellite Pictures Show Another Revolution Waiting to Happen In Bahrain," *Business Insider*, May 24, 2013, http://www.businessinsider.com/bahrain-satellite-photos-of-inequality-2013-4?op=1; Mahmood Nasser Al-Yousif, "Google Earth Blocked in Bahrain," blog post, Mahmood's Den, August 7, 2006, http://mahmood.tv/2006/08/07/google-earth-blocked-in-bahrain/.

that the contrast with Kuwait—with its virtual absence of reclamation projects—is particularly vivid.[131] The very wealthy Bahraini prime minister, Khalifa bin Salman, controls an extensive patronage network and is deeply involved in business; he was also one of the family's hard-liners in the Arab Spring and its aftermath.[132]

Bahrain, like Oman, is a middling rentier, and this is apparent in its labor market. Yet Bahraini politics are inescapably shaped by its sectarian divide, and as a result of this divide, the reaction of the Bahraini regime to the employment problem in Bahrain has differed sharply from that of the regimes of both Oman and Saudi Arabia. Bahrain, before the Arab Spring, initiated the most creative approach to labor market reform found in any of the Gulf monarchies. The effort was led by the LMRA, under the protection of the crown prince and as part of his efforts to construct a set of institutions parallel to those controlled by the prime minister.[133] The centerpiece of the reform (discussed in chapter 1) was a tax imposed on employers of foreign labor. The tax was intended to raise the cost of foreign labor and earned the enmity of Bahraini employers. The beneficiaries were to be the Bahraini workers who relied on private-sector jobs; because Sunni Bahrainis tend to have privileged access to public-sector positions (many of which, in Bahrain and the rest of the Gulf, are in the security services and military), the beneficiaries of the LMRA scheme were primarily Shi'i.

The reaction of the Bahraini authorities to the Arab Spring, in terms of the labor market, did not echo that of Oman or, for that matter, Saudi Arabia. Rather than pressing forward with reforms that benefited citizen labor at the expense of capitalists, the Bahraini authorities backpedaled, responding to merchant criticisms of the reforms.[134] This occurred in the context of much wider upheaval in Bahraini politics in which the Sunni ruling family crushed the primarily Shi'i protests; at the same time, hard-liners in the ruling family sidelined members of the family who supported dialog with the Shi'a, including the crown prince. The failure of labor market reforms was just one part of the regime crackdown on Shi'i Bahrainis.

Bahraini population figures reflect the bias toward business owners, even in the period before the Arab Spring. In a country in which many citizens—especially Shi'a—cannot find employment in either the public or private sector, the number of foreigners in the country nearly doubled between 2000 and 2010, increasing

131. The Kuwaiti government reclaimed land off the coast of the city early on, resulting in the Gulf Road along with a seafront that provides abundant public access to the Gulf.

132. For an outstanding analysis of intrafamily politics in the Al Khalifa, see Gengler 2013. See also Gengler 2011, 218.

133. Wright 2008, 2–3; Niethammer 2006, 9–10.

134. Hasan Tariq Al Hasan, "Bahrain Bids Its Economic Reform Farewell," *openDemocracy*, July 8, 2012, http://www.opendemocracy.net/hasan-tariq-al-hasan/bahrain-bids-its-economic-reform-farewell.

from 630,000 to 1.2 million. As a share of the population, expatriates went from just over one-third to over one-half.[135] The overall picture here is of a regime that has decisively turned its back on those citizens who, because of lack of opportunities in the public sector, must find private-sector employment.

Saudi Arabia. Saudi Arabia resembles Oman much more than Bahrain in terms of the approach of the regime to the labor market. The Saudi ruling family, to be sure, has many business interests and has made vast sums of money from the sale of state land.[136] Access to the bureaucracy is organized around princes of the ruling family, and these princes and their clients have overlapping interests in government bureaucracies and the private sector.[137] Clients have, and can offer to others, access to the bureaucracy that allows individual businesses to evade Saudization mandates. But the senior members of the family appear to take labor market issues seriously and have been—at times—willing to impose major costs on the private sector to coerce capitalists to hire Saudi citizens. The regime has not been consistent in this. The number of expatriate workers in the kingdom has grown over time, and there were proposals in the midst of the boom years of the 2000s to weaken Saudization requirements in the new economic cities. These cities were seen as the response of the Saudi regime to the rise of Dubai, although in practice they tended to lean much more toward heavy industry.[138]

Steffen Hertog, in his work on the Saudi bureaucracy, makes Saudization one of his main case studies. He paints a picture of a bureaucracy that was highly segmented around the powerful princes of the ruling family, with the consequence that policymakers at the top of the regime had a great deal of difficulty effectively implementing policies. The general intent of senior members of the ruling family, however, over the past several decades has been to impose increasingly strict demands on the private sector to hire Saudi nationals. The entourages of the senior princes, of course, also had a hand in undermining these same policies by helping individual companies evade the Saudization requirements. In 2010, while Saudization had made very modest progress, "the situation was more hopeful than in the early 2000s."[139]

135. Central Bank of Bahrain, "Economic Indicators," March 2005, (no. 7), page 2, and September 2013 (no. 41) page 3. Available at http://www.cbb.gov.bh/page-p-economic_indicators.htm.

136. Hertog 2010c, 296.

137. Hertog 2010b, 47–48, 110, 126. On the segmented nature of the Saudi state, see also Al-Rasheed 2005; Hertog 2010b, 27, note 52.

138. Tomlinson 2007; "Industrial Cities," *MEED: Middle East Economic Digest,* September 29, 2012, 77–79.

139. Hertog 2010b, 218

In the wake of the Arab Spring, the regime redoubled these efforts, investing them with a seriousness that reflected the evaluation by the regime of the potentially catastrophic (for the Al Saud) combination of youth unemployment and the spirit of uprising prevalent in neighboring Arab states. The private sector hired more citizens under direct pressure from the government, and the business press reported higher wages for Saudis as businesses bid up the price of Saudi labor (increased public-sector hiring had something to do with this as well).[140] The Al Saud also put in place a system of payments to unemployed Saudis. The regime, in another move that directly addressed labor market imbalances, began deporting thousands of expatriate workers, with a total of some 800,000 deported by spring 2013.[141]

Overall, the response of the Saudi regime suggests that the senior princes of the Al Saud saw the world—at least after the Arab Spring, but also before it—through the prism of the needs of an embattled elite to avoid street demonstrations rather than through the eyes of a capitalist elite determined to promote economic growth despite the consequences for the demographic balance in their society. This bodes well for the long-term development of the kingdom as a polity responsive to its citizens.[142] It is perhaps ironic that Saudi policies—in this regard at least—compare favorably to those adopted by the ruling family of Bahrain.

★ ★ ★

The Gulf absolutisms have diverse approaches to the opportunities and challenges of rentier labor markets. The Saudi and Omani regimes seem to take seriously the labor market problems faced by their citizens, although their responses have not always been particularly effective. Bahrain abandoned its reforms, which would have benefited its Shi'i citizens. In two extreme rentiers, UAE and Qatar, most citizens who want a job can find one in the public sector. This has freed the rulers to pursue capitalist growth based on low-cost labor imported from abroad. The result has been dizzying change in these societies as their economies grow and diversify, and become ever more dependent on foreign labor, foreign tourists, and foreign business.

In the next chapter I turn to again to Kuwait which, like the UAE and Qatar, is also an extreme rentier. Kuwait, however, has a powerful National Assembly, and this has led to a very different pattern of economic development because the Kuwaiti middle class has imposed its own preferences on the economic model pursued by the Kuwaiti state.

140. Gavin 2012.

141. Martin 2013; Dudley 2012.

142. Limiting the share of foreigners in its workforce is a goal that Saudi Arabia shares with other richer countries. The massive deportations, however, have had a deep human cost.

Chapter 5

The Consequences of Participation

It is generally agreed that Kuwait has accomplished little by way of diversifying its economy. Although most observers trace this failure to the Kuwaiti political system, there is much less agreement on the specific ways in which the political system affects the economy. Thus in this chapter, I have two tasks: to show how the Kuwaiti political economy differs from that of the UAE (and the other Gulf monarchies) and also to show which aspects of the Kuwaiti political system are to blame for the lack of diversification. I open the chapter by setting out several explanations for the comparatively poor economic performance of Kuwait, drawn from the political science literature and other sources. I then consider six areas in the Kuwaiti economy: land, tourism, logistics and trade, petrochemicals, the financial industry, and housing. In each I compare the performance of Kuwait with that of the other Gulf monarchies.

Explanations for the Lack of Diversification in Kuwait

Explanations for the economic problems of Kuwait focus on what is seen as the broken Kuwaiti political system.[1] This is because the economic problems of Kuwait are almost always defined in contradistinction to the perceived successes

1. The aftereffects of the Iraqi invasion, for example, are rarely cited to explain the poor economic performance of Kuwait compared to the other extreme rentiers of the Gulf.

of other Gulf countries, especially the UAE and Qatar. What sets Kuwait apart from its neighbors is its political system rather than its culture, history, entrepreneurial traditions, or other variables. Kuwait does not differ from the UAE in its oil wealth, of course, which saps the explanatory viability—in this specific comparison—of the usual villain of the resource curse literature, which is of course Kuwait's oil wealth itself.[2]

Most explanations of Kuwait's relatively poor economic performance are found in the press rather than in the academic literature. The most prominent exception is a *World Politics* piece by Steffen Hertog in which he asks how it is that the Gulf monarchies—with the exception, of course, of Kuwait—have "defied the resource curse" by creating successful SOEs, such as SABIC in Saudi Arabia and DP World in Dubai.[3] His central puzzle—as is clear from the title of his article—is the success of the Gulf monarchies in light of the dismal expectations of the resource curse literature. But he devotes a fair amount of attention to the puzzle within a puzzle of the failure of Kuwait to develop successful SOEs in face of the successes in each of the other five Gulf monarchies.[4] Hertog argues that what makes Kuwait different from the other Gulf monarchies is the absence of "substantive regime autonomy in policy-making." Kuwait has difficulty creating successful SOEs, Hertog argues, because its ruling family is not autonomous: Kuwait "is the one regime that has been much less autonomous in economic decision making. . . . The Kuwaiti leadership has experienced strong pressure from electoral politics and organized bureaucratic interests that it has not been able to contain." [5] He attributes this lack of autonomy directly to the Kuwaiti parliament.[6]

Hertog's argument is restricted to SOEs, and his definition of *autonomy* ("a coherent regime core that can make economic decisions independent of larger interest groups") is not synonymous with a lack of democracy.[7] His argument, however, roughly resembles (or is in the same category as) a common explanation for the contrasting economic records of Kuwait and the UAE. In this argument,

2. Sachs and Warner 1995. See also Brunnschweiler and Bulte 2008; Stijns 2001.

3. Hertog 2010a. The title of the article is "Defying the Resource Curse: Explaining Successful State-Owned Enterprises in Rentier States."

4. For Hertog, the economic failures of Kuwait lie primarily in the failures of its SOEs. Kuwait, he notes, "has a number of very successful companies in sectors in which Dubai's SOEs have excelled, but all of which are outside of the public sector." He cites as examples Agility, a warehousing and logistics firm, and Zain, a telecom provider (2010a, 288, note 103).

5. Ibid., 263. There is a second variable in his larger argument—a "populist-mobilizational history." This is, however, absent in all the Gulf monarchies (290, table).

6. Ibid., 287–88.

7. Ibid., 282.

the UAE has a potent fusion of the political regime with the capitalist elite, one that results in a developmental state laser focused on capitalist growth.[8] Kuwait, on the other hand, suffers from too much democracy—the government, beset by distributional and sectional demands, is not able to diversify the economy.

One version of this argument might lead us to the conclusion that authoritarianism is generally better for economic development than democracy. Of course, there are a lot of rich democracies, so this is not very satisfying. A more nuanced version of the argument is, instead, that Kuwait has moved away from the authoritarian development state but has not yet put in place a state, and political system, responsive to the needs of its citizens and capable of generating economic growth. This is a hard task; arguably it is harder than the creation of Dubai Inc.

We can get a sense of the problems facing Kuwait by considering the political rhetoric surrounding corruption. What is corruption in Kuwait is—as we have seen in the last chapter—an integral part of the developmental state in Dubai and, to a certain extent, the remaining Gulf monarchies. Thus, concerns about corruption are a sign of progress in Kuwait toward a different model of economic development, one that better serves the interests of the middle class rather than the economic and political elite. In Kuwait, the National Assembly has worked hard to establish the norm that the wealth of the state should be distributed through a regular process governed by law. This effort, however, is far from complete. What has emerged is a political dynamic in which the National Assembly, to avoid corruption, blocks most initiatives put forward by the government for fear that the benefits will go disproportionately, and unfairly, to the traditional economic elite.

In some cases, these fears of corruption are well founded. But allegations of corruption also appear in contexts in which there is no particularly good evidence of corruption. The effect, however, is the same. The most prominent example is the 2008 deal between the Kuwaiti government and Dow Chemical, which failed after the threat of an interpellation of the prime minister.[9] Accusations helped scuttle what would have been a profitable deal for Kuwait, and Kuwait exposed itself to enormous liability in the British courts for terminating the deal in violation of the terms in the contract. An editorial in *Al-Qabas* identified these unsubstantiated accusations of corruption as one of the main ways in which the National Assembly contributes to the frustration of development in Kuwait: "What adds insult to injury is constant suspicion of the actions of ministers and the executive branch . . . on the grounds that it harbors some sort of profiteering,

8. For arguments in this general vein, see Hvidt 2009; Sampler and Eigner 2008, 128–29, 159.

9. This debacle is still debated in Kuwait, and perhaps evidence will eventually come to light of actual corruption.

such as the Dow Chemical deal, the fourth refinery, the clean fuels project, development of the islands, and improvements of the public infrastructure."[10] Deputies in the National Assembly tend to see corruption in every single contract, and the safe default position for bureaucrats is to do nothing—and that, in fact, is what they often do.

A counterfactual helps make my argument clear.[11] If the 1962 constitution had never been put in place, and the Kuwaiti National Assembly were as weak as the FNC in the UAE, we would expect that the Kuwaiti political economy would generally resemble those of the UAE and Qatar, with a political regime responsive to the needs of the capitalist elite. This is not to say that Kuwait would be the same as Dubai; the confederal nature of the UAE has made the Al Maktoum particularly focused on economic diversification. But we would expect the Kuwaiti ruling family to react to the Dubai model in the same spirit as the ruling families of Abu Dhabi and Qatar. Expatriates would make up a larger share of the population, and the ruling family would pursue the sort of projects found in Abu Dhabi and Qatar, driven by the same combination of vanity and desire for profit.

The National Assembly makes the Dubai model impossible in Kuwait, but this does not mean that the Kuwaiti economy has no available path toward growth. Economic diversification, even in rentiers, can occur along multiple paths (put differently, it is characterized by equifinality, in that different sets of causes can produce the same result).[12] Some of these paths are available to democracies, and my argument here is *not* that the greater level of political participation in Kuwait dooms its economy. What is true, however, is that, even though the Dubai model of development is not the only way that a state in the modern world can effectively pursue economic development, the Dubai model is the one most obviously available to Kuwait and the one that has worked in a country that, in many respects, resembles Kuwait. The inability—or lack of desire—of Kuwait to follow the Dubai model does not mean it cannot diversify its economy, but it does mean that it must find a different path. Given the difficulties that many countries around the world have faced in creating richly productive economies, Kuwait faces a daunting task.

The interests of the Kuwaiti middle class are systematically affected by extreme rentierism; the middle class has less to gain from diversification than would be the case if more Kuwaiti citizens relied on the private sector for jobs or for taxes to pay for public services. This has a crucial effect on the Kuwaiti political economy

10. Unsigned front page editorial representing the views of the newspaper and its owners, "Da'u iqtisadna li-ya'ish!" [Let our economy live!], *al-Qabas*, July 27, 2011, 1.

11. Morgan 2007, 7, 277.

12. George and Bennett 2005, 63.

and helps explain its failure to diversify its economy. The link between extreme rentierism, the strength of the National Assembly, and economic outcomes in Kuwait has been much discussed in the Kuwaiti press. Kuwaiti business leaders often bemoan the degree to which the National Assembly has become "a large union for the employees of the government and its enterprises."[13] The National Assembly represents the majority of Kuwaiti voters; this majority is composed of state employees dependent on oil revenues with little immediate stake in diversification, which would provide them neither with jobs nor with tax revenues. Diversification away from oil imposes costs on citizens—a need to tolerate foreign mores and an influx of foreigners—that citizens have little incentive to put up with. So they do not, and the National Assembly makes sure they are not forced to. The result is the failure of the Kuwaiti state to take serious steps to promote diversification.

This is a theory favored by Kuwaiti capitalists. In a survey by a Kuwaiti newspaper, businessmen were asked what they thought prevented candidates for seats in the National Assembly from offering ideas that would aid the private sector. The most popular reply, by far was "state employees are a majority of the voters and no voice is louder than theirs."[14] A former deputy in the parliament—a member of the opposition from a venerable merchant family—explained the failures of the National Assembly to promote the private sector in an interview, "I tried as far as possible, with a small number of deputies. . . , to undertake a role in supporting the demands of the private sector and to raise its issues in the parliament, but we were a minority."[15] Jassem Zainal, the head of a finance company, wrote in *Al-Qabas*, "The executive and legislative branches do not take into account the views of the private sector, for the government's hands are tied and it is directed by the National Assembly, to whom the government looks before taking any step, out of fear of some of the deputies, while most of the National Assembly is suspicious of the role of the private sector. The concern of the deputies is satisfying the desires of voters. . . ."[16]

13. Saud al-Fadhali and Ali al-Khalidi, "Al-Haroun: Majlis al-Umma niqaba kabira hammha al-awwl al-difa' 'an masalih muwaththafi al-dawla" [Al-Haroun: The Majlis al-Umma is a large union whose main concern is defending the interests of state employees], *al-Qabas*, April 20, 2008, 52.

14. Saud al-Fadhali and Ali al-Khalidi, "Ma al-su'ubat allati tahul dun tahqiq tarh da'am al-qita' al-khass li-murashshahin fi al-intikhabat?" [What are the difficulties that prevent candidates raising the issue of support for the private sector in elections?], *al-Qabas*, April 20, 2008, 53.

15. Saud al-Fadhali and Ali al-Khalidi, "Al-Sager: Fi al-wilayat al-muttahida wa al-dimuqratiyat al-mutaqaddima takattulat iqtisadiyya tuda'im murashshahin yatabannun qadayaha" [Al-Sager: In the United States and advanced democracies economic blocs support candidates who adopt their issues], *al-Qabas*, April 20, 2008, 52.

16. Jassem Zainal, "Hukuma musayyara min majlis la yathiq bi-l-qita' al-khass" [The government is directed by a Majlis that does not trust the private sector], *al-Qabas*, September 2, 2011; Kuwait Stock Exchange, "International Finance Company," December 31, 2012, www.kse.com.kw/Stock/Stock.aspx?stk=212&V=0 (accessed December 31, 2012).

The 'no jobs, no taxes' theory predicts that diversification will be more successful in those areas in which the costs (for citizens) of diversification are less and the benefits to citizens greater, given that citizens are unlikely to be employed in the non-oil sector or to receive much in the way of government benefits paid for with tax revenues levied on the non-oil sector. Tourism has many negative externalities for citizens, but downstream diversification in the petroleum industry has fewer. Regardless of the severity of the externalities, the relative lack of need among citizens for either jobs or tax revenue should mean that the National Assembly finds it relatively free to indulge in class politics, killing projects on the suspicion that the merchant class will make money on contracting that could instead be spent directly on income support for citizens.

Other causes have been proposed to explain the failure of Kuwait to diversify its economy. One has to do with the peculiarities of monarchical political institutions. The Kuwaiti political system attempts to share power between the National Assembly and the ruling family—that is, between two not easily compatible principles of political authority, one democratic and the other hereditary. The constitution, under current practice, gives the National Assembly what amounts to a soft veto on government policy, a veto expressed through the threat of interpellation and withdrawal of confidence. In a fully democratic parliamentary system, the use of this negative power would be limited by the fact that a majority party (or a majority coalition of parties) would form the government and would have a powerful incentive to demonstrate its competence. In Kuwait, by contrast, the parliament has little stake in the success of the government because the government is appointed by members of the ruling family, not by a majority coalition in the National Assembly. The National Assembly can stop the government from acting, but it does not have the responsibility of forming a government and providing coherent rule.[17] Hertog, in his discussion of SOEs in the Gulf, cites the "halfway democratization" of Kuwait as one explanation for its economic failures.[18]

Of course, Kuwait is not the first monarchy to split power between an elected legislature and a government beholden to the monarchy, although in the modern world it is now rare. Heinz Eulau presents a fascinating discussion of how similar problems were dealt with in Germany in the first half of the nineteenth century: "A natural state of war was assumed to exist between the government and the people. Continuous conflict between the governments and the representative assemblies characterized the early decades of German constitutional development."[19]

17. Brown 2002, 135.
18. Hertog 2010a, 294.
19. Eulau 1942, 45.

As a consequence, by 1848 there was "almost universal acceptance of the principle of parliamentarism by all parties, even by the conservatives," which was "a natural reaction to the disheartening picture of the German dualistic constitutional experience."[20] The comparison with Kuwait might seem a stretch, but it is worth making—the institutional resemblance is striking, and the problems are similar.

Increasingly in Kuwait, too, it is thought that parliamentarism (*al-hukuma al-shabiya*) will help alleviate some of the economic problems and the political paralysis of the country (a point also made by Hertog[21]). In the long run, this is likely to be the direction in which Kuwaiti politics will head. Parliamentarism would certainly make Kuwait more democratic, and it is probably a necessary condition for the development of a state that effectively represents the interests of the Kuwaiti middle class and promotes economic diversification. It is not, however, a sufficient condition. Parliamentarism might well replace one set of political problems with another. It is easier to imagine a fractious party system in Kuwait than a stable party system; it is easier to imagine a democratic government in Kuwait more focused on distributing oil revenues to its clients than one focused on furthering economic diversification.

Another possible cause of Kuwait's failure to diversify is found in the quality of its political leadership. It is common in Kuwait to hear criticism of the government (though most still hesitate to criticize the emir himself). Some of this criticism of the government is voiced by the opposition and is predicated on the presumption that the ruling family should get out of the way and let the National Assembly rule, which pretty much restates the problem of the incompatibility of the two principles of political authority. Others argue that the two principles of political authority could coexist if the ruling family adopted policies that were both wiser and earned more popular support. An *Al-Qabas* editorial gives us a flavor of this sort of criticism. The editorial—on the front page above the fold—starts by pointing out that the "populist approach" to politics in the National Assembly, with its demagoguery, has crippled the economy but continues, saying that "it is the successive governments since 2006 which bear the largest responsibility."[22] There is probably something to this explanation for the problems of Kuwait. At the same time, there are powerful structural forces (as previously discussed) that make it difficult for the Kuwaiti leadership to effectively diversify its economy.

In October 2012, the emir (Sabah al-Ahmad) issued a decree changing the electoral system. The opposition boycotted the next two elections (held in December 2012

20. Ibid., 48.
21. Hertog 2010c, 294.
22. *Al-Qabas* editorial, "Hukumat mashlula" [Paralyzed governments], *al-Qabas*, July 10, 2012.

and July 2013), and the government as a result has faced a less obstructionist National Assembly. This led to the passage of a number of laws long delayed in the National Assembly, and some signs of reform in the bureaucracy. This is hardly a permanent solution to governance problems of Kuwait, but the government now faces a more direct test of whether the problems in the political system lie in the obstinancy of the opposition or in the incapacity of the government.[23]

A final factor (although it probably does not rise to the level of an explanation for the economic performance of Kuwait in its own right) is that identity divisions in Kuwait correspond with class divisions, and the two mutually reinforce each other. One of the two main identity cleavages in Kuwait is between *hadhar* and *bedu* (the other is between Sunni and Shi'a, but the sectarian distinction does not have a strong class component in Kuwait). The *hadhar* are Kuwaitis who descend from families who have long been settled in Kuwait town; the *bedu* are more recently settled Kuwaitis of tribal origin, almost all of them Sunnis.[24] One group within the *hadhar*, the traditional Kuwaiti merchant elite, make up the bulk of the large business class in Kuwait. The *bedu*, by contrast, enjoyed fewer commercial and educational opportunities in the earlier days of the oil boom and today tend to rely on state employment more than the *hadhar* do. Deputies in the National Assembly who hail from the less affluent *bedu* districts push for policies that directly benefit state employees—most obviously with across-the-board increases in salaries paid to state employees but also policies such as the forgiving of consumer debts. This meets with staunch opposition from the Kuwaiti economic elite, who argue that this commits the government to unsustainable spending in the future and further distorts Kuwaiti labor markets. It also reinforces a more general prejudice among many *hadhar* against the *bedu*. This discourse has several elements, including an assertion that the *bedu* are not real Kuwaitis (because their ancestors did not live in Kuwait town) and the accusation that the *bedu* drain state resources without giving much back to the Kuwaiti nation. The prejudice has a cultural component also. The *bedu* are seen as uncouth, and their more traditional attitudes are resented by Kuwaiti liberals, who are mostly *hadhar*. These prejudices are held, of course, in varying degrees; some members of the elite Kuwaiti families fairly seethe with contempt for the *bedu*, whereas others assert a much more inclusive view of Kuwaiti identity. The *bedu*, for their part, do not reflect the same degree of hostility back toward the *hadhar* as a group (and see the lines as less clear between the two groups), but many *bedu* do resent the accusation that they are

23. Herb 2013; Michael Herb, "A Respite in Kuwait?" *Foreign Policy* blogs, December 21, 2012, http://mideast.foreignpolicy.com/posts/2012/12/21/a_respite_in_kuwait.

24. Longva 2006.

parasites on Kuwaiti oil wealth.[25] And it is not hard to find an element of hypocrisy in the accusations of the merchant elite, many of whose families enriched themselves in the early days of oil by manipulating land purchases.

The tension between the *hadhar* and the *bedu* exacerbates class politics in Kuwait. But it is not clear that Kuwait stands out from the other Gulf monarchies in having an identity cleavage that roughly corresponds to class divisions. In the UAE, there is tension between those who come from richer and from poorer emirates (and, because Emiratis typically belong to a tribe, this potentially sets off a more privileged group of tribes from a less privileged group). And in Bahrain, the divide between Sunni and Shi'a is far more severe than any identity division in Kuwait. Moreover, it also appears that the Kuwaiti class division has helped to make the *hadhar-bedu* divide deeper and more politically salient; the causal arrow goes in both directions.

The line between *hadhar* and *bedu* is not insurmountable. The traditional Sunni elite merchant families, after all, trace their descent to the tribes of the Arabian peninsula, and this is a point of pride among them.[26] The cleavage, which used to be less important in Kuwaiti politics, is not exacerbated by international politics (in contrast to the Sunni-Shi'i cleavage), and it does not have the same importance in the politics of other Gulf monarchies as it does in Kuwait. In short, although the *hadhar-bedu* cleavage in Kuwaiti politics is important for understanding how class politics plays out, it is probably not a sufficient explanation, on its own, for the severity of class politics in Kuwait.

Issues in the Kuwaiti Economy

Kuwait does not uniformly, to a constant degree, lag behind the UAE in all economic sectors. In some cases, it lags far behind; in others, it is surprisingly competitive. In some other ways, the Kuwaiti political economy is simply structured quite differently from those of its Gulf neighbors. I consider here a number of economic areas, starting with land. This is one area in which the differences between Kuwait and the UAE are particularly stark and illustrate the impossibility of adopting the Dubai model in Kuwait while also showing the influence of the National Assembly. I follow with a consideration of other sectors: tourism, the entrepôt economy, petrochemicals and refining, the financial industry, and housing. These are the main areas in which other Gulf economies have pursued

25. Ibid., 173.
26. Al-Rumi 2005, especially the table of contents, which is organized by tribe.

diversification, as evidenced by discussions in the press, by the academic literature, and by the economic data.[27]

Land

In Kuwait, undeveloped land is owned—both nominally and effectively—by the state, not by the ruler or the ruling family. Moreover, the state owns something like 90% of the total land area of Kuwait. While other Gulf rulers sell land to promote development, the Kuwaiti National Assembly jealously guards against what it sees as alienation of the national patrimony through sale to the private sector. Thus, much of the 90% of the land owned by the Kuwaiti state is unavailable for development by the private sector, and the private sector complains about this frequently and loudly. In 2008, *MEED (Middle East Economic Digest)* reported that land prices in Kuwait were more expensive than in Dubai or Abu Dhabi because the governments of those emirates play a "lead role . . . in developing land." In Kuwait, by contrast, "developers . . . face a chronic shortage of private land coming to market. . . ."[28] The IMF, in a report on Kuwait, cited "limited access to land" as one of three impediments to foreign direct investment.[29] A 2008 report by the Oxford Business Group said that the largest challenge to the Kuwaiti industrial sector "is the lack of appropriate land required to develop industrial plants or expand already-existing facilities. . . ."[30] In a survey of businessmen conducted by *al-Qabas,* the top concern expressed was privatization, followed by "breaking the grip of the state over land"; 90% of respondents said that this was a priority. According to the newspaper, "Those surveyed agreed that the bottleneck in Kuwait is hidden in the monopoly of the state over approximately 90% of real estate, and the small remainder has increased in price to crazy levels, and it is land for speculation more than development. . . . The private sector, to put it simply, waits for land to be released for real estate investment (housing and commercial), tourism (hotels, resorts and entertainment complexes) and industry (parcels meeting the demand of serious

27. Statistics on the export performance of Gulf economies are often wanting. It is particularly problematic that many GCC states classify a great deal of their exports in a catch-all "other" category (SITC code 931 "Special transactions and commodities not classified according to kind"). United Nations, "United Nations Commodity Trade Statistics Database (UN Comtrade)," UN Statistics Division, comtrade.un.org (accessed January 2, 2013).

28. Redfern 2008.

29. International Monetary Fund (IMF) 2009a, 15. The other two factors were the slow pace of structural reforms and heavy bureaucracy.

30. Oxford Business Group 2008.

investors)."[31] The emir himself, at a meeting with deputies and ministers in 2008, "mentioned the complaints of some citizens who were not able to acquire a plot of industrial land in Kuwait, so they went to Dubai where they were able to acquire a very large piece of land and built a factory on it." [32]

The system of land ownership in the pre-oil era in Kuwait did not differ much from that in the rest of the Gulf; individuals gained ownership over undeveloped land largely through grants from the ruler or a member of the ruling family.[33] The Municipality, at its founding in 1930, took responsibility for documenting and approving land transfers, although members of the ruling family continued to distribute undeveloped land as grants in the 1930s.[34] Najat Abd al-Qadir Al-Jasim, in her authoritative history of the Kuwait Municipality—one of the first governmental institutions in Kuwait and more important than its title implies—writes that "When a member of the ruling family granted land to a citizen, the citizen would go to the Municipality, bringing with him the paper giving the grant, and then would go with the director [of the Municipality] to place markers on the land granted to him. . . ."[35] Those who wanted to purchase land from the state made a request to the Municipality, which then decided whether to accept the request and the price. Proceeds from these sales went to the coffers of the Municipality.[36]

By the late 1940s and early 1950s, land had become valuable, both because of the oil boom and because the government began purchasing large amounts of privately owned land. Shaykhs of the ruling family took advantage of their existing authority to seize lands outside the city. Crystal quotes the political agent in Kuwait, who in 1948 was complaining about "land-grabbing" by the shaykhs; he thought that "the Al Subah are without peers, even in the Gulf, in the exercise of rapacity and selfishness."[37] In his memoirs, Ahmad al-Khatib says that a National Assembly committee in 1971 discovered that the shaykhs had claimed virtually the entire country, from Iraq in the north to Saudi Arabia in the south.[38] Al-Khatib writes that, after the closing of the Majlis in 1939 and the consolidation of the rule of the al-Sabah family, the shaykhs took on the attitude that land

31. "Matha yurid mujtama' al-a'mal min majlis al-umma al-muqbil?" [What does the business community want from the upcoming National Assembly?], *al-Qabas*, March 30, 2008, 45.

32. Ibrahim al-Saidi and Muhammad Sandan, "Al-Amir: Al-khalal bayn al-sultatayn yash'urni bi-l-qalaq wa la niyya li-hall al-majlis" [The emir: The imbalance between the two powers fills me with worry, and there is no intent to dissolve the Majlis]," *al-Qabas*, September 8, 2008, 16.

33. The other means were purchase or simple occupation of the land. Al-Jasim 1980, 190.

34. Before 1931, there were no official form for land transfers, and titles were often lost or destroyed. Ibid., 197.

35. Ibid., 191.

36. Al-Jasim 1980, 191–92 gives an account of several transactions of this sort.

37. Crystal 1990, 64.

38. Al-Khatib 2007, 264.

was "their private property according to the traditional tribal understanding, and according to the understanding of conquest and the traditions common in the [Arabian] peninsula.[39]

Initially, in the 1940s, the emir appears to have approved of the land seizures as a way to preserve peace within the family.[40] This seems to have generated unhappiness in the Municipality. In 1943, the Municipality placed a limit on the size of plots that could be owned outside the town, and in 1947, it required that grants made by members of the ruling family of land outside the city be referred to the emir.[41] It is not clear how effective this was; the political agent's complaint about rapacity of the shaykhs was made in 1948. Nonetheless, merchant influence against the ruling family lived on, to some degree, in the Municipal Council, despite the overall absolutism of the Kuwaiti political system.

After Abdullah Salim came to power in 1950, he sought to curb land seizures by his relatives and reestablish the ruler's control over land in the emirate. He was encouraged to do this, Ghanim Al-Najjar says, by a group of merchants who went to him to complain about land policies. Their unhappiness was shared by some members of the ruling family because only a few members of the family had seized the most land.[42] In October 1954, the High Executive Committee—a new body set up by the emir—declared that all lands outside the planning boundaries of the city were emiri land that could not be owned privately (the term *emiri* itself illustrates the traditional conflation of property owned by the emir and owned by the state).[43] The decree prohibited anyone from owning, buying, or registering the land.[44] The planning line—outside of which fell well over 90% of the land of Kuwait—continues to be important. In 1970, a U.S. urban planning firm wrote in a report that the planning line defines "the areas within which the Government is prepared to recognize claims to private land ownership. The land outside the line is virtually all in Government ownership."[45] A court case in 2011 referred to the planning line when the court ruled on a land transfer involving three shaykhs of the ruling family.[46]

39. Ibid., 259.
40. Crystal 1990, 63–64.
41. Al-Jasim 1980, 193–4.
42. Al-Najjar 2000, 46.
43. Schumpeter 1954.
44. Al-Jasim 1980, 198; Al-Najjar 2000, 61.
45. Colin Buchanan and Partners 1970, 60, 67. A map showing the line appears on page 58.
46. Muhammad Sandan, "'Al-mal al-'amm' tulzim majlis al-wuzara' bi-taf'il qanun B.O.T." ["Public money" forces the council of ministers to activate the B.O.T. law], *al-Qabas*, October 28, 2011, 12.

Thus, before independence Abdullah Salim established the principle that members of the ruling family could not grant or seize land on their own authority and that land outside the boundaries of the town would be, by default, state land. Several decades later, the National Assembly asserted its control over this land, cementing its status as the property of the state and not of the ruling family. In the intervening decades, the Kuwaiti political elite enriched itself via land ownership by selling it to the state rather than by developing it.

Tathmin. In 1952, the Kuwaiti state initiated a policy of assessing (*tathmin*) and purchasing land in Kuwait town from its owners at inflated prices. This helped to define the attitude of the economic elite toward land for several decades. While in recent years across the Gulf land has been valuable largely for its development potential, for many years in Kuwait land was valuable because the state was willing to purchase it at inflated prices.

The ostensible original purpose of the policy of *tathmin*—apart from making land available for government uses—was to provide Kuwaitis with enough money to build modern houses. Traditional construction was of mud brick and had a dangerous tendency to collapse in the occasional heavy rains in Kuwait.[47] Very quickly, *tathmin* became a way for the government to distribute Kuwaiti oil wealth, and it did so in a spectacularly unequal fashion. Those who had land and political connections at the opening of the oil age made vast fortunes. Ghanim al-Najjar estimated that in the first two years 60% of the payments for land went to members of the ruling family itself—and the vast majority of that to only a few members of the family.[48] After protests from merchants the circle of beneficiaries broadened, at least to some extent. From the beginning of the policy, in 1952, through 1982, the state paid out half of the total sum to members of the ruling family and to prominent merchant families. The share of the ruling family was 339 million KD and the merchants' share around 783 million KD.[49] To put this into perspective, *tathmin* accounted for 35% of all government expenditures in 1961–1962 and typically fluctuated between 5 and 10% of all government expenditures up to the early 1980s (see figure 5.1). One Kuwaiti writes, "The land purchase program, which was established in 1952, was used as a distributing mechanism for the oil revenue. But unfortunately the program was corrupt and information was used by influential individuals who had prior knowledge and influence inside the committee making the decisions. Those individuals used

47. Al-Jasim 1980, 206–7; Al-Sabah 1980, 56–57.
48. Al-Najjar 2000, 46.
49. Al-Dekhayel 1990, 374–76, see also 293; Salih 1991, 48.

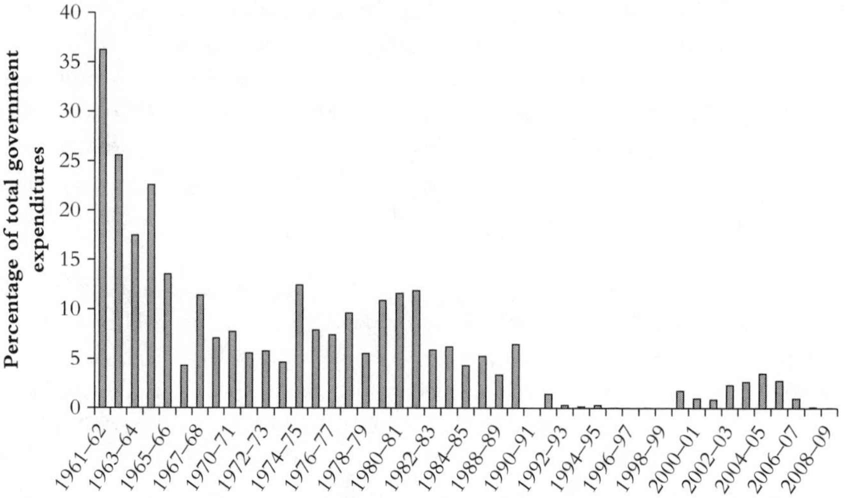

Fig. 5.1 Land purchases as percentage of all Kuwaiti government expenditures, 1961–2009. Years with no expenditures on land purchases are shown in the chart; years with no data are omitted. Central Bank of Kuwait, "CBK Quarterly Statistical Bulletin," 1995 Q4, 1999 Q4, 2005 Q4, 2011 Q2, www.cbk.gov.kw (accessed October 14, 2011); Al-Dekhayel 1990, 177; Al-Sabah 1980, 56.

their power and information to increase their own wealth tremendously." He also points out that the policy "made it risky for people without inside information to invest or deal in land."[50] It does appear that over time the distribution of wealth through *tathmin* became somewhat wider, both early on an again in the mid-1960s. The overall effect, however, was to enrich much of the traditional elite.[51]

In other ways, too, land policy in the first decades of independence helped the elite merchant families. A 1965 law gave Kuwaitis engaged in industry the right to request from the government a plot of industrial land at a nominal rent in places such as Shuwaikh, to the west of downtown.[52] The idea was to provide industry with access to land, and in fact the "overwhelming majority" of industrial projects in Kuwait are built on "industrial plots" (*al-qasa'im al-sina'iya*), which are "state owned lands rented to citizens so that they can use the lands [for industrial purposes]. These parcels remain the property of the state, the state allows citizens to use [the parcels]."[53] The intent of the law was to encourage the private sector

50. Al-Fraih 1993, 154–55, 156.
51. Al-Ebraheem (1975, 111).
52. Al-Tabtabai (1988, 13, 14–15).
53. Al-Tabtabai (1988, 11, 13).

to undertake approved projects. Companies that applied for land were required to specify the use that they would make of the land. Yet the land was valuable, and many leaseholders sold their leases to others for amounts vastly larger than the nominal price paid to the government for the lease. Others subleased their properties. These transfers were of questionable legality, and a substantial amount of law and legal interpretation has grown up around them.[54] Nonetheless, those who leased the plots—by reputation, they were mostly from the larger merchant families—gained a windfall at the expense of the state. Despite the legal doubt surrounding the legal status of the lands, the leases are bought and sold for prices approaching the value of the land.[55] A similar alienation of state lands, although less well documented, occurred along the shoreline south of Kuwait cities. These are the "chalets" along the shore on which well-off Kuwaitis have built homes—notwithstanding, again, the legal uncertainty over title.[56]

The National Assembly and Land. In early years, the National Assembly did not closely supervise the disposal of state land with the same urgency it does today. This did not distinguish land from other economic issue areas; up to the mid-1980s, the National Assembly did not exercise a strong role in most economic issues, with the main exceptions being Kuwaiti contracts with international oil companies and the employment of citizens in the oil industry. Nevertheless, deputies did not wholly ignore the issue. The very first interpellation, held in 1963, concerned the distribution of land in one of the new residential districts—but, in keeping with the early, mostly nonconfrontational attitude of the National Assembly, the deputies dropped the matter after receiving a reply from the minister in question.[57]

In 1975, a deputy from a tribal district, Sa'd Tami—who, unusually for a *bedu* representative at the time, voiced opposition to the government—did try to point out to his fellow *bedu* deputies that the policy of *tathmin* harmed their interests but to little avail.[58] A bill in parliament to equalize *tathmin* payments for properties inside the old city walls (where *hadhar* lived) and in the villages (where mostly *bedu* lived) failed in the National Assembly, and in its wake Sa'd Tami called on

54. Al-Tabtabai (1988).

55. Kuwait Financial Centre—Markaz (2008, 30).

56. The merchant elite's use of state power to enrich itself was not limited to land. Pete Moore (2004, 52–57) has an excellent discussion of merchant collusion through the Chamber of Commerce focused on business and import licensing.

57. Kuwait National Assembly, "Tarikh al-istijwabat" [History of interpellations], 2011, www.kna.kw/research/all_interpullations-v8.pdf.

58. The deputy was Sa'd Tami al-Ajmi. See Michael Herb, "Sa'd Tami al-Ajmi," Kuwait Politics Database, http://www2.gsu.edu/~polmfh/database/DataPage240.htm (accessed January 3, 2013).

his fellow representatives to vote against the budget. He did not expect them to actually do this, however, saying, "The budget is coming up, and the deputies of the villages [mostly tribal deputies living outside the town of Kuwait] should vote against it. The government does not respect us because we do not respect ourselves; we are the henchmen of the government."[59]

It was only after 1985, when the opposition won a majority in the National Assembly, that the National Assembly used its constitutional powers to seriously address the distribution of oil revenues by the government. This opposition included deputies from tribal areas; the "henchmen of the regime" in 1975 began to move, in part at least, toward the opposition. Initially, the National Assembly focused on the vast expenditure of funds that followed the Suq al-Manakh stock market collapse; the ruling family responded by shutting down the National Assembly in 1986 and did not open it again until 1992.

In the 1990s, following the Iraqi invasion and in the context of a more powerful National Assembly, the ruling family scaled back the *tathmin* program. By the time this program wound down, much of the land in Kuwait was in the hands of the state, by some accounts, 90% of the total land area of Kuwait. This included substantial tracts in what had been the traditional city center of Kuwait, which lay vacant.[60] Since the resumption of parliamentary life in 1992, the National Assembly has kept a close watch on land issues.[61] A 1997 interpellation—which resulted in the resignation of the minister of finance a month after a successful vote of confidence—dealt with a decrease in the rents charged to owners of industrial plots and the chalets during the period (following the 1986 suspension) when the National Assembly was not in session.[62] In a 2003 interpellation, a deputy accused a minister of selling land to a private company in "a new style of fraud aimed at taking possession of the land of the people and state for very low prices or without money, and reselling it at high prices to make outrageous profits," a practice that was and is common, of course, in the rest of the Gulf.[63] An interpellation in 2004 focused on the sale of 150,000 square meters of land for a fraction of the market price to a single investor. Musallam al-Barrak, one of the leaders of the interpellation in the National Assembly, pointed out that the minister should have followed the build-operate-transfer (BOT) mechanism in making

59. *Al-Qabas* June 11, 1975.

60. Muzafar Abdallah, "Milyar al-istimlakat mas'uliyya al-hukuma wa majlis al-umma wa al-baladi" [Billion in land purchases are the responsibility of the government, the National Assembly, municipal council], *Al-Taleea* (Kuwait), May 11, 1994.

61. Salem 2007, 15.

62. Salih 2006, 45.

63. "Kuwaiti MP Wants to Quiz Minister over Land Deal," AFP, January 12, 2003.

land available to investors because the land would revert back to the state.[64] A 2006 interpellation over BOT contracts led to the resignation of the minister of information—his company, it was alleged, had violated the law on public land before he became minister.[65] Yet another interpellation in 2012 involved, among other things, allegations that the minister allowed the law to be violated in a deal that transferred leased state lands from one company to another.[66]

The BOT Mechanism. State control of the bulk of Kuwaiti land poses a problem for economic development. Yet the prevailing political attitude toward land in Kuwait is that land is a part of the national patrimony, not to be alienated through sale to the private sector. In the face of this strong opposition to the sale of state land to private investors, Kuwait turned to the BOT mechanism to make land available for development. The BOT mechanism is found outside Kuwait; it is typically used in the construction of major public works projects. For example, a private company builds a roadway with private funds. In exchange, the state gives the company the right to collect tolls from the roadway for a fixed period of time. After an agreed-upon time has passed the project returns to public ownership. The overall goal is typically to facilitate the construction of public infrastructure by contracting with the private sector to provide financing and to manage the complexities and risks of construction.[67]

In Kuwait, the BOT mechanism has taken on a quite different role. The state uses BOT to make land available—if only temporarily—to the private sector. As the Kuwait Chamber of Commerce observes, the concentration of BOT projects in the real estate sector is a direct consequence of the state ownership of more than 90% of land in Kuwait.[68] One discussion, published under the auspices of the State Audit Bureau, summed up the attraction of the mechanism with a direct reference to class resentment directed toward the *tujjar* (merchants). The single

64. "Mulhaq khass: Istijwab al-na'ib Mussalam al-Barrak li-wazir al-maliyya Mahmoud al-Nuri" [Special supplement: Musallam al-Barrak's interpellation of the minister of finance Mahmoud al-Nuri], *Aldostoor* (Kuwait), March 10, 2004, 2.

65. "Clamping Down," *MEED: Middle East Economic Digest*, December 22, 2006; "BOT Saga Continues," *Kuwait Times*, January 8, 2007. He resigned before the interpellation was actually held on the floor of the National Assembly.

66. Ahmad ʻAbd al -Sitar, Mishaʻl al-ʻUtaybi, Tariq al-ʻAydan and Muhammad Sandan, "Al-Shamali istiqal baʻda istijwab marathuni" [Al-Shamali resigns after a marathon interpellation], *al-Qabas*, May 25, 2012, 14.

67. What in Kuwait is called a BOT might better be called a "concession." See World Bank, "Concessions, Build-Operate-Transfer (BOT) and Design-Build-Operate (DBO) Projects," World Bank: PPP in Infrastructure Resource Center, www.kna.kw/research/all_interpullations-v8.pdf (accessed January 2, 2013).

68. Kuwait Chamber of Commerce and Industry (KCCI) 2007.

most important reason that the state uses the BOT mechanism to develop public facilities on state owned land is that

> the state does not lose its ownership of these facilities [i.e., projects built on state land] and for that reason this mechanism is accepted in both public and official circles. Many members of the Kuwaiti society would object to the privatization of these facilities if the consequences of that was transferring ownership of these facilities, in that they would fear that that would lead to a weakening of state supervision over these facilities, and they fear that this would result in the hegemony of a minority of the merchants [*tujjar*] over services and vital installations, and would leave individuals at the mercy of these merchants.[69]

The details of the BOT law illustrate just why it earns such opprobrium from the private sector. When the BOT period ends, the private investor must turn over to the state the land on which the project was built and all buildings and improvements on the land. The private investor receives no compensation. The contract to manage the property is put out to bid, and the existing management receives no preference in the bidding. Thus, for example, a private-sector investor who builds a mall on state land under the BOT mechanism must earn a high enough return to pay for the project within the period of the BOT.

The BOT mechanism appeared in Kuwait as far back as the 1970s, when it was used to build several multistory parking garages in downtown Kuwait. In subsequent years, the BOT mechanism was used to develop projects as varied as retail developments, sports complexes, slaughterhouses, tourist facilities, industrial plots, labor camps, and recreational facilities.[70] Some projects were not of the sort that would typically be built via a BOT mechanism in a country in which private land was more widely available; these included the two largest malls (at the time that they were built) in Kuwait, Souq Sharq and Marina Mall.[71]

A company led by the emir's son (and majority-owned by the ruling family) developed Marina Mall and earned the close attention of the deputies in the National Assembly. In 2006, Musallam al-Barrak demanded that the BOT contract

69. Al-Salama and Al-Mubaraki 2006, 4. This is one of a series of very detailed reports on the BOT mechanism issued by the State Audit Bureau as part of "the seventh competition of reports at the level of all departments of the State Audit Bureau" (ibid., 1).

70. KCCI 2005; "*MEED* Special Report on Kuwait—Construction—First BOT Schemes Go Down Well," *MEED: Middle East Economic Digest*, February 19, 1996.

71. Melanie Britto, "Govt Keen on BOT Projects," *Arab Times* (Kuwait), February 14, 2006; KIPCO Kuwait Projects Company (Holding), "Annual Review 2011," 14; KIPCO Kuwait Projects Company (Holding), "Ownership Structure," 2012, www.kipco.com/InvestorCentre.asp?q_pageid=163 (accessed December 31, 2012).

be canceled for irregularities, which would have resulted in the entire project reverting back to the state, and asked why the hotel in the development did not have a proper license.[72] In the 2008 election campaign, a candidate in the fourth district (a less affluent, tribal district) complained that the Ministry of Public Works had wasted public money by building infrastructure for the mall.[73]

The accusations of corruption at Marina Mall were part of wider concerns about corruption in the BOT mechanism as a whole. In 2006, the State Audit Bureau—a powerful and prestigious government agency charged with, among other things, conducting audits to detect corruption—issued a report on BOT projects, finding a large number of violations. The Chamber of Commerce itself acknowledged that there had been corruption in the BOT process.[74] (In 2010, Adel al-Subaih, former minister of oil, more or less blamed the corruption on scarcity of land: "it was the state monopoly of land that drove some to fraud to secure land, and thus generated a major reaction from the government."[75]) The State Audit Bureau report resulted in the cancellation of several existing contracts, which in turn led to the immediate transfer of the entire project back to the government, with no compensation to the investor. One such project, owned by the very prominent Kuwaiti company Agility (and its parent company) had already invested "several millions of dollars" when its BOT contracts two free-trade zones were cancelled.[76] Although the decision was eventually reversed, a European commercial attaché quoted in *MEED* asked, ""How can you expect companies to think about investing when they could see their investments wiped out in a flash and their stock collapse?"[77] That said, it was also true that Agility had initially been a state-owned warehousing company and, after its privatization, wound up in control of much of the warehousing capacity in Kuwait while land scarcity created a major barrier to entry for potential competitors.[78]

72. In a conversation in 2013, a representative of the company insisted that the hotel had been licensed all along. The board of directors of KIPCO, the holding company of which the developer, United Real Estate, is a subsidiary, includes Hamad, the emir's son (as chairman), and two of the emir's grandsons, Abdullah Nasser Sabah Al Ahmad and Sabah Nasser Sabah Al Ahmad. B. Izzak, "MPs Maul Marina Mall," *Kuwait Times*, December 6, 2006; KIPCO Kuwait Projects Company (Holding), "Annual Review 2011," 14; "Government Probes Private Sector," *MEED: Middle East Economic Digest*, October 27, 2006.

73. Dhahi Al-Ali, "Al-Barrak: Wasf al-dawawin bi-l-i'tida' ala amlak al-dawla nukta" [Al-Barrak: Describing diwaniyas as infringements on public property is a joke], *al-Qabas*, April 8, 2008, 22.

74. KCCI 2007.

75. Fathi Naha, "Al-Sabih: Al-kuwayt al-dawla al-wahida allti tukhbiz wa ta'jin wa ta-bi' al-biskut" [Al-Sabih: Kuwait is the only country that bakes and kneads and sells cookies], *al-Qabas,* May 10, 2010, 56.

76. "Clamping Down," *MEED: Middle East Economic Digest*, December 22, 2006

77. James 2008b.

78. Rania El Gamal, "New Warehousing Firm Takes On Kuwait's Fierce Market," *Kuwait Times*, August 20, 2007, www.kuwaittimes.net/read_news.php?newsid=NTU0MDg2NjAz.

The State Audit Bureau report—along with threats of interpellations—have also had a chilling effect on the willingness of the state bureaucracy to approve future BOT projects and, indeed, projects of all types. The president of a major project consulting firm told *MEED* that "previous decision-makers have found themselves in the prosecution office being accused of squandering public funds."[79] *MEED* reports that "those involved with Kuwait's landmark infrastructure schemes are happy for every possible avenue to be explored before making decisions"; this is a result, says another businessman, of the fact that "Nobody wants to be the one to make the decision because they are fearful of the consequences."[80]

The ultimate result of the State Audit Bureau report was the suspension of new BOT projects until the National Assembly passed a new law regulating the BOT mechanism in 2008. This had long been a wish of the private sector, which sought a more liberal legal regime governing land. In some respects, the law did meet some private-sector demands; for example, the maximum period of a BOT agreement was extended from twenty to forty years, giving investors more time to recoup their investments before turning the project over to the state.[81] Not long after the law passed, however, the deputy president of the Chamber of Commerce complained that it had been written by deputies with little expertise in the matter and that hostility toward the private sector was driving capitalists out of Kuwait.[82] In late 2008, *al-Qabas* interviewed several businessmen involved in real estate. They generally agreed that the new law imposed punitive conditions on the private sector and blamed the National Assembly. One said that "continuous pressure from deputies in the National Assembly on the government created a climate of fear in the state sector, and this fear is reflected in the new law on BOT projects which has drawbacks in need of immediate correction." Another said that "Kuwait has become an exporter of investment to outside—in fact it expels local investments to the other countries of the region, which embrace this money and open avenues for investment without complications."[83] At a conference in May 2010 on the BOT law, the law itself received somewhat more mixed reviews, with some saying that the problem lay not so much in the law as in its application in Kuwait. One businessman gave a stark portrayal of these problems, saying that "we have an administration that

79. McClenaghan 2007.

80. "Kuwait's Malaise," *MEED: Middle East Economic Digest,* February 23, 2007.

81. Sell 2008.

82. Hasan Malak, "Al-Mutairi: Rijal al-a'mal majmu'a ara' wa ahwa'. . . la ra'y wahidan yujammi'hum" [Al-Mutairi: Businessmen have a range of opinions and inclinations . . . one opinion does not unite them], *al-Qabas,* April 27, 2008.

83. *Al-Qabas* 31 December 2008, 32. "Tashih 'uyub al-B.O.T. yusa'id fi al-khuruj min al-azma" [Fixing the deficiencies in B.O.T. will help in escaping the crisis], *al-Qabas,* December 31, 2008, 32.

is hostile to the private sector, for the government monopolizes all of the land. We ask 'Why is there no growth in manufacturing and we speak only of health and education?' We must understand that the private sector has a vital role in development in all economic sectors, and that we not malign it and cast aspersions on the intentions of the private sector, and avoid describing them as 'thieves.'"[84]

Although before independence the politics of land in Kuwait strongly resembled those in the other Gulf monarchies, by the real estate boom of the 2000s, land in Kuwait had a fundamentally different role in its political economy. Abdullah Salim's reforms of the 1950s are in part responsible, as is the policy of *tathmin*, which focused the elite on selling land back to the state rather than collecting it in their own hands. But it was the rise of the National Assembly that solidified citizen control over land. In the 1990s, after liberation, the National Assembly asserted its control over land, and the political elite could no longer expropriate land for private purposes. This has had direct and wide-ranging consequences for the ability of Kuwait to follow the Dubai model—indeed, it has made any direct imitation of the Dubai model of development impossible.

Tourism

The Gulf states—with the exception of Kuwait—have made determined efforts to build a tourism industry in recent years. Dubai, of course, has led the Gulf in this field, improbably turning a flat, barren, and (for much of the year) extraordinarily hot expanse of desert into a popular tourist destination. Bahrain, too, has long made tourism one of the pillars of its economy, although it has traditionally drawn its tourists from other Gulf countries, mostly Saudi Arabia. (One of the main attractions in Bahrain has been its more lenient laws governing alcohol.) Oman, another middling rentier, has developed several large projects aimed at upscale tourists. The successful bid of Qatar to host the 2022 World Cup was, in part, an effort to attract tourists, and Abu Dhabi has sought higher-end tourism to its newer cultural attractions.

Kuwait is the exception in the Gulf, the country that has failed to attract tourists in any substantial numbers. The data on this are quite conclusive, as figure 5.2 shows.[85] This state of affairs seems unlikely to change anytime soon. Kuwait's ambitious

84. Isa Abd al -Salam, "Ta'akhkhur al-dawla fi tarh al-'aradhi ahamm mu'awwiqat tanfith al-mashari'" [Delays by the state in releasing land is the most important obstacle to carrying out projects], *al-Qabas*, May 11, 2010, 57.

85. The natural environment of Kuwait does not explain its failure to develop a tourism industry; Dubai is also a patch of (often, blisteringly hot) desert next to the sea—as is Qatar and, in most respects, Bahrain. Oman benefits from a spectacular setting but receives only a modest number of tourists. Foreigners visit Saudi Arabia mostly on pilgrimage to the holy places in the Hejaz.

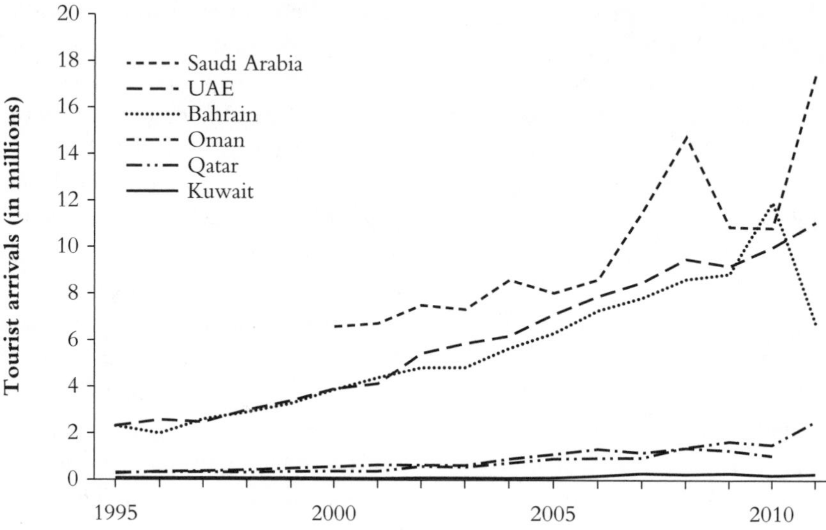

Fig. 5.2 Annual tourist arrivals in the Gulf monarchies, 1995–2011. (The earliest year for which *World Development Indicators* data are available for any GCC country is 1995.) World Bank, 2011, "International tourism, number of arrivals," *World Development Indicators*; for the UAE after 2005, Ruggles-Brise and Aimable 2012, 5.

2010 Development Plan, passed by the National Assembly with great fanfare, makes much mention of various strategies that might be adopted to diversify the Kuwaiti economy and strengthen the private sector but tourism hardly warrants a mention in the document.[86] A separate "National Strategy for Tourism," drawn up in 2005, garnered little attention.[87]

The explanation for the lethargy of the Kuwaiti tourist sector is clear. The National Assembly is unwilling to make the concessions necessary to attract tourists to Kuwait. One of these concessions is legalizing alcohol, without which Kuwait cannot be a major tourist destination or, for that matter, a really competitive business hub. The lack of legal alcohol in Kuwait—it is officially dry with no exceptions for hotels—is the work of the National Assembly, which banned alcohol, even on the national airline, in its second session, which adjourned in July 1964. The ban did not please the emir, who sent the law back to the assembly. On its reconsideration, no fewer than forty-two deputies voted for the ban, achieving the two-thirds majority needed to pass the law without the assent of the emir.[88] The

86. State of Kuwait 2010. There is a brief mention on page 46.
87. Discussed in KCCI 2009.
88. Al-Rifai 1996, 10–11; Jarman 2002, 181, 186.

ban has stood to the present day, and there is no serious discussion in Kuwait of liberalizing the laws on alcohol.

The alcohol issue is part of a larger concern on the part of Kuwaitis and their representatives in the National Assembly that the concessions necessary to attract tourists also threaten the traditional mores of Kuwaiti citizens. Thus, one firebrand deputy, Faysal al-Muslim was quoted in 2008 as saying, "The message of the Kuwaiti people is clear: this is a conservative country that will not tolerate harming values and morals. He who wants tourism of the islands and hotels built on alcohol and prostitution, we will confront him and hit him on the head, and we know these names but we will confront them anyways." He went on to deliver a pointed warning to the minister of information, a shaykh of the ruling family.[89]

Efforts by the National Assembly to safeguard morality have extended to the entertainment offered in Kuwaiti hotels and other venues. In 2004, the prime minister—at the time, Sabah al-Ahmad—asked the minister of information to allow a Star Academy show at the Kuwait fairgrounds. (Star Academy is an internationally franchised singing competition, along the lines of the Idol franchise). Thousands attended the event, and hundreds protested it. Islamists threatened to interpellate the minister of information over the concert, and the minister responded with a set of restrictive guidelines for such shows, strengthening existing prohibitions. This did not mollify the Islamists (although it generated much unhappiness among liberals). The controversy festered for months and resulted in a new interpellation. The minister resigned in January 2005 rather than face an interpellation and vote of confidence.[90]

Entertainment, and the morality of it, has continued to be an issue in Kuwaiti politics. In 2008, the minister of commerce, Ahmed Baqer—an Islamist who had previously won election to the National Assembly six times—threatened to fine and close a Kuwaiti hotel that held a private party, with singing, for a mixed-gender audience. The deputy minister, speaking on behalf the ministry, said that the ministry was "determined to protect authentic Kuwaiti traditions

89. Muhammad Sandan, "Al-Muslim: Man yurid tahwil al-bilad ila juzur wa khumur fasanadribuh ala ra'sihi [Al-Muslim: He who wants to turn the country into islands and alcohol, we will strike him on his head], *al-Qabas*, May 23, 2008, 8

90. As is the norm, other issues also contributed to the fall of the minister. Hamad Al-Jasir, "Al-Kuwayt: Hifla li-nujum 'star akadimy' qad tuthir muwajaha bayn al-hukuma wa al-islamiyin [Kuwait: Concert for the "Star Academy" stars could provoke a confrontation between the government and the Islamists], *Al-Hayat*, May 8, 2004, 4; Hamad Al-Jasir, "Al-hukuma al-kuwaytiyya ankathat wazir al-i'lam wa al-libraliyun ya'tabirun al-thaman bahizan" [The Kuwaiti government saves the minister of information and liberals consider the price to be high], *Al-Hayat*, May 20, 2004, 2; Hamad Al-Jasir, "Star akademi yatih wazir al-ilam al-kuwayti" [Star Academy topples the Kuwaiti minister of information], *Al-Hayat*, January 3, 2005.

and practices, and to preserve the Islamic identity of the society." The ministry would therefore "strike with a hand of steel" to prevent these sorts of infractions and hold accountable those who commit them.[91] A member of the National Assembly, responding to the same event, demanded that the license to operate of the hotel be revoked.[92] It does not appear that further action was taken, but the threats give a good indication of the sort of political climate faced by the tourist industry. A 2011 report on the state of the hotel industry in Kuwait—especially compared to other Gulf states—noted the complaints of hotel owners about the difficulties they faced in securing licenses to hold events. They emphasized that "what hotels face completely contradicts any intention on the part of government agencies to attract tourists to the domestic market or energize domestic tourism."[93] Kuwaitis now routinely travel to the UAE—by the thousands—to attend the sorts of events that hotels in Kuwait cannot hold.

Finally, the Kuwaiti tourism industry, like other industries in Kuwait, suffers from a lack of access to land.[94] As Waleed Hazbun puts it, "Land and its location are a critical resource for most aspects of tourism development. . . ."[95] This is a particular problem for Kuwait because the state controls access to the seashore, and there is not much else about the physical location Kuwait that would be attractive to tourists. Over the years, there has been talk of developing Failaka Island as a tourist destination; it has plenty of shoreline and is somewhat removed from the rest of the city. But nothing has come of it, and the stance of the National Assembly suggests that major tourist facilities are unlikely to be built on Failaka in the future.

In the past decade or so, all the Gulf states—except Kuwait—have taken steps to allow foreigners to purchase real estate (this was typically not allowed from the earlier days of the oil boom). Purchases are typically limited to specific developments marketed to foreigners, usually upscale mega-projects. As Omar Al-Shehabi documents, the practice emerged early in Dubai and was an integral part of its effort to build, and profit from, the tourist industry. In Kuwait, however, foreigners are not allowed to purchase, or lease long term, any real estate.[96] No

91. Layla Al-Saraf and Fahd Al-Qabnadi, "'Al-tijara': Sanudrib bi-yad min hadid li-hafiz al-'adat wa al-huwiyya ["Commerce": We will strike with a hand of steel to preserve customs and identity], *al-Qabas*, August 27, 2008, 8.

92. "Al-Harbush: Ghayr mutafa'il bi-muhasiba al-mutajawizin fi hafla al-funduq" [Al-Harbush: Not optimistic about holding accountable those who committed violations in the hotel party], *al-Qabas*, August 27, 2008, 27.

93. Naha Fathi, "Alaf al-ghuraf al-funduqiyya al-jadida . . . masirha al-shughur" [Thousands of new hotel rooms . . . their future is vacancy], *al-Qabas*, October 24, 2011, 50.

94. KCCI 2009.

95. Hazbun 2008, 217–18; compare also his discussion of Jordan (142–52).

96. Al-Shehabi 2012, 85–89; England 2012.

serious efforts have been made to change this by either the government or the National Assembly. The lack of public discussion about changing the property laws is not so much a result of a lack of desire in some quarters to do so but, instead, a recognition that (like liberalization of the alcohol laws) the National Assembly, reflecting public sentiment, will not allow it.

The best explanation for the dismal performance of Kuwait in the tourist industry, compared to its GCC neighbors, is its extreme rentierism. In an economy in which the tourist industry provided jobs and tax revenue, we would expect capitalists to meet with more success in arguing that Kuwaiti mores ought to bend, at least a bit, in response to the need to provide employment for Kuwaiti citizens. The complete divorce of the tourist industry from the economic fortunes of the Kuwaiti middle class makes it relatively costless for the National Assembly to actively discourage tourism.

The Entrepôt Economy

Several Gulf states have sought to exploit their first-world infrastructure and central geographical location in Asia to become major logistics and trading hubs. They have sought to attract business with a potent combination of low taxes, investment in infrastructure such as airports and seaports, SOEs in the transportation and logistics sectors, and a business-friendly regulatory climate. Tourism feeds the entrepôt economy, and Dubai has become a shopping destination popular throughout Africa, the Middle East, and much of Asia. The development of an entrepôt economy is entirely in keeping with the economic history of the Gulf, including that of Kuwait. Many Kuwaiti merchant families in the pre-oil period had extensive links with India, for example, and often a branch of the family would live in India to facilitate trade. Other Gulf shaykhdoms, especially Bahrain, Dubai, and Oman, had extensive trade links as well.

In recent years the UAE—and especially Dubai—has become a major logistics and business center. Today the UAE exports more non-oil goods than it does oil; most of these non-oil goods are imported from elsewhere, but this attests to the vibrancy of the entrepôt trade in the UAE. As the 2010 Development Plan of Kuwait points out, the "extremely modest" reexport trade in Kuwait is an indication of its failure to develop as a trading center (figure 5.3).[97] Dubai had the 9th busiest container port in the world in 2010; Kuwait ranked 116th. The Dubai ports handled sixteen times as many containers as the main Kuwaiti (civilian) port at

97. State of Kuwait 2010, 22.

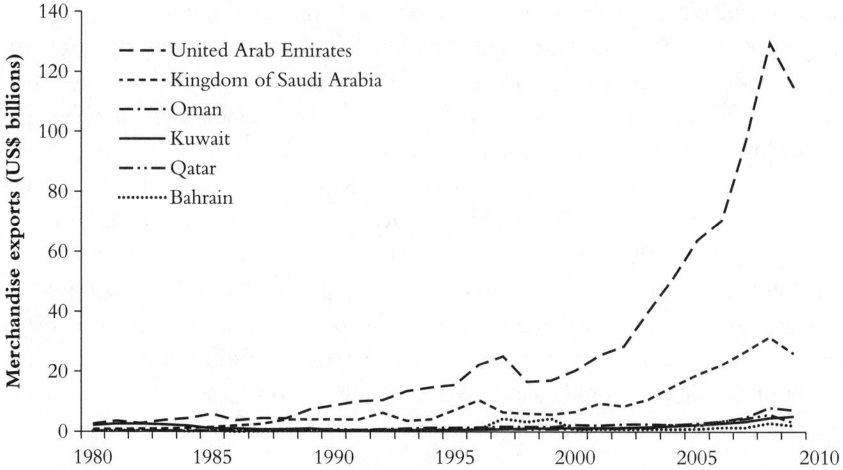

Fig. 5.3 Value of merchandise exports from the Gulf monarchies, except fuels ([exports of fuel and mining products] minus [exports in total merchandise trade]), 1980–2009. World Trade Organization, "Statistics Database," http://stat.wto.org/Home/WSDBHome.aspx?Language=.

Shuwaikh.[98] The contrast in air freight was just as sharp. Kuwait's airport handled 3% of the total air freight handled by UAE airports in 2009, and 12% of that of Qatar (figure 5.4). By 2010, Qatar had developed its airport into the twenty-seventh busiest cargo airport in the world, and Dubai was the eighth busiest.[99] Both the UAE and Qatar have seen sharp increases in the number of passengers coming through their airports in recent years. Passenger traffic at the Kuwaiti airport in 2010 was 6% of the passenger traffic at UAE airports as a whole and 22% that of Qatar (figure 5.5).

The main distinction of Kuwait in logistics has been its role as a staging area for U.S. military operations in Iraq.[100] Apart from this, however, Kuwait has largely failed to develop as a logistics hub. The failure of Kuwait to develop itself as an entrepôt can be traced to three main factors. First, an entrepôt economy requires a degree of openness to the outside world—an openness that includes some of

98. American Association of Port Authorities, "World Port Rankings—2010," http://www.aapa-ports.org/ (accessed October 26, 2012).

99. World Bank, "Air Transport, Freight," *World Development Indicators*; Airports Council International, "Cargo Traffic 2010. Final," August 1, 2011, http://www.aci.aero/Data-Centre/Annual-Traffic-Data/Cargo/2010-final.

100. Agility (a Kuwaiti warehousing firm) profited from supplying the U.S. military and built an international logistics business. In 2009, however, the firm was indicted in the United States for what amounts to defrauding the U.S. military.

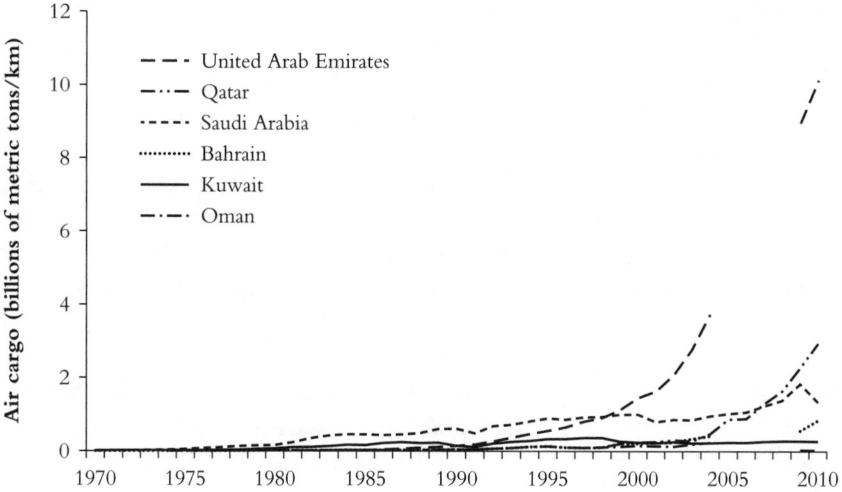

Fig. 5.4 Air freight in the Gulf monarchies (in metric tons times kilometers traveled), 1970–2009. World Bank, 2013, "Air Transport, Freight," *World Development Indicators*.

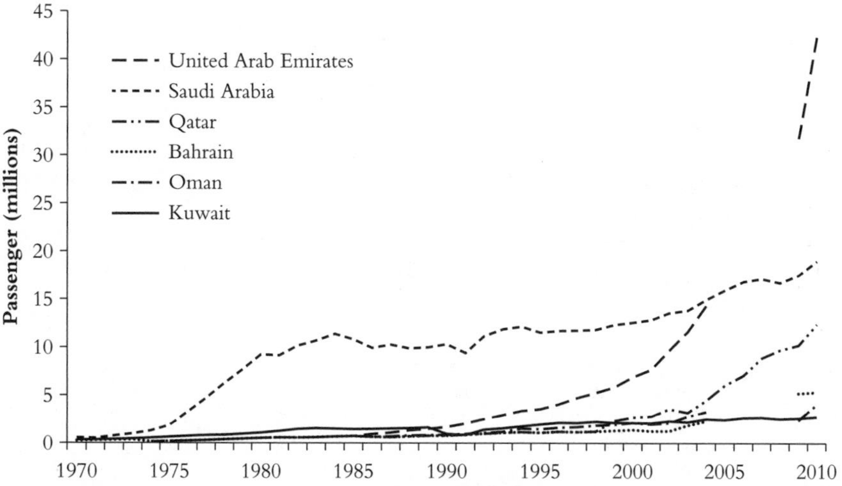

Fig. 5.5 Air passengers carried in the Gulf monarchies, 1970–2010. World Bank, 2013, "Air Transport, Passengers Carried," *World Development Indicators*.

the aspects required to attract tourists, and Kuwait has made few efforts to attract foreign visitors. The ban on of alcohol matters more, in this regard, than might be immediately apparent; the lack of legal alcohol colors the perceptions of the international business community about the attractiveness of Kuwait as a place to do business. This is reinforced by the modest Kuwaiti tourist infrastructure and—certainly compared to some of its Gulf neighbors—its lack of effort to adjust its social mores in a direction accommodating to foreigners.

Second, successful entrepôts create an attractive business environment, and Kuwait has not done this. The cost of exporting a container from Kuwait is the highest of all the six Gulf monarchies, almost double the cost of exporting a container from the UAE (see table 5.1). And the quality of the Kuwaiti port infrastructure in 2009 was also the worst in the Gulf, coming in at sixty-second in the world; the UAE was eighth and Qatar twenty-seventh (see table 5.2). It is clear that the quality of the infrastructure in the UAE is the result of deliberate decisions on the part of the state to attract business. The 2010 Development Plan of Kuwait identifies trade as a crucial area of focus in efforts to strengthen the private sector and diversify away from oil. The plan proposes several steps to improve the dismal Kuwaiti performance in rebuilding its trading sector, chief among them being the construction of a vast new port facility on Bubiyan Island along the

TABLE 5.1.
Cost to export a container, 2010

	World ranking	Cost (US$)
UAE	4	$521
Saudi Arabia	7	$580
Qatar	30	$735
Oman	35	$766
Bahrain	65	$955
Kuwait	84	$1,060

Sources: World Bank, 2011, *World Development Indicators*, "Cost to Export (US$ per container)," http://data.worldbank.org/data-catalog/world-development-indicators.

TABLE 5.2.
Quality of port Infrastructure, 2010

	Infrastructure world ranking
UAE	8
Bahrain	13
Qatar	27
Oman	32
Saudi Arabia	35
Kuwait	62

Sources: World Bank, 2011, *World Development Indicators*, "Quality of Port Infrastructure," http://data.worldbank.org.

Shatt al-Arab, north of Kuwait city.[101] If the port is completed it will be a crucial component of the efforts of Kuwait to diversify its economy.[102]

Finally, an entrepôt needs strong SOEs, and Kuwait (as Hertog observes) lacks the strong SOEs that play such a central role in the entrepôt economies of other Gulf states. Dubai's DP World has the ethos of a private company and not only runs the Dubai ports but has also grown into an international heavyweight in the business of operating ports around the world. In contrast, the Kuwait Ports Authority is a state bureaucracy that has made little progress developing the logistics sector. The starkest failure of Kuwait, however, is its national airline. Emirates airline has helped to grow passenger traffic at the Dubai airport and has brought customers to the burgeoning malls and markets of Dubai. Qatar Airways, following this example, has developed a reputation as one of the world's best airlines, a reputation it shares with Emirates and Ittihad (the state-owned airline of Abu Dhabi).[103] By contrast, Kuwait Airways is famed for its poor service and unreliability. Kuwaitis view it as a national embarrassment, and savvy travelers avoid it.

Petrochemicals and Refining

To varying degrees all the Gulf states have attempted to diversify their economies by exploiting their comparative advantage in hydrocarbons. Historically, Kuwait has done well in this regard. Kuwait exports more refined petroleum products—as a percentage of crude exports—than Saudi Arabia, Oman, or the UAE (figure 5.6).[104] Kuwait also exports a good deal of petrochemicals, many of them manufactured by Equate, a cooperative venture with Dow Chemical; this venture accounts for the bulk of Kuwaiti exports apart from crude and refined petroleum. The main Kuwaiti partner of Equate is the state-owned Petrochemical Industries Company; the Kuwait Projects Company (KIPCO), which is controlled by the emir's family, owns a share through a partially owned subsidiary.[105]

101. State of Kuwait 2010, 46, 51.

102. The project ran into fierce resistance from Iraqi politicians, which was eventually overcome after Kuwait agreed to cancel a fourth phase of the project. But it was not a propitious start because one of the largest potential markets for a Kuwaiti logistics and trade hub is Iraq itself. Layla Al-Saraf, "Al-'iraq yu'akkid ahaqqiyya al-kuwayt fi mina' Mubarak" [Iraq confirms Kuwait's legal claim at Mubarak Port], *al-Qabas*, February 29, 2012, 1; Ali al-Sharuqi, "Safar: Ilgha al-marhala al-rabi'a li-mina' Mubarak" [Safar: Cancelation of the fourth phase of Mubarak Port], *al-Qabas*, July 6, 2012, 2; Tony Blair Associates 2009, 50.

103. Skytrax World Airline Awards, "World Airline Awards 2012," http://www.worldairlineawards.com/Awards_2012/Airline2012.htm (accessed January 20, 2013).

104. Bahrain exports only refined petroleum products, and Qatar exports a great deal of liquid natural gas, which requires an expensive infrastructure. United Nations, "United Nations Commodity Trade Statistics Database (UN Comtrade)," UN Statistics Division. comtrade.un.org (accessed November 27, 2011).

105. Equate, "About Equate," www.equate.com/En_EQUATE_fact_Sheet.cms (accessed January 21, 2013); Qurain Petrochemical Industries Company, "Annual Report 2011–2012," n.d., 3, www.qpic-kw.com.

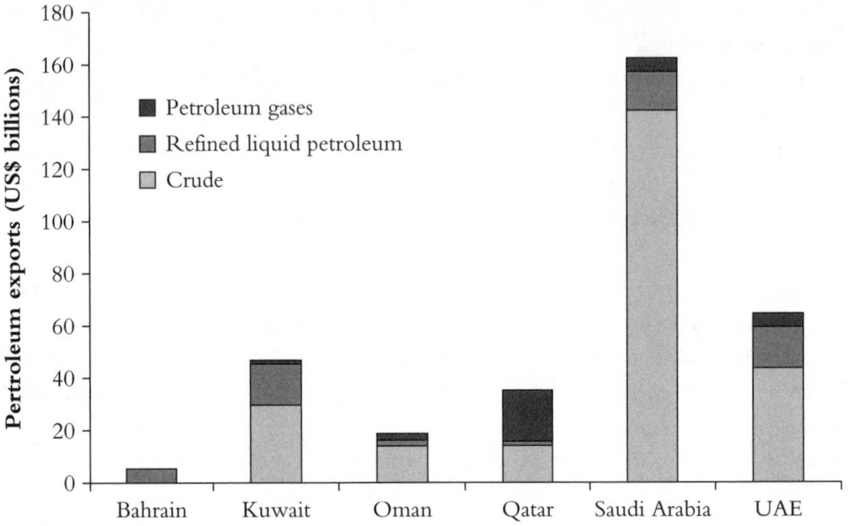

Fig. 5.6 Value of petroleum exports, 2009. UN Statistics Division, "United Nations Commodity Trade Statistics Database (UN Comtrade)," http://comtrade.un.org/db/default.aspx (accessed November 27, 2011).

Petrochemicals are an area in which Kuwait could be expected to diversify with fewer of the obstacles faced in sectors such as tourism and trade. The industry workforce includes a fairly large percentage of Kuwaiti citizens (Equate claims that its workforce is 55% Kuwaiti), and the industry does not pose the sorts of challenges to Kuwaiti norms found in the tourism industry. There are multiple international companies eager to partner with Kuwait, and Kuwait, of course, enjoys some profound comparative advantages resulting from its combination of abundant petroleum resources, advanced infrastructure, and surplus capital.

Despite all of these advantages, and despite a promising history, Kuwait has experienced some spectacular failures in developing new petrochemical export ventures with foreign multinationals—failures that have cast serious doubt on the reliability of Kuwait as a business partner. The most prominent setback occurred in late 2008, when Kuwait signed a deal with Dow Chemical in which Kuwait was to purchase a 50% share in the Dow Chemical basic petrochemicals business (the joint venture was dubbed K-Dow).[106] The logic of the deal lay in its combination of Dow technical expertise with Kuwaiti petroleum feedstock. One business publication said that the deal was about an opportunity for Kuwait

106. Esposito 2009.

to work with "an experienced market leader, whose technical expertise and infrastructure could have allowed Kuwait to make significant strides in diversifying its economy."[107] Although the deal itself would not have directly resulted in the construction of new petrochemicals capacity in Kuwait, it would have put Kuwait in a very strong position to further develop the industry in the future by making it co-owner of one of the world's leading basic petrochemical companies.

But a few weeks after the Kuwaiti government signed the deal, at the end of December 2008, the Kuwait government canceled the contract. This left Kuwait vulnerable to a claim by Dow for $2.5 billion for breaking the contract. Ostensibly, Kuwait pulled the plug on the deal because the global economic crisis and the consequent decline in the price of oil made the price that Kuwait was to pay for its share of the Dow petrochemical business too high.[108] In retrospect, the price was low. The politics of the Kuwaiti withdrawal, moreover, pointed to more serious problems. The Kuwaiti government pulled out of the deal as a direct response to a threat by members of the National Assembly to interpellate the prime minister over the deal.[109] In late 2008, the Kuwaiti ruling family had not yet consented to allow the prime minister to be interpellated on the floor of the National Assembly, fearing that this move would set the precedent that the prime minister and his government relied—as a whole—on the support of a parliamentary majority. Yet because each National Assembly deputy has the authority to call an interpellation (and the agreement of only ten deputies is required to call a vote of confidence) the ruling family gave a parliamentary minority in the National Assembly the ability to essentially veto government policy—the mere threat of an interpellation caused the government to surrender whatever policy it sought to pursue.

Ultimately, of course, this proved to be utterly unworkable—the government could not function if every deputy had a veto over government policy. In early 2009, faced again with demands to interpellate the prime minister, the emir dissolved the National Assembly and called new elections. The elections results were favorable for the government, which in the Kuwaiti context means that deputies who favored cooperation with the government did noticeably better than they had in the previous election. This reflected public sentiment, which had grown

107. "State Is Missing Opportunities," *MEED: Middle East Economic Digest* 53(3), January 16, 2009, 6.

108. Salisbury 2009.

109. "'Al-Sha'bi': Al-mudi fi 'daw kimikal' ya'ni istijwab ra'is al-wuzara' mubasharatan" ["The Popular Bloc": Continuing with "Dow Chemical" means immediate interpellation of the prime minister], *Al-Jarida* (Kuwait), December 22, 2008; "Al-Salaf yudkhilun khatt rafdh 'daw': Sanuharrik al-musa'ala fi hal tawqi' al-safqa [The Salafis join in the repudiation of "Dow": We will launch an interpellation if the contract is signed], *Al-Jarida* (Kuwait), December 23, 2008.

tired of political paralysis. Later in 2009, on December 8, the ruling family allowed, for the first time in the history of Kuwait, an interpellation of the prime minister and a vote of confidence. The prime minister won with thirty-five votes in favor of confidence, thirteen against, and one abstention. His win demonstrated that he had the support—at least for the moment—of a parliamentary majority.[110]

Winning the vote of confidence strengthened the hand of the prime minister and the government and led to an outbreak of optimism in Kuwait that the political paralysis would end and development would proceed. International oil companies took note. Chevron, which had shut down its Kuwait office after the failure of K-Dow, reopened its office after the vote of confidence in late 2009.[111] Yet this was a brief window of optimism indeed; by mid-2011, Kuwait had descended again into a series of political crises that can be traced directly to the failure of the prime minister to maintain a reliable majority in the National Assembly and to the refusal of the ruling family to admit this and find a new prime minister who could.

The resignation of Ahmed al-Fahad al-Sabah in June 2011 had a particularly dispiriting effect. He is a younger shaykh who had been associated with the authoritarian wing of the ruling family but who also had a reputation as a man who could get things done. He took up the planning portfolio in the government in May 2009 and led a high-profile (and successful) effort to pass into law a major development plan.[112] In a notable success, the National Assembly approved the plan in February 2010. His resignation—under threat of interpellation—cast into doubt the ability of the government to continue its development efforts. The consulting firm, PFC Energy, called his resignation "the last nail in the coffin" of efforts to develop the oil sector.[113]

The failure, thus far, of plans to build a fourth refinery also illustrates the barriers facing the efforts of Kuwait to add value to its crude exports. The refinery, if built, would add 615,000 barrels per day of refining capacity of Kuwait, bringing

110. Ibrahim al-Saidi and Badr al-Muhana, "10 nuwwab waqqa'u "adam ta'awun' wa 30 dhidd: Ra'is al-wuzara' sa'id al-minassa fi sabiqa tu'akkid an dimuqratiyatna bikhayr [10 deputies sign "no confidence" and 30 are against: The prime minister ascends the podium in a precedent that affirms that our democracy is healthy], *al-Qabas*, December 9, 2009, 1; Ibrahim al-Saidi and Badr al-Muhana, "Al-Muhammad: La-natwi safaha al-madhi wa nantaliq lil-mustaqbal: Awwal ra'is wuzara' yahza bi-thiqqa al-majlis—35 ma'a al-ta'awun—13 dhidd—1 imtina'" [Al-Muhammad: Let us turn the page on the past and look to the future: First prime minister to secure the confidence of the assembly—35 for cooperation—13 against—one abstention], *al-Qabas*, December 17, 2009, 1.

111. Salisbury 2010a.

112. Salisbury 2010b.

113. Mai Mamoun, "Tadwir qiyadat al-qita' al-nafti sayyi' jiddan lil-mashari'" [Leadership change in the petroleum sector is very bad for projects], *al-Qabas*, August 3, 2011.

the total to 1.4 million. (A related project would modernize other Kuwaiti refineries so that they could produce fuel that meets newer, and stricter, environmental standards in the consumer countries.) The first round of bids, in 2006, came in far above budget.[114] The oil company then asked for a new set of bids, signed contracts, and ran into a barrage of complaints from the National Assembly. Among other accusations, it was alleged that deputies with ties to the oil minister (himself associated with the Muslim Brotherhood) had met with a company that was awarded a contract to solicit benefits for themselves.[115] The government asked the Audit Bureau to look into the contracts and then cancelled the project altogether in 2009.[116] In 2012, the state oil company tried again, for the third time, to get the project off the ground, asking again for bids to build the refinery and provide the related modernization of existing refineries.[117] There is, still, some hope that the project might be built, eventually.

And these are not the only problems that Kuwait has had in its oil industry. Failure to further develop the oil fields in the northern part of Kuwait—known as Project Kuwait—has caused enormous frustration among international oil companies that wish to participate in the development of these fields. The effort goes back to 1997 and is motivated by the need of Kuwait for the help of international oil companies to pull the remaining oil from its giant oilfields in the northern part of the emirate. Project Kuwait has, thus far, failed because the National Assembly suspected fraud in the contracts and was extremely suspicious of any agreement with international companies that would give them a share in the Kuwaiti oil industry.[118]

This sensitivity has historical roots. In the 1960s and 1970s, the chief arena in which the National Assembly participated in shaping public policy was oil policy. The Arab nationalist minority in the assembly found it possible—in several separate episodes—to convince deputies in the conservative, pro-government majority to vote against agreements that the government had negotiated with international oil companies. The chief complaint of the National Assembly was,

114. James 2008a.

115. Ibrahim al-Saidi, "Makhawaf min t'arradh al-'ulim li-sinariyu al-humaydhi" [Fears that Olaim will be subjected to the Al-Humaidi scenario], *al-Qabas*, August 23, 2008, 1; Hamad Al-Jasir, "Al-Mu'aridha tahaddathat 'an 'shubhat athira' . . . al-Kuwayt: Al-hukuma taqarrar al-tahqiq fi mashru' al-misfat al-rabi'a [The opposition speaks of "many suspicions" . . . Kuwait: The government decides to investigate the fourth refinery project], *al-Hayat*, August 26, 2008.

116. "Ilga' al-misfat al-rabi'a" [Cancellation of the fourth refinery], *al-Qabas*, March 21, 2009, 1.

117. Mirza 2012.

118. James 2005; Hamad Al-Jasir, "Jalsa barlamaniya khassa li-'iqrarih wa istithmaratih 8.5 bilyun dular" [A special session of parliament to pass it, and an investment of 8.5 billion dollars], *al-Hayat*, June 9, 2005.

of course, the price, but the assembly also pushed for the full nationalization of Kuwaiti oil resources. And, perhaps more remarkably, the National Assembly also pushed the government to pump less, rather than more, oil.[119] This seems counterintuitive but the deputies argued that Kuwait generated a surplus in any case (which is still true today) and that the oil was potentially more valuable in the ground than produced and sold.[120] It was in this context that the government attempted to develop the northern fields. The National Assembly had fought hard to nationalize the oil company and the oil resources of Kuwait, and the various agreements with international oil companies were seen to threaten those achievements, despite the technology, marketing, and other expertise that the foreign companies offered Kuwait. Historically, the National Assembly had not pushed hard to increase production. And the newer concerns about corruption in the contracts further reduced any incentive felt by deputies to push for the development of the fields.

The Financial Industry

Kuwait has historically had a leading position in the financial industry in the GCC; the abyss that separates Kuwait from its Gulf neighbors in terms of tourism, logistics, transport, and other measures of diversification is absent in the financial sector. The emir has promoted the idea that Kuwait should focus its energies, in terms of economic development, on the financial industry, and there is much to recommend it as a focus of efforts by Kuwait to diversify its economy, beyond its historical leadership role. In Kuwait, and throughout the Gulf, citizens compose a relatively high percentage of the workforce in the financial sector, so new jobs in the financial sector are more likely to go to citizens than are, for example, jobs in the tourist sector. Pay is high, as are skill levels, and well-educated Gulf citizens can often compete for positions in the sector without the overt government intervention required for less-skilled parts of the workforce.

The historical preeminence of Kuwait (among the Gulf monarchies) in finance dates back to the founding of the National Bank of Kuwait in 1952. The bank was the first local publically traded corporation in the Gulf.[121] Other publically traded companies followed, and over the years, a stock market emerged, along with a legal structure governing the market. In most of these developments,

119. Al-Sabah 1980, 35–37.

120. For example, "Huqul al-shamal . . . bu'ra al-tawattur al-kamina bayn al-hukuma wa 'suqur' al-barlaman" [The northern fields . . . focus of simmering tension between the government and the hawks of the parliament], *al-Qabas*, July 3, 2006, 39.

121. Al-Zumai 2006, 66.

Kuwait led the region. In the late 1970s and early 1980s, an alternative stock market, trading in shares of Gulf companies, emerged in Kuwait, the Suq al-Manakh. The exchange operated outside any government regulations, and the result was a very impressive asset bubble. The exchange traded in shares of companies located—in theory—in other Gulf countries, especially the less-developed emirates of the UAE.[122]

The 1982 stock market crash left behind a series of debts, in the form of postdated checks, equaling US$90 billion.[123] The government wound up picking up the pieces, proposing a plan that would have bailed out investors with state money. Many members of the National Assembly opposed this. In the elections of 1985, candidates who opposed a bailout did well, and the 1985 National Assembly took a harder line against government efforts to rescue those who had suffered from the crisis.[124] Indeed, the crisis gave rise to the first sustained use of parliamentary power to criticize and change the distributional choices of the Kuwaiti government on populist grounds and helped usher into office the first real opposition majority in the history of the Kuwaiti National Assembly. Although the largest players in the Suq al-Manakh were not from the traditional merchant elite, the Chamber of Commerce favored a government rescue, and the opposition to the bailout took on an increasingly populist tone. It did not help that one of the larger traders was a shaykh of the al-Sabah and that he and some others "in deference to their social and trading status" had not been sent to bankruptcy court.[125] The National Assembly forced the resignation of a minister—who was closely related to the ruling family—whose son had received millions in the Suq al-Manakh bailout, and the National Assembly set up a committee of investigation to look into the books of the Central Bank to see if money had been distributed beyond that authorized by the National Assembly.[126]

The government took the issue to the Constitutional Court, which ruled in favor of the National Assembly. The ruling family—partly but not wholly in response to these developments—then unconstitutionally dissolved the National Assembly. With the National Assembly out of the way, the government approved the plan favored by the Chamber of Commerce to bail out—to some degree—those who had suffered losses.[127]

122. Darwiche 1986, 21–30, 78.
123. Ibid., 60–63.
124. Al-Ghazali 1989, 106–9.
125. Darwiche 1986, 133, 107, 127.
126. Crystal 1990, 105. *Al-Qabas,* May 16, 1986. and February 19, 1995.
127. Moore 2004, 133–34.

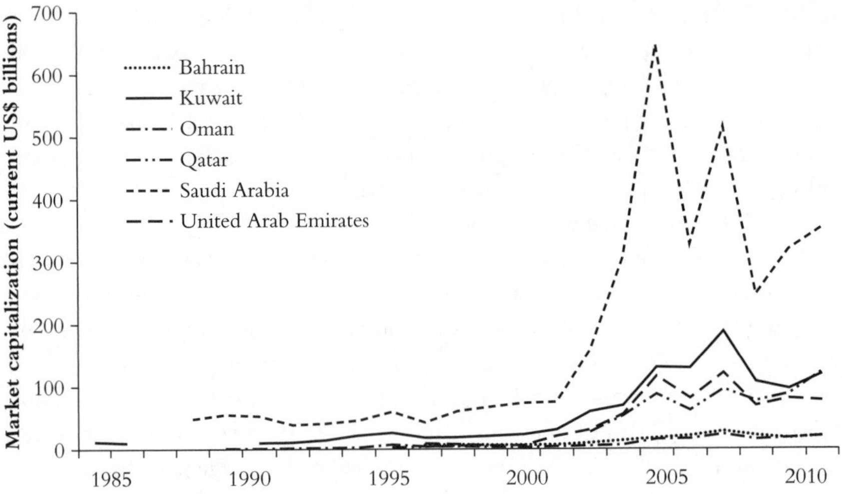

Fig. 5.7 Value of total GCC stock market capitalization of banks and financial firms, 1988–2010. World Bank, 2014, "Market Capitalization of Listed Companies," *World Development Indicators*.

The early leadership of Kuwait in the financial industry has positive legacies as well. Kuwait has a large wealth-management industry that stands out in the region.[128] Kuwaiti investment companies administer more assets than those of any other GCC country, save the much larger Saudi Arabia. The Kuwait Financial Centre, in a rough calculation, estimated that Kuwaiti firms accounted for over one-third of the total assets under management in the GCC.[129] The relative strength of Kuwait in the financial industry extends to its stock market, the first in the Gulf. For many years, the total valuation of all companies listed on the Kuwaiti exchange far exceeded the value of those on any other GCC bourse, except Saudi Arabia. The UAE (with two stock markets, one in Abu Dhabi and another in Dubai) and Qatar have caught up in recent years, but Kuwait still enjoys a strong position (see figure 5.7). In 2011, financial and banking companies made up more than half of the market capitalization of the Kuwaiti bourse; among all the Gulf states, the market capitalization of Kuwaiti financial-sector firms was, in

128. Tony Blair Associates 2009, 182.

129. Raghu, Al-Ammar, and Soothanan 2011. The report notes that the Central Bank of Kuwait publishes a monthly report that provides "by far the most transparent break-up of assets in the asset management industry available in the GCC region" (ibid., 13). Nevertheless, in other respects the quality of the Kuwaiti regulatory structure is often criticized (as, for example, the lack of a good bankruptcy law for investment companies).

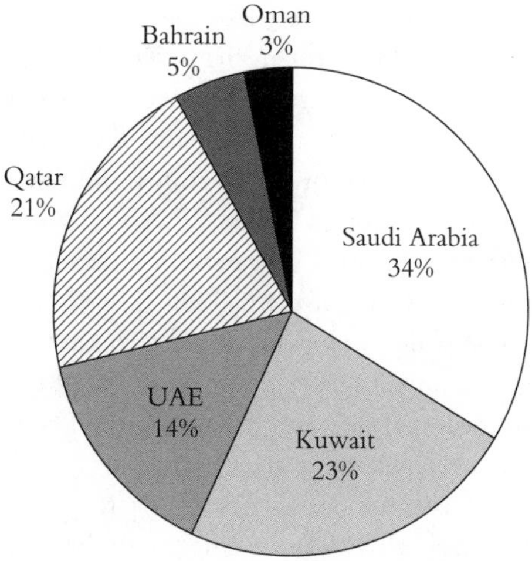

Fig. 5.8 Market capitalization of banks and investment firms on GCC stock markets, October 2011. KAMCO Investment Research Department, *GCC Equity Markets Monthly Review*, www.kamconline.com/ResearchReport.aspx?language=en (accessed December 9, 2011).

total, behind only that of Saudi Arabia (figure 5.8). That said, the 2008 economic crisis dealt a hard blow to Kuwaiti investment companies, a number of which were essentially wiped out during the crisis.[130]

In recent years, Kuwaiti investment companies have invested increasingly large percentages of their total assets abroad, and their foreign assets have become substantially larger than their domestic assets.[131] The choices of investment companies have reflected the grievances of the Kuwaiti private sector, which loses few opportunities to complain about how government policies in Kuwait have encouraged Kuwaiti money to find investment opportunities abroad.

The financial crisis of 2008 revived the sort of class politics seen in the Suq al-Manakh crisis. Many investment companies and banks suffered severe losses, and the government felt compelled to intervene to stabilize the financial system. This generated a round of populist rhetoric in which the term *hitan* ("whale") was used to refer to the investment companies; one member of a venerable merchant family said that the term "had no meaning or purpose other than to provoke."[132] The

130. IMF 2012a, 5–12.

131. IMF 2011a, 27.

132. The interview was with Tarek Sultan, the head of Agility. Muhammad al-Itribi, "Sultan: Sharikat al-istithmar fashilat . . . wa masarif al-kuwayt fi khatar" [Sultan: Investment companies fail . . . and Kuwait banks are in danger], *al-Qabas*, March 15, 2009, 38.

government proposed a financial stability law that would, at least potentially, allow a government bailout of failed investment firms. The National Assembly initially refused to pass the law, and the emir issued it by decree when the National Assembly was not in session, after a dissolution and before the elections.[133] The financial stability law then became an issue in the elections, and few candidates made an effort to defend the bailout (although the IMF advised it was necessary to preserve the solvency of the financial system and prevent a more expensive rescue later on).[134] One tribal candidate said that the bailout "is nothing but an effort by the government to save companies that do nothing to serve the Kuwaiti economy." These companies, he continued, "have never contributed to the development of the economy or have been partners in growth as would be expected from them in exchange for the large benefits that the government has given them for many years."[135] Another candidate, also in a tribal district, said that the government should address the financial crisis by addressing the problems of "simple" citizens, "pointing out that the private sector is not a pillar of the economy in Kuwait in the way that it is in America." He continued that "the country does not benefit from the private sector because it does not help at all with development projects, and the state does not tax it in order to build Kuwait's infrastructure." He then said that if there were, in fact, Kuwaiti employees harmed by the financial crisis that the government should address their problems through any means other than bailing out the "whales."[136] A former minister of finance came to the defense of the government efforts to rescue the financial industry, pointing out that it would not lead to immediate handouts to the investment companies. His defense of the role of the private sector in Kuwait more or less conceded the critics' point about taxation; he said that "if some mean by 'whales' the Kuwaiti private sector . . . this sector had a basic role in supplying most of the revenues of the state before the appearance of oil in the 1950s. . . ."[137]

In the end, the law did not result in the transfer of huge sums from the Kuwaiti treasury onto the balance sheets of private companies in the financial industry. It

133. Mubarak al-Abd al-Hadi, Zakaria Muhammad, and Ibrahim al-Sa'idi, "'Al-istiqrar al-mali' fi marsum al-dhurura wa 3 asabi' li-la'iha al-tanfithiyya" ["Financial stability" in an emergency decree and three weeks for implementing regulations], *al-Qabas*, March 27, 2009, 1.

134. IMF 2009a, 10–11.

135. "Al-'Utaybi: Qanun al-istiqrar muhawala li-inqath kubar al-mutnaffithin" [Al-Utaybi: The financial stability law is an effort to rescue the highly influential], *al-Qabas*, March 31, 2009, 18.

136. "'Ayad Abu Khosa: Al-balad lam yastafid min al-qata' al-khass" [Ayad Abu Khosa: The country does not benefit from the private sector], *al-Watan (Kuwait)*, March 28, 2009, 14.

137. "Al-Humaydhi: Nastaghrib istikhdam 'ibarat ghayr la'iqa dhid qanun al-istiqrar al-mali" [Al-Humaidi: We are surprised by the use of inappropriate language against the financial stabilization law], *al-Qabas*, March 30, 2009, 11.

appears that only one investment company restructured under the law, with a first set of payouts of 82 million KD to individual investors and small institutions.[138] In a research report, one of the larger investment companies complained that "Government assistance, in the form of stimulus packages, lines of credit, equity injections, repurchase agreements etc have been the most visible of responses to the global financial crisis. Yet, nothing substantial happened along these lines in Kuwait."[139]

As a result of the crisis, the Kuwaiti financial sector incurred serious losses, and major losses were absorbed by the "whales" without threatening the stability of the financial system in Kuwait as a whole.[140] In this case, parliamentary vigilance probably had a salutary role. The Kuwaiti government, in sharp contrast to its previous practice, did not spend with abandon to absorb the private losses incurred by the financial industry. This avoided the spending of money in a way that, in the past, had exacerbated distributional inequalities and class resentments between the merchant elite and the salaried Kuwaiti middle class.

Other Forms of Development: Housing

The term *development* is commonplace in Kuwaiti political rhetoric, but what is meant differs from one context to another. Some see development in terms of diversification away from oil. In Kuwaiti political discourse *development* also denotes the improvement of public services. Middle-class citizens support these development projects—the construction of houses, schools, hospitals, and so forth—for the straightforward reason that these projects are built for them. The merchant elite, wary of direct cash payments to citizens, also like these projects because the private sector receives the contracts to build the projects. Budgetary constraints are essentially absent. The problem in Kuwait is not a lack of money to spend on development projects but an incapacity to spend the available funds. Given the wide political support for these projects, this failure suggests a problem with the capacity of the Kuwaiti state to act, a sort of sclerosis not seen in the other extreme rentiers of the Gulf.

138. IMF 2012a, 11–12.

139. Raghu and Al-Ammar 2012. Earlier, in 2009, Musallam al-Barrak voiced suspicions that the government was using state money to prop up investment firms, although it appears that this in fact did not happen, or did not happen much. There is no doubt there were no bailouts on the scale of those following Suq al-Manakh or the 1977 stock market crisis. "Al-Barrak: Hukuma al-muqara'a bi-al-hujja harabat min jalsa al-istijwab" [The government fled from the interpellation], *al-Qabas*, March 29, 2009, 15; Darwiche 1986, 13.

140. IMF 2012a, 7, 9.

The issue of housing provides a useful example of the problem of development in Kuwait. The Kuwaiti state, for most of the period since the start of the oil era, has provided housing aid of three types to citizens: (1) free houses built by the state and given to citizens; (2) interest-free loans (currently around US$250,000) to build a house, sometimes accompanied by a free plot of land, with utilities provided, on which to build it; and (3) a monthly housing stipend (around US$500) for those who rent rather than own.[141] The Kuwaiti state has displayed the necessary competence to distribute the loans and rent subsidies. The state's record of building houses and preparing plots for houses, however, has not been impressive. This is, in part, because of overpromising by the state. The working assumption is that the government should provide each citizen with a house (and a large one at that). Thus, each male citizen, when he qualifies, registers his name with the Public Authority for Housing Welfare. The Authority, as it builds houses and develops plots, works through the list. And because the Authority does not build enough houses to satisfy the understandably high demand for free houses, it has fallen very far behind. In 2013, it was building houses for those who had put their name on the list in the mid-1990s.[142]

The problem, however, is not limited only to overgenerous promises by the government. Because the state monopolizes most of the land in Kuwait, the supply of single-family residences (the only sort of interest to citizens) cannot increase in any substantial way without the direct involvement of the state.[143] The state need not supply ready-built houses, but it must supply at least plots of land. It must ensure that these plots are supplied with comprehensive public services, including electricity, water, and schools. Although the state can and does hire private-sector contractors to do the work, the state must still take the initiative in organizing the provision of these services. Because the municipality of Kuwait covers the entire country, this effectively means that the central state must develop plots of land for residential use.

Over the years, the Kuwaiti state has, in fact, built a great many houses for its citizens, more than 48,000 houses, 28,000 plots of land, and 1,000 apartments from 1974 through 2010. It has also built 115 primary schools, 241 mosques, 20 police stations, and a multitude of other public buildings in new

141. An overview can be found in Freeman and Sudarsanan 2012.

142. Ahmad Al-Masudi, "'Al-Sakaniyya': Tawzi' 96651 wahda sakaniyya munthu bada' al-iskan al-hukumi" ["Housing Authority": 96651 housing units distributed since the beginning of government housing], *al-Qabas*, March 4, 2013, 7.

143. Some substantial plots of land inside the planning boundary, and thus available for development, have been held by private owners, some from the ruling family. This includes land around the site of the U.S. Embassy in Bayan.

neighborhoods.[144] In recent years, compared to pre-invasion years, the state has built many fewer built homes and developed somewhat more plots of land.[145] In the earlier years of the housing program, the government built houses of differing levels of quality for Kuwaitis of different income levels, which in effect meant that the newly settled *bedu* received houses that were much below the standard of those inhabited by the *hadhar*.[146] This practice ended in the 1980s. The expectation that the government would provide a house, however, did not end; instead, it became the expectation that the government would provide quite a large house.

Given the widespread political support for the housing program and the lack of fiscal constraints, the state ought to do better than it has. There is little disagreement between the National Assembly and the government on the need for more housing, so the explanation for the failure of the state to provide housing seems to lie in some combination of inattentiveness to the problem at the top and bureaucratic inertia at the bottom. An analysis of the problem in *al-Qabas*—which focused on precisely this issue—concluded that the specific cause for the delays lay in the inability of the Housing Authority to secure land to build on from other state agencies, including the state oil company, the municipality, and the military.[147] That, of course, does not explain the failure of the Council of Ministers to solve the problem. This is, perhaps, the result of the distractions caused by the long series of crises growing out of the struggle over authority between the National Assembly and the ruling family. Others argue that it is simply the result of a lack of political and management acumen in the senior leadership of the government.

There are some signs that the government may manage to perform better in the housing sector in the future. In 2010, the National Assembly passed a major five-year development plan (following a lull in the battle between the ruling family and the National Assembly).[148] A number of targets were set for the Public Authority for Housing Welfare, and there are some indications that the state is beginning to build more houses and, especially, develop more plots of land. The

144. Public Authority for Housing Welfare, "'An Al-mu'assasa" [About the Authority], http://www.housing.gov.kw/AboutPHW.aspx (accessed February 17, 2013).

145. State of Kuwait 2012a.

146. Al-Dekhayel 1990, 307, 311.

147. Ahmad Al-Masudi, "100 alf talab iskani bi-intizar al-hasm" [100 thousand housing requests await resolution], *al-Qabas*, June 20, 2012, 4. See also "Ma misaha al-aradhi allati sallamatha wizara al-naft lil-iskan wa kam wahda sakaniyya tastaw'ib?" [What area of land has the ministry of oil given to the housing (authority) and how many housing units will it accommodate?], *al-Qabas*, November 17, 2008, 15.

148. State of Kuwait 2010, 79; Salisbury 2010b.

difficulties of the housing authority in securing public land appear to have been addressed. Following the elections of July 2013, the issue of housing received an enormous amount of attention from newly elected deputies and the press. The issue remains, however, an important test of the capacity of the Kuwaiti state to implement policies that enjoy widespread political support.

★ ★ ★

It is clear that the Kuwaiti National Assembly makes it impossible for Kuwait to follow the development model that is currently the vogue in the other Gulf extreme rentiers. The National Assembly would not tolerate the sort of fusion between public and private interests that is at the heart of the Dubai model. Kuwaitis have declared, in no uncertain terms, that public funds and public resources—including, and most important, land—should be controlled by the National Assembly and distributed only in a way that does not further enrich the ruling family and the traditional merchant elite. Because this sort of arrangement is at the core of the political economy of the other extreme rentiers of the Gulf, Kuwait needs to find an alternative model of development.

The economic problems of Kuwait, however, are not due wholly to its rejection of the Dubai model of the developmental state. As we have seen in the discussion of the five economic sectors, there are several additional obstacles. The fact that diversification does not generate jobs or tax revenues for Kuwaiti citizens helps to explain the overreliance of Kuwait on oil revenues. This is especially true of the lack of a tourism industry. Kuwaitis today have little reason to put up with the negative externalities (as they see them) of the tourist industry. If their jobs depended on this industry, citizens would need to strike some balance between jobs and traditional mores. The same sort of adaptation to foreign norms that would be necessary to encourage a tourism industry is also important in making Kuwait into a major international trading entrepôt. Even the problems in the Kuwaiti oil industry can be attributed, at least in part, to the fact that it is an extreme rentier; at the moment, the Kuwaiti state earns more money than it spends on its citizens, so the immediate cost incurred by the National Assembly in blocking projects in the oil industry is very low.

The one relatively bright spot in the non-oil economy of Kuwait is the financial sector, and it is not coincidental that this is the sector that has the fewest negative externalities for Kuwaiti citizens. It employs a fair number of citizens (especially compared to, say, tourism), and it fits with citizen mores. The financial-industry complaints about the miserliness of the government bailout are not evidence of government failure; the Kuwaiti middle class does not benefit from a financial industry that requires massive bailouts every decade or two. Instead, the middle class needs a financial industry that is well regulated, economically productive, and generates jobs for citizens.

The "no jobs, no taxes' thesis, however, has its limits in explaining the problems of the Kuwaiti economy. The cancellation of the Dow Chemical deal was a direct result of the monarchical form of government, which—at that particular time in Kuwait—gave a handful of deputies in the National Assembly the power to force the cancellation of the project by merely threatening an interpellation of the prime minister. Parliamentarism would not necessarily bring good government to Kuwait, but it would remove a prominent obstacle to the emergence of an effective government.

The travails of the Kuwaiti state in providing housing to citizens require a different explanation altogether. The state's record, to be sure, is not one of unremitting failure. Kuwait has built a great many houses for its citizens and is still building. Yet there is agreement in Kuwait that the performance of the state has been lacking in recent years, in housing and in the provision of other public services to citizens. This relatively poor performance cannot be blamed on the absence of the Dubai model in Kuwait because the benefits of building houses (and other similar public services) accrue directly to the Kuwaiti middle class. Nor can it be blamed on the fact that the construction of houses does not generate many (if any) jobs for citizens; Kuwaitis have no compunction whatsoever about hiring foreigners to provide goods and services for themselves, such as building free houses—that is why there are so many foreigners in Kuwait. Nor is there much evidence that concerns about corruption or problems arising from monarchical gridlock have had a major role in slowing the pace of housing construction. Poor leadership in senior government posts may have exacerbated the problem, perhaps partly as a consequence of the general distraction posed by the interpellations and other manifestations of the ongoing battles between the government and the opposition. The more worrying possibility, however, is that the problems faced by the Kuwaiti state in providing houses to its citizens are a sign of a lack of effectiveness and capacity of the state itself, manifested not only in housing but also in health, education, and other public services. Rectifying these problems is a necessary part of creating a Kuwaiti model of development that can meet the needs of the Kuwaiti middle class.

Chapter 6

What Resource Curse?

In this chapter, I discuss the implications of my argument for the literature on the resource curse and draw comparisons with rentiers outside the Gulf. In the next (and concluding) chapter, I discuss the economic and political future of the Gulf monarchies.

The literature on the resource curse predicts authoritarianism and the lack of economic growth. The literature boasts a large number of causal mechanisms that connect rents to these outcomes. Rents are thought to discourage democracy because of the autonomy of the rentier state, a rentier mentality among citizens, rentier social contracts, the dependency of the bourgeoisie, an absence of class politics in rentiers, the overweening repressive power of the state, and so forth. My argument in this book does not start from any of these causal mechanisms. Instead, I argue that rents have made possible, in all three extreme rentiers, the emergence of badly distorted labor markets in which citizens are employed largely by the state at wages higher than market wages while foreigners compose the bulk of the private-sector workforce and sell their labor in a market with lower labor prices. I set out this argument in detail in chapter 1. Such labor markets are unique to extreme rentiers; the sort of wealth that allows the state to offer essentially full employment to citizens, at a wage that is reasonably generous by world standards, is possible only in extreme rentiers.

How, then, do these bifurcated labor markets affect political and economic outcomes? Their effect is mediated by the level of political participation. Where the level of political participation by citizens is high, as in Kuwait, the state adopts policies that do not encourage non-oil economic growth. This is because citizens do not benefit from most varieties of this sort of diversification. Tourist facilities, for example, employ many, many foreigners and hardly any citizens, and they do not generate tax revenues needed by citizens for the provision of public services. In the medium term, at least, Kuwaiti citizens might reasonably think they are better off without a large tourist industry. Such industries, however, potentially generate large profits for local capitalists, who have a strong interest in encouraging this sort of development. In Kuwait, local capitalists do not have a majority in the National Assembly, and the National Assembly has effectively frustrated capitalists' ambitions in this direction. (This is the core argument of chapter 5.) In the UAE, by contrast, middle-class citizens (those dependent primarily on state salaries for income) have little political voice, while capitalists—who are led by the ruling families—have a great deal of political power. For reasons specific to the federal structure of the UAE, this has led to the emergence of the Dubai model of development, a model that has been influential elsewhere in the Gulf. (This argument is made in chapter 4.)

From the vantage of the resource curse literature, one immediately notable aspect of my argument is that source of the difference in outcomes—that is, the existence of a powerful National Assembly in Kuwait and its absence in the UAE—is *not* related to variations in the level of rents. Instead, (as I argue in chapter 3) the key difference between the experiences of the UAE and Kuwait lies in the threat that Iraq posed to Kuwait at crucial points in its political development, in the early 1960s and again in the early 1990s. This threat generated and then reinforced the power of the National Assembly and put Kuwait on its current path, a path that is moving it toward greater political participation and away from the type of political and economic system found in Qatar and the UAE.

Rentiers elsewhere

Extreme rentierism makes these distorted labor markets possible. Does it make them necessary? Put differently, do we find these kinds of labor markets in extreme (and middling) rentiers outside the Gulf? As it turns out, we do find bifurcated labor markets in some other rentiers, but not all of them.

The extreme rentier with labor markets that most closely resemble those of the Gulf is the ill-fated island micro-state of Nauru, a country with a miniscule population even by Gulf standards (it had a citizen population of around 8,000 in 2003). In the 1970s, phosphate exports gave the citizens of Nauru per capita incomes among the highest in the world. Nauruans—or 95% of those with a job—worked in the public sector and developed a poor work ethic. Foreigners made up the bulk of the workforce in the phosphate mines and amounted to around half the residents of the island in the 1980s.[1] Then the phosphates petered out, and the government frittered away Nauru's overseas savings. By 2006, the result was an economic collapse that made observers question whether Nauru could survive as a sovereign state. In 2003, the country lost its telecommunications links to the outside world except when a ship with a satellite phone visited.[2] Throughout all this, Nauru was a parliamentary democracy, with a parliament of 18 members chosen by an electorate that numbered 2,000 in 1980.[3] This is, if nothing else, a sobering example for the Gulf states, particularly Kuwait.

Today the richest rentier outside the Gulf appears to be Brunei, a small oil exporter that is the only Malay sultanate to become an independent state. The Brunei labor markets broadly resemble those of the middling Gulf rentiers. The population is legally divided into three groups: citizens, permanent residents, and temporary residents. In 2010, some 268,000 citizens made up about 65% of the population, permanent residents 8%, and temporary residents (i.e., foreigners) 27%.[4] These percentages are more comparable to Saudi Arabia or Oman than to Qatar or the UAE. Many of the permanent residents are stateless, and many are ethnic Chinese (most Bruneians are Malay). With the exception of foreign women who have married Bruneian men and a few permanent residents born in Brunei, the government grants citizenship to few foreigners or permanent residents, in line with the rentier logic of citizenship found in the Gulf. Naturalizations in Brunei have averaged a few hundred annually in recent years.[5] It also appears to be difficult for foreigners to become permanent residents.

As in the Gulf rentiers, the private sector hires mostly foreigners. According to figures released by the Brunei government (and the government is stingy with its data), citizens made up 25% of the private-sector workforce in 2009, permanent residents made up 6%, and foreigners made up the remaining 67%.[6] The government does not release data on public-sector employment by citizenship status.[7] By reputation, however, Bruneians are concentrated in the public sector, although not so much so that a significant number do not need to find work in the private

1. Connell 2006, 49; *The Economist*, "Paradise Well and Truly Lost" 361, December 22, 2001, 39–41.
2. Connell 2006, 58–59.
3. Taylor and Thoma 1985, 150.
4. Brunei Economic Development Board, "Brunei Darussalam Key Indicators 2011," Department of Statistics, Department of Economic Planning and Development, Prime Minister's Office, http://www.bedb.com.bn, 1.
5. Ubaidillah Masli, "283 Granted Brunei Citizenship," *Brunei Times*, April 25, 2010; Fitri Shahminan, "294 Get Brunei Citizenship," *Brunei Times*, January 25, 2011; Fitri Shahminan, "New Citizens Told to Uphold Bruneian Identity," *Brunei Times*, February 1, 2012.
6. Nation of Brunei Department of Economic Planning and Development 2010, 44–45.
7. Ibid., 52.

sector. Unfortunately, the political consequences of this sort of bifurcated labor market are not easy to discern in any detail. Brunei is an absolutist monarchy, more closed even than Qatar. In the words of the Economist Intelligence Unit, "Brunei remains one of the only countries in the world to have no real political scene. . . ."[8] The sultan has pursued a policy of promoting economic development and diversification, but there is little evidence of the sort of boom—with an accompanying deluge of foreign labor—seen in Gulf countries such as Qatar and the UAE. Instead, the closer analog might be Oman. The Malay character of the state and the demographic predominance of Malays are not challenged even though the labor market, especially in the private sector, includes a large number of foreigners.

Norway, in sharp contrast to other countries with its level of rent income, has experienced little labor market distortion. Immigration has been modest (and net immigration has been even lower), although there has been a noticeable upswing in immigration since 2007.[9] Unlike other rich rentiers, however, Norway provides immigrants with a clear path to citizenship, and naturalizations in recent years have approached 12,000 annually. This is not much less than net immigration up to the mid-2000s.[10] The state employs one-third of the total workforce, a figure well within Scandinavian norms, between Sweden (with a slightly smaller public sector) and Denmark (with a slightly larger one).[11] This is remarkable given the substantial rents received by the Norwegian state. Although some efforts have been made to identify political traces of the resource curse in Norwegian politics, it is hard to escape the conclusion that oil wealth has failed to make Norwegian political problems different in scope or kind than those faced by other advanced democracies.[12] The strong institutions of Norway, as many have noted, seem to have insulated it from serious political and economic distortions arising from its oil wealth.

The next tier of middling rentiers includes the three not-so-wealthy Gulf monarchies—Oman, Bahrain, and Saudi Arabia—along with Trinidad and Tobago, Equatorial Guinea, and Libya. The economy of Trinidad has long relied primarily

8. "Brunei Politics: The Sultanate Remains in Political Limbo," Economist Intelligence Unit ViewsWire, March 26, 2012, http://viewswire.eiu.com/index.asp?layout=VWArticleVW3&article_id=988907483.

9. Statistics Norway 2011, 109.

10. Ibid., 113.

11. Ibid., 205; Statistics Sweden 2012, 243; Statistics Denmark 2011, table 109. Data is for 2009 (Denmark), 2010 (Norway), and 2011 (Sweden).

12. Listhaug 2005. Much the same can be said of efforts to find the resource curse in Australia (Goodman and Worth 2008). For an interesting micro-level discussion of how the oil boom helped the Norwegian economy, see Fagerberg, Mowery, and Verspagen 2009.

on exports of oil, although in the mid-2000s it benefited from a natural gas boom that propelled it into the ranks of the middling rentiers.[13] Foreign-born residents accounted for only 3.7% of the population in the 2011 census, compared to 3.3% in 2000.[14] The public sector (including SOEs) employed 27% of all workers in 2011.[15] It is not clear how Trinidad has so successfully escaped the labor market consequences of rentierism, although this appears to be partly due to a relatively lower level of rents before the mid-2000s. Its success also bears comparison with Norway. Trinidad and Norway are the two established democracies among the richer rentiers, and it is notable that both have avoided a division of the labor market between foreigners and citizens (Nauru, although a micro-democracy, did not manage this). Trinidad, with its relatively positive outcomes, deserves more attention than it has received from scholars of the resource curse.[16]

Equatorial Guinea releases very little good data on its economy or otherwise. The United Nations estimates that the population is 700,000, whereas the government claims a population of 1.6 million, and it is said that the discrepancy helps the regime to steal elections.[17] There are no available data on labor markets, although the U.S. State Department says that "irregular residents from [neighboring countries] represented a significant portion of the labor force."[18] Citizens, however, do not constitute a privileged caste of the sort found in the Gulf. The ruling family of Equatorial Guinea displays a singular unwillingness to share the oil wealth with citizens, and there are few signs of the sort of distributional impulses that led to the widespread employment of citizens in the public sector in the Gulf monarchies. Observers criticize the regime for leaving its citizens in "abject poverty"[19] and note that, well into the oil boom, it was spending less on health and education than the African average.[20] The IMF pointedly observes that the per capita GDP of Equatorial Guinea is close to that of Hungary but that three-quarters of the population lives on less than $2 per day.[21] The private sector of the country "remains extremely limited outside the hydrocarbon sector," and the business climate is "unwelcoming." These problems are related to the horrific

13. U.S. Energy Information Administration, "Country Analysis Briefs: Caribbean," May 1, 2012, http://www.eia.gov/EMEU/cabs/Caribbean/pdf.pdf (accessed October 5, 2012).

14. Trinidad and Tobago 2012, 23.

15. Trinidad and Tobago, "Labour Force Bulletin for the 3rd Quarter 2011," Central Statistical Office, http://www.news.gov.tt/index.php?news=10801 (accessed June 9, 2013).

16. For an exception, see Smith and Kraus 2005.

17. International Monetary Fund (IMF) 2013, 4; Wood 2004, 549.

18. U.S. Department of State 2011.

19. McSherry 2006, 36. Also see Silverstein 2002.

20. Frynas 2004, 543.

21. IMF 2013, 4, 8.

political history of the country, which included the murder or exile of one-third of the citizen population during the rule of the uncle of the current president.[22] Oil has not solved the problems of Equatorial Guinea, but neither is oil their cause. The legacy of the dismal political history of Equatorial Guinea appears to be a rentier state that feels no need strong urge to "buy off" its own citizens—and whatever pressure it does feel comes from the outside, not from any internal dynamics rising out of rentierism.

Data on the Libyan economy are also scarce, although it appears that something like three-fourths of formal employment was in the public sector before the fall of Muammar Gaddafi in 2011. A parallel informal sector employed about the same number of people as were employed in the formal labor market. Some of these were, in fact, the same people because underpaid public-sector employees also held positions in the informal economy.[23] Many of those with public-sector positions did not in fact show up for work.[24] Thus, although the Libyan state clearly sought to distribute wealth via government employment, most citizens also relied on the private sector (which was largely informal) for all or part of their livelihoods. The state lacked the funds to support its citizens in the style of the extreme rentiers of the Gulf. Despite this, the private sector in Libya before the revolution faced obstacles higher than those in any of the other rich rentiers, with the exception of Equatorial Guinea. In the later part of the 1970s and first half of the 1980s, Gaddafi's regime largely destroyed the existing private sector, which was "virtually eliminated."[25] Much of the prerevolutionary economic and social elite fled into exile.[26] Reforms in following years did not revive the private sector, largely because of the systematic undermining of state institutions by the regime. The Monitor Group, which became notorious during the Arab Spring for its lobbying on behalf of Gaddafi's regime, published in 2006 a study of the economy that was as perceptive in its economic analysis as it was toadying in its politics; the report declared Libya to have one of the least friendly business environments in the world.[27]

All told, the rent-abundant countries are a disparate lot. Norway and Trinidad have managed to avoid the widespread use of state employment to distribute oil revenues; so too has Equatorial Guinea, for very different reasons. Brunei and

22. Wood 2004, 548–49.

23. St. John 2008, 87; Monitor Group and Cambridge Energy Research Associates 2006, 37–38, 109, 131.

24. Monitor Group and Cambridge Energy Research Associates 2006, 38.

25. St. John 2008, 77.

26. Lacher 2011, 142–43.

27. Monitor Group and Cambridge Energy Research Associates 2006, 42–65. See also Chami et al. 2012, 17.

Libya look more like the Gulf countries. In some countries (Norway and the UAE), the private sector flourishes. In other countries, the private sector has done much more poorly, although it is only in Kuwait that we find economic development frustrated by a legislature that represents a state-employed middle class dependent on oil rents.

The usual assumption made by researchers analyzing the political and economic consequences of rent wealth is that the consequences are monotonic—an increase in rentierism (however measured) results in an increase in authoritarianism or economic stagnation.[28] Rents, however, might better be thought of as having a conjunctural causal impact. That is, rents in conjunction with one variable may cause one outcome but in combination with another variable may cause an entirely different outcome.[29] Taking the Gulf rentiers alone, we can devise a very simple model. Extreme rentierism and a weak representative assembly produce an extraordinarily imbalanced labor market and, to some degree, economic diversification; extreme rentierism combined with an influential parliament results in little economic diversification and, consequently, not quite so severe a demographic imbalance. If we broaden the cases to include middling rentiers and countries outside the Gulf, the picture becomes less clear, but we still can find some possible regularities. In two democracies, Norway and Trinidad, rentierism did not produce extremely distorted labor markets; in Nauru, also a democracy (albeit an extraordinarily small one), rentierism did produce a distorted labor market. None of the extreme or middling rentiers that started out authoritarian have escaped distorted labor markets and a sizable influx of foreign labor, and the problem seems to be roughly in proportion to the per capita amount of oil revenues—although the demographic imbalance in Kuwait is not quite so skewed as that of its more authoritarian neighbors.

In a recent piece on the resource curse, David Waldner and Benjamin Smith categorize approaches to the theory into three groups: the view that the relationship between rents and outcomes is unmediated (monotonic); the view that the relationship is "heterodox," in which the effects of rents are mediated by other variables and can be positive or negative; and the view that there simply is no relationship.[30] The sheer profusion of outcomes among the most rent-abundant states of the world strongly supports the second view: the political consequences

28. Gerring describes monotonic causality as existing where "an increase (or decrease) in the value of X causes an increase (decrease) or no change in Y," where X is the causal variable and Y the outcome (2012, 224–26).

29. Ragin 2008, chap. 1. To give a different example, rents combined with dynastic rule produce very durable monarchies; rents without family rule, as in Libya, produce a fragile monarchy.

30. Smith and Waldner (in press).

of rents are decisively shaped by the political contexts of the countries that receive rents.[31] There can be no doubt whatsoever that rents have had extraordinary consequences for the politics and economics of all of the Gulf states, and it could hardly be otherwise. And there are very clear ways in which rents decisively shape the nature of political participation and economic diversification. But, when we take a step back and look at the larger political and economic outcomes in these states, rents do not always push these states toward common outcomes, be they authoritarianism or economic stagnation.

Leviathan and the Extreme Rentiers

At the center of much of the literature on rents and democracy lies the argument that democratization is a competition between state and society and that rents tip the balance of power toward the state, making democracy less likely. This argument is not limited to rent wealth. Milton Friedman, writing on the consequences of socialism, writes that "if economic power is joined to political power, concentration seems almost inevitable. On the other hand, if economic power is kept in separate hands from political power, it can serve as a check and a counter to political power." One of the obstacles to freedom in a socialist society, he observes, is that "all jobs are under the direct control of political authorities."[32] Extreme rentiers are not socialist, by any means. But the role of the state as the default employer of citizens appears to provide yet another causal mechanism through which rents increase the power of the state. Only socialist economies can match the near-monopsony position of the extreme rentier state in employment of citizens.

As my discussion earlier in this book makes clear, however, Kuwait is perceptibly moving in a democratic direction. Given what seems to be the overwhelming concentration of state power in the hands of the ruling family, this is indeed a remarkable result. A full explanation for this lies outside the scope of this book.[33] The Kuwaiti experience, however, does suggest that political institutions can constrain state power more effectively than is usually thought, even when the state

31. See for example Smith 2007, 8–9. Michael Ross does not make this point, but he does observe that "countries are only hurt by oil wealth under certain conditions—some of them fairly restrictive" (2012, 230).

32. Friedman 1982, 16.

33. It would require tracing the historical relationship between the government and the National Assembly to determine the specific processes by which the National Assembly has usurped some of the authority of the ruling family.

enjoys a great deal of economic power. The economic influence and weight of the state in modern developed democracies is immense, but these states are constrained by democratic political institutions. Rentier states typically start from an authoritarian status quo, but rents do not make the task of constraining the state impossible. That Kuwait is an extreme case of rentierism—a spectacularly rich exporter of oil, in which the consequences of rentierism should be felt more profoundly than virtually anywhere else—reinforces this thesis.

★ ★ ★

The extreme rentiers of the Gulf display the consequences of rentierism in their clearest form. In these countries, rentierism is not a by-product of poverty but, instead, a result of the extraordinary ratio of rent wealth to number of citizens. The Gulf extreme rentiers make up the entire current universe of extreme rentiers; the remaining three Gulf countries make up a substantial share of the universe of middling rentiers. But, even among these cases, the political and economic consequences of oil wealth are decisively shaped by other existing factors, enough so that very different results can be seen in countries that otherwise share much in common. In the next chapter, I turn from the political science literature on rentier states and consider the future of the Gulf monarchies.

Dilemmas of Development and Democracy in the Gulf

It is as if these governments told the citizens of these states: 'We will drown you in a flood of humanity so that you aspire to no more than not drowning, and we will stay on our thrones dividing the spoils with those in our circles and those who applaud our policies.'"

—*Yousif Khalifa al-Yousif*

In recent years Kuwait and the UAE have pursued contrasting models of political and economic development. In this book I have explained how the two countries, initially much more similar, have grown so different, and I have explored some of the consequences for their politics and their economies. In this chapter I look to the future, asking where these divergent paths are likely to lead and tracing out the likely consequences of these models for the other Gulf monarchies. I start with a discussion of the stability of these monarchies in light of the Arab Spring in order to provide the necessary context for understanding the future of the Gulf.

The Continuing Resilience of the Gulf Monarchies

The Arab Spring, not surprisingly, has led to a resurgence of arguments that the days of the Gulf monarchies are numbered. Until recently, this view had been in retreat.[1] Christopher Davidson has set out the most forceful and prominent argument that the end is nigh for the Gulf ruling families. In his book *After the Sheikhs:*

1. Herb 1999; Gause 2000; Lucas 2004; Anderson 1991.

The Coming Collapse of the Gulf Monarchies,[2] he discusses a number of "mounting pressures" on the ruling families, many of which overlap with the themes I have discussed here. Stability, he argues, rests on "unwritten, unspoken ruling bargains or social contracts"[3] between rulers and citizens; these include an implied promise to provide jobs and an elaborate welfare state for citizens. To varying degrees, this social contract is fraying across the Gulf monarchies. As it frays, citizens have grown ever more vocally opposed to corruption, to the theft of national resources by the ruling families, and to vanity projects. The Dubai model (he does not call it that) generates yet more dissatisfaction among citizens: "efforts to diversify their economic bases away from hydrocarbons … have precipitated the development of new economic sectors geared towards foreign investors, tourists, or simply an increased number of expatriates." The pursuit of economic growth has led to "top-down changes and relaxations in the Gulf monarchies' societies, especially with regard to cultural and religious practices."[4] He highlights citizen concerns about alcohol and prostitution.[5]

Davidson's accounting of the difficulties faced by the Gulf ruling families is comprehensive, detailed, and well informed. Much less clear are the mechanisms by which these pressures will cause the collapse of the Gulf monarchies. He is right to highlight the seriousness of the exogenous shock of the Arab Spring for the Gulf monarchies. The fall of seemingly durable Arab regimes elsewhere, even though they were all republics, changes the political environment for the Gulf monarchies in a way not favorable to the ruling families. But it does not follow that their collapse is imminent.[6]

To understand why the regimes will survive, it is necessary to think through the ways in which they might be brought down.[7] Until recently, the chief threat to the survival of Arab monarchies came from their militaries. It was the militaries that did away with the monarchies in Libya, Iraq, and Egypt; street protests had very little or no role in these republican revolutions. The family character of the Gulf monarchies—what I have called dynastic monarchism—makes these regimes

2. Davidson 2012.

3. Ibid., 49.

4. Ibid., 155.

5. Davidson 2012, in chapters 4 and 5, discusses a fairly lengthy list of additional pressures on the ruling families including stateless populations, sectarian tensions, increasing censorship, foreign policy issues, and internal tensions within the ruling families.

6. Davidson avoids providing much in the way of a description of how complete the collapse of the monarchies will be or the process by which they will fall. The tenor of his discussion, however, suggests, at minimum, an end to the effective power of the ruling families and probably the creation of republics. See also Davidson 2013.

7. These are, of course, small rich countries with covetous neighbors. I deal here with domestic, not international, threats to the ruling families.

resistant to coups, and none has ever been seriously threatened by a military coup.[8] The uprisings that broke out across the Arab world in spring 2011 pose a different and more serious threat to the monarchies. To be sure, the monarchies, including the dynastic monarchies, did a much better job than the Arab republics in keeping their citizens off the streets during the Arab Spring, and this no doubt had something to do with their monarchism. These regimes have many resources—ideological, monetary, political, and institutional—available to deflect such protests. That said, there is no reason to think that dynastic monarchism can avoid street protests with the same success with which they have avoided military coups.

The long-term stability of the Gulf monarchies thus depends on their ability to respond effectively to street demonstrations. These regimes are different from the regimes that fell during the Arab Spring in two crucial ways. First, the Gulf ruling families can credibly reform without ending the monarchy—and to do this, they need to set up something like the National Assembly of Kuwait.[9] Second, the ruling families will retain the loyalty of the military, police, and security forces much longer than did the presidents of Tunisia and Egypt—long enough so that, if need be, they could reform rather than risk civil war.[10]

Let us start with the second point first. In Tunisia and Egypt, the lack of close links between the presidents' families and the military helped make possible the clean decapitation of the regimes in 2011. In many respects, these events are best understood as military coups provoked by mass demonstrations. Similar military coups (whether ending in elections or not) will not happen in the Gulf monarchies: dynastic monarchism is particularly well suited to the prevention of coups.

What, then, of reform? Bahrain was the only Gulf monarchy to experience widespread protests during the Arab Spring, and it did not reform at all. Bahrain, however, also had Saudi assistance, and it suffers from a sectarian divide that makes its situation different from that of the other Gulf monarchies. Sectarianism reinforced the loyalty of the security forces, which are almost entirely Sunni, and it made reform much more difficult because the Shi'i majority is alienated from the ruling family to a degree not found elsewhere in the Gulf.

The other Gulf monarchies have more flexibility to reform (though this is more the case in Saudi Arabia and Oman than in the UAE and Qatar, for demographic reasons). The resilience of the dynastic monarchies is buttressed by their ability to depose a ruler should he become a lightning rod for the sort of vitriolic hate directed at Hosni Mubarak or Bashar al-Asad (or, for that matter, the shah of Iran).

8. Herb 1999.

9. On the prospects for reform in the Gulf monarchies generally, see Ehteshami 2003; Kéchichian 2004, 53; Nonneman 2006, 37; Ehteshami and Wright 2007; Herb 2002.

10. On the role of the military in the Arab Spring, see Barany 2011.

When Ali Abdullah Saleh of Yemen finally resigned the presidency (or when one of his resignations finally took), he was replaced by someone outside his family. In a dynastic monarchy, the ruler is very likely to be replaced by another member of the family with a reputation for being a reformer. Hosni Mubarak could not reform by resigning in favor of his son Gamal; the prospect of Gamal's ascendance to the presidency was an aspect of Mubarak's regime that his opponents found particularly offensive.[11] None of the Gulf ruling families has reached this level of unpopularity, with, again, the partial exception of Bahrain. All of the dynasties currently have—or could conjure up—a member of the family with a reputation as a reformer. Such a figure could bring together the many supporters of the dynasty while earning a honeymoon of sorts from moderates in society. In this case, the political dynamics of monarchism differ in a basic way from the dynamics of the would-be hereditary republican regimes of the Arab world before the uprisings.

The Gulf dynastic monarchies have a reform path open to them, one that preserves the monarchical nature of the regime but increases citizen political participation. It is true that, today at least, the Gulf monarchies have led the counterrevolution in the Arab world and have generally moved away from reform in the aftermath of the Arab Spring. This does not mean that reform—the Kuwait model—is unavailable to these regimes. Faced with a vital threat, the Kuwaiti ruling family—which is not unlike those of its neighbors—put in place a liberal constitution. It is not hard to imagine that a different sort of threat, one from within, could induce one or more of the Gulf monarchies to take similar steps. Davidson argues that "the window of opportunity for the region's autocratic rulers to agree to some sort of compromise solution—possibly constitutional monarchies with elected legislatures—seems to be closing."[12] But a compromise solution—along the Kuwaiti model—is still available to the regimes, albeit in varying degrees. Constitutional reform certainly is not a path any of the ruling families wants to take. But the Kuwaiti path remains very much a live option.

Labor Markets, Expatriates, and Participation in the Extreme and Middling Rentiers of the Gulf

The crucial questions concerning the future of the Gulf monarchies, then, are not how and when they will be overthrown, because their overthrow is unlikely. Instead, the political and economic future of the Gulf states will be decisively

11. Lynch 2012, 86–87.
12. Davidson 2013.

shaped by the issues raised in previous chapters. Will the ruling families continue to seek growth at the expense of concerns over demography? Can the UAE and Qatar expand political participation for citizens while continuing to diversify their economies? Can Kuwait develop an economic model that will allow it to combine political participation with economic diversification? What are the consequences, both political and economic, of the increasingly large role of expatriates in the economies of most Gulf monarchies?

A Dystopia in the Making? The United Arab Emirates

If the UAE continues the policies pursued by its rulers over the past decades, the country will arrive at a truly remarkable place: it will consist of a small caste of citizens surrounded by millions of expatriates, all ruled by several families unaccountable to anyone but themselves. This presumes economic growth continues; the remarkable economic diversification seen in the UAE—and particularly in Dubai—seemed for a while to be imperiled by the catastrophic collapse of the Dubai real estate market that began with the 2008 world financial crisis. But the economic foundations of the increasingly diversified Dubai economy are sounder than they sometimes appear. Dubai—and the UAE generally—offers first-world infrastructure, an aggressively pro-business political climate, low-cost labor, low taxes, abundant capital in the region, and a favorable geographical location. These factors (except the last two) are in place because those with power want them to be. The state is controlled by a family that has a vital interest in creating a positive business environment, not least because of the ruling family's investments in real estate and other growth-oriented business enterprises. The result of this has been a very impressive entrepôt economy based on logistics and trade. This entrepôt economy grew even while the real estate market collapsed, and it is likely to continue to grow. As it grows, it will bring the other emirates of the UAE—except, perhaps, Abu Dhabi—into a large UAE conurbation centered, at least economically, on Dubai. Absent political problems, there is little reason to think that this urban complex will not continue to add millions more to the already substantial UAE population.

As the UAE economy grows, more immigrants will move to the UAE, further reducing the percentage of citizens in the total population. Citizens will become an ever more privileged Arab caste in a largely non-Arab population, marginalized politically, socially, and economically but still enjoying the benefits of their exclusive caste status in an increasingly diversified economy. Middle-class expatriates, for their part, will find the UAE to be a good place to improve their economic lot and that of their families, as will perhaps the less-skilled expatriates who manage to avoid the worst exploitations of the sponsorship system. The implicit condition of expatriate prosperity, of course, will be political exclusion. The result will be the dystopia that al-Shehabi sees in the Gulf future: "a society 'without an identity' of multiple ethnicities, with a common denominator amongst them only a focus on growth in GDP, consumption, and the English language."[13]

What actors might push the UAE onto a different path, one leading to a different sort of political and economic future? There are three possibilities: the ruling family of Abu Dhabi, Emirati citizens, and foreigners.

The Al Nahyan. The one political institution in the UAE that has the political power to fundamentally constrain the Dubai development model is the ruling family of Abu Dhabi. The 2008 world financial crisis bankrupted Dubai, and Abu Dhabi—which is to say the Al Nahyan ruling family of Abu Dhabi—bailed it out.[14] The abrupt renaming of the world's tallest building from Burj Dubai to Burj Khalifa—after the ruler of Abu Dhabi—drove home the change in the balance of power between the emirates. Given the long history of tensions over the consequences of the Dubai economic model in the UAE—especially (as we have seen in chapter 4) in the constitutional debates in the 1970s—it might be expected that Abu Dhabi would take advantage of the economic problems of Dubai to rein in its distinctive development model. But unhappiness with the Dubai model, which emerged so forcefully in the 1970s, has apparently disappeared among the senior shaykhs of the Al Nahyan. In the 1970s, Zayed fought to strengthen the federation, equalize opportunity across the various emirates, and give citizens a voice in how they were governed. By the 2010s, the ruling family of Abu Dhabi had major investments in real estate and other business ventures both inside and outside the emirate of Abu Dhabi. And the ruling family has embraced projects which give foreigners a central role in the emirate's future. How else can we explain the investment of hundreds of millions of dollars in building a university (NYU Abu Dhabi) whose inaugural class included only a modest number of Emirati students?

All that said, the wealth of Abu Dhabi gives its ruling family latitude in choosing a development model. No ruler can go against the core interests of the ruling family, but those interests might be interpreted in different ways. A turn toward the inclusion of citizens, and away from the excesses of the Dubai model, cannot be ruled out. Such a change would not be easy and would generate dissent from the other ruling families of the UAE and from members

13. Al-Shehabi 2012, 135.
14. International Monetary Fund (IMF) 2011b; 2012c, 27.

of the Al Nahyan family. But the sheer abundance of hydrocarbon wealth in Abu Dhabi gives its ruling family a freedom to maneuver that is a source of uncertainty.

Citizen Democracy. How likely is it that Emirati citizens could effectively demand that their rulers grant them a greater degree of political participation? Up to 2011, the answer seemed clear—not very likely at all. But the Arab Spring changed the calculations of both the rulers and the ruled, not only in the Arab republics but also in the monarchies.[15] Borrowing Charles Kurzman's memorable turn of phrase, the Arab Spring made the "unthinkable thinkable."[16] Davidson documents an increase in opposition in the UAE (even before spring 2011) that culminated in petitions sent to the ruler in March 2011.[17] One of these petitions, signed by 133 Emiratis, called for all members of the FNC to be elected by an electorate consisting of all citizens and for the FNC to be given "complete legislative and supervisory powers."[18] The regime responded with repression rather than conciliation, arresting several signatories of the petitions. The repression continued into 2013 with a widely watched trial of dozens of citizens who were charged with belonging to an organization—affiliated with the Muslim Brotherhood—that was accused of seeking to overthrow the regime.

What sort of changes do Emirati citizens want? The regime would have us believe that its opponents are chiefly interested in a Muslim Brotherhood republic. The signers of the petitions—and many other Gulf citizens—instead demanded elections to an empowered national legislature and the eventual transition to constitutional monarchy. By focusing on the chimera of a Muslim Brotherhood revolution, the ruling families distract the citizens and outside powers from demands for constitutional reform. It is very difficult to imagine exactly how the Muslim Brotherhood—or any other domestic political force—could forcibly remove the ruling families of the UAE.[19] The Kuwaiti

15. On the Arab Spring in the monarchies, see Yom and Gause 2012; Michael Herb, "Monarchism Matters." *Foreign Policy* blogs. November 26, 2012, http://mideast.foreignpolicy.com/posts/2012/11/26/monarchism_matters.

16. Kurzman 2004, ix.

17. Davidson 2012, 220–26; Kristian Coates Ulrichsen, "The UAE: Holding Back the Tide," openDemocracy blog post, 2012, http://www.opendemocracy.net/kristian-coates-ulrichsen/uae-holding-back-tide.

18. The petition, titled simply "The Petition," and dated March 3, 2011, can be found at http://www.ipetitions.com/petition/uaepetition71/ (accessed April 3, 2013).

19. The most relevant point of comparison is the performance of the Muslim Brotherhood in Kuwaiti elections. The political organization has never captured more than a modest fraction of the fifty seats.

model might be a distant prospect, but a Muslim Brotherhood revolution is even more so.

The recent demands for reform in the UAE are the most positive indications of possible change in a more democratic direction in many years. That said, it is hard to be optimistic. The Kuwaiti model faces high obstacles in the UAE, obstacles greater than in the other GCC states save for perhaps Bahrain. First, the federal nature of the UAE makes it difficult to accomplish a serious expansion of political participation without a corresponding increase in the authority of the federal institutions. This imposes, on potential reformers, two tasks: an increase in the authority of the FNC within the political institutions of the federation and also an increase in the power of the federation against the constituent emirates of the UAE. A strengthened FNC in a weak federation would accomplish little. Expanding the power of the federation against the emirates would be resisted by many of the ruling families; if history is any guide, the Al Maktoum of Dubai would vehemently resist an expansion of federal power.

Second, the geographic dispersion of citizens poses its own obstacle. Although a national identity has emerged in the UAE in recent years—an identity that transcends the individual emirates—the citizens who live in the heart of political and economic power in the UAE (i.e., the citizens of Abu Dhabi) are also the most privileged group of citizens in the UAE. Less-privileged citizens, those who are the rough equivalent of the *bedu* in Kuwait, do not live in the suburbs of Abu Dhabi but, instead, in more distant Ras al-Khaimah and the other, poorer emirates. But these emirates are further removed socially, geographically, and politically from the centers of power in Abu Dhabi than are the *manatiq al-kharajiya* ("outer districts") where most of the Kuwaiti *bedu* live.

Finally, the spectacular demographic imbalance and the increasingly central role of foreigners in the UAE economy make constitutional reform on the Kuwaiti model difficult to achieve. It is not simply that a strong representative assembly along the lines of the Kuwaiti National Assembly would oppose the Dubai economic model—that would be a potential consequence of political participation, not an obstacle to it. The obstacle to democracy lies in the possibility that the ruling families could mobilize foreigners as a counterbalance to citizens—even the hint of such a mobilization would raise the specter of the loss of citizen privileges. To be sure, mobilizing expatriates is a risky strategy for the ruling families and one that they have only hinted at thus far. Nevertheless, it is a basic political fact that citizens compose only 11% of the population and falling. The other 89% (foreigners) run most of the economy and have important roles throughout all parts of the state, the media, and virtually all other Emirati institutions including, for example, the police.[20] The interests of this very large expatriate population are much more closely aligned with those of the rulers than with those of citizens,[21] at least when it comes to the sort of economic, political, and social policies that an empowered citizen parliament would be likely to adopt. Neha Vora points out that the Indian middle class in Dubai often praises the Emirati leadership for creating "an environment where foreigners have many opportunities to accumulate wealth" or embrace Dubai as "a 'clean Bombay.'"[22] It is hard to imagine how expatriates would benefit from a more influential citizenry in the UAE—and this makes expatriates a potential reservoir of support for the ruling families. This balancing need not be overt, although it could be, and it would not require that expatriates be given the right to vote in political institutions; expatriates need only be allowed to organize associations of various sorts and express their views. Their presence throughout the state and the media and their dominance in many economic sectors give expatriates a latent influence that can be exploited by the ruling families.[23]

The ruling families benefit from the demographic imbalance even when they do nothing in particular to mobilize expatriates. The favored weapon of the people during the Arab Spring was the street demonstration. Demonstrators have more difficulty claiming to represent "the people" when the people make up 11% of the population. The prospect of underprivileged masses taking to the streets to protest frightens citizens.

The ruling families can create a solid foundation for their rule by protecting the interests of the expatriates from the citizens while, at the same time, encouraging citizens to cling to the ruling families as the defenders of Emirati identity in a country populated largely by expatriates. As citizens become more marginalized, the UAE ruling families portray themselves as defenders of Emirati identity—and

20. The Dubai police employed more foreigners than citizens in 2010. "Foreign Police Officers Here to Make Expats Feel at Home," *The National* (Abu Dhabi), April 4, 2010, http://www.thenational.ae/news/uae-news/foreign-police-officers-here-to-make-expats-feel-at-home; Government of Dubai, Dubai Statistics Center, *Statistical Yearbook—Emirate of Dubai 2010*, fig. 3.5, http://dsc.gov.ae/EN/Publications/Pages/PublicationsList.aspx?PublicationId=1. A comparison with the situation in Kuwait is telling. Kuwaiti citizens are also a minority, but the key institutions in Kuwait—economic, political, and social—remain firmly in the hands of Kuwaitis, and the ruling family lacks the ability to change this. It is here where we can see starkly the effects of path dependency; Kuwaitis are now in charge of the Kuwaiti state—and through their influence in the National Assembly, they can ensure that they stay in charge of the state. Emirati citizens, by contrast, have no political levers with which to prevent the ruling families from taking steps that gradually, and perhaps not always intentionally, further marginalize citizens.

21. Davidson 2012, 12.

22. Vora 2008, 380, 383.

23. Al-Shehabi 2012, 25.

citizen privilege—against the foreign majority. This is hardly less effective because the ruling families are responsible for the demographic imbalance in the first place. In short, the maintenance of the status quo, in the long run, works against the possibility that citizens in the UAE can effectively demand real political participation following the Kuwaiti model.

Expatriate Inclusion. Students of democratization generally assume that the franchise is sufficiently broad for a country to be considered democratic if all competent adult citizens have the right to vote. Thus, the checklist used by Freedom House in constructing its well-known democracy index requires, apropos of who can vote, "universal adult suffrage for all citizens."[24] Political theorists, however, have given the issue of noncitizen voting rights much more thought than have scholars of democratization. The conclusion of political theorists is that citizenship, as defined by governments, is not an adequate basis on which to define the set of people in a territory who ought to have voting rights. One political theorist writes that "perhaps all contemporary political theorists" accept that "long-term residency in a democratic state is what should entitle people to full political rights. . . ."[25] Robert Dahl writes, "The citizen body in a democratically governed state must include all persons subject to the laws of that state except transients and persons proved to be incapable of caring for themselves."[26]

No country meets this standard in full. But in most democracies, long-term residents compose a modest share of the population, and many enjoy at least a potential route to citizenship. As a consequence, scholars of democratization (as opposed to political theorists) appear to have set the issue of the resident noncitizen aside as falling into the category of ways-to-perfect-democracy rather being among the preconditions for considering a country to be democratic in the first place.

This is not good enough when we consider the Gulf rentiers. Eight out of every nine residents of the UAE are not citizens. It is true that many of the noncitizens live in the UAE only temporarily and would not, by any reasonable measure, have a right to political participation. (In the UAE, and elsewhere in the Gulf, caps on the number of years that expatriates can stay in the country have been discussed; the adoption of such a cap would help discourage the emergence of a permanent less-skilled expatriate population). Nevertheless, many more noncitizens are

24. Freedom House, "Methodology | Freedom House," 2012, http://www.freedomhouse.org/report/freedom-world-2012/methodology.

25. Lopez-Guerra 2005, 216–17. See also Beckman 2008; Carens 2008, 422.

26. Dahl 1998, 78.

long-term residents of the UAE, especially those in the middle class; many were born there, and indeed fewer citizens than noncitizens are born in the UAE.[27] There is no real pathway to citizenship for these noncitizen residents or their descendants, even for those who were born in the UAE and spend their entire lives there. Given this demographic imbalance, a citizen-only democracy in the UAE would be a deeply flawed, partial democracy.[28]

Although full democracy in the UAE requires the naturalization of long-term expatriates, there is virtually no chance that this will occur in the foreseeable future. In part this is because the interests of foreigners are the same, in some respects, as those of the more business-oriented members of the ruling families; most foreigners come to the UAE to do business or find employment, and the ruling families profit from accommodating them. At the lower end of the wage scale, there has been labor unrest, usually motivated by employers' broken promises. Among the more-skilled labor and longer-term middle-class foreigners, political malcontents can be dealt with through the straightforward expedient of deportation or the nonrenewal of residency permits. This is a remarkably effective threat that ensures the political quiescence of expatriate labor.

In the much longer term, however, the UAE will increasingly fall out of step with world norms. If anything, the Arab Spring was a powerful indication of the continued attraction of democracy. The prospect that really frightens Emirati citizens is the possibility of being forced by the international community to naturalize expatriates. This is a specter raised frequently in the UAE but hardly at all in Kuwait. For example, al-Shahin writes, "The cries have risen warning of the possibility of a retreat of the border [of the Arab world]—or part of it—to behind the oil wells, as a result of the implementation of the right of self-determination. . . . "[29] Ebtisam Al Ketbi, a professor at the leading UAE state university, told a U.S. reporter, "And those people are coming from democratic countries. They cannot be ruled with undemocratic way[s]."[30]

The sense of crisis felt by Emirati intellectuals grows out the realization that in the future the UAE may face a direct choice between democracy and its current Arab and Muslim identity. This concern, in some cases, has a nativist undertone

27. United Arab Emirates 2009, pt. 26, 27.

28. Discussions of democratization in the Gulf give the role of expatriates less attention than it deserves, and this is a difficult omission given the demographic weight of expatriates in many Gulf states. Ahn Nga Longva makes this point about Kuwait; she notes that "few analysts react to the total absence of linkage between studies of Kuwaiti politics and studies of Kuwaiti labour relations" (2005, 118).

29. al-Shahin 1997, 341.

30. In CBS News, "A Visit to Dubai Inc.," *60 Minutes*, October 14, 2007, http://www.cbsnews.com/stories/2007/10/12/60minutes/printable3361753.shtml.

to it, one that should be recognized. But the concern about identity should not be dismissed out of hand as merely xenophobic. Democratic societies are often cosmopolitan and accepting of immigrants; democratic societies, however, do not allow themselves to be wholly replaced by another identity, as Al-Shehabi points out.[31] There is a good reason that the 5 million or so citizens of Norway allowed 74,000 immigrants to settle in Norway in 2010[32] and not ten times that number. A few more decades of economic growth in the UAE will create a situation in which any real transition to democracy would result in a country with a basically South Asian (rather than Arab) identity. There is nothing, to be sure, wrong with such an outcome, but it is not what most Emirati citizens would choose if they had a say in the matter. There is, in fact, an allure to the idea of a truly cosmopolitan country, one unmoored from any narrow identity and adopting a neoliberal "multinational modernity."[33] And certainly we should hope that the UAE, in the long run, will forge a tolerant, Arab–South Asian inclusive identity for all those who permanently call it home. This is the best possible outcome. But the society being created in the UAE today is not that society—it is, instead, a society of national cantons isolated by citizenship laws and wracked by mutual suspicions. People in democratic nations can build tolerant, inclusive societies welcoming of immigrants, but they do not do so by adopting the sort of policies we see today in the UAE.

Can the demographic dilemma of the UAE be resolved by naturalizing the Arab noncitizen residents, at least preserving the Arab character of the country? A few Emirati intellectuals are more open to the idea of naturalizing Arabs than we might expect—and certainly more open to it than are Kuwaitis of all political stripes; in Kuwait, naturalizing anyone (other than the stateless *bidoon* and the children of female citizens) is an idea with no supporters.[34] Naturalizing Arabs in the UAE, of course, runs into the logic of extreme rentierism, in which naturalization harms the interests of the existing citizens because a fixed sum of oil resources would have to be shared among a larger number of citizens. It is striking, too, that Emiratis appear to be very uneasy about the role of Arabs who have already been naturalized, including Yemenis who worked in the police force.[35]

The naturalization of long-term foreign residents in the UAE may be hard to avoid in the future and it is a requirement for any real democratic transition. Nevertheless, there is little international pressure in this direction today. There is no

31. Al-Shehabi 2012, 34–35
32. Statistics Norway 2011, 66.
33. Kanna 2011, 135.
34. Ghubash 1999, 21.
35. Two interviews with UAE intellectuals in Dubai in 2007.

indication that the major Western powers are inclined to criticize the UAE for its refusal to grant citizenship to South Asian residents of long standing. U.S. diplomats seem to admire the prodigious economic growth, cooperative foreign policies, relatively liberal social atmosphere, and (at least until recently) velvet-glove approach to repression of the UAE. International organizations see the problems of expatriates in the UAE as one of human rights and economic exploitation rather than one of denial of political rights. The notion that long-term residents have a right to participate in politics is commonplace among political theorists but remains largely restricted to them. Neither foreign powers nor international nongovernmental organizations advocate granting political rights to long-term nonresidents.

This may not be the case, however, in the very long term. Let us imagine a world, decades in the future, in which democracy has become the predominant political system both in the Arab world and internationally and in which India has become a major world power. Long-term trends point in this direction. In such a world, it is not hard to imagine the UAE being pressured to naturalize its long-term noncitizen residents and democratize. The signal advantage of this outcome—if and when it comes about—is that the resulting democracy would encompass the political community as a whole.

We may reasonably conclude that the UAE is unlikely to find an easy path toward greater political participation, with or without including expatriates in the political community. Thus, existing trends are likely to carry forward, at least in the short and medium terms. The ruling families will continue to pursue growth. Citizens will become an ever smaller minority, a privileged and mostly powerless caste in a diversified economy. The ruling families will continue to put off movement toward democracy by balancing a fearful citizen minority against an increasingly large and permanent expatriate population pursuing a middle-class life. And, we should recognize, such an outcome would have many positive elements, despite the singular lack of democracy. The Dubai model opens up opportunities for millions of expatriates, especially from South Asia, to create better lives for themselves and their families.[36] Emirati citizens benefit from their membership in a privileged caste, and we can perhaps suppose that the loss of their political rights will be compensated by their high status and wealth—especially when we compare the citizens' circumstances to those of most noncitizens working in the

36. And the Gulf acts as a regional economic dynamo, driving economic growth in the parts of Asia, the Arab world, and even Africa; see Chorin 2010; Saifur Rahman, "Senegal Welcomes Dubai Developers with Open Arms," *Gulf News*, April 19, 2007, http://gulfnews.com/business/property/senegal-welcomes-dubai-developers-with-open-arms-1.173006.

UAE, many of whom face poverty and exploitation. But UAE citizens did not ask to be a politically powerless minority in their own country, deprived of real political rights and deprived, increasingly, of a country to call home.

Dilemmas of Democracy in Kuwait

While the problems of the UAE are more political than economic, the problems of Kuwait are both. Still, it is easier to imagine a future in Kuwait that combines both political participation and economic diversification than it is to imagine the UAE abandoning its current path.

Absolutism or Parliamentarianism. The Kuwaiti political system pits two principles of political authority—one monarchical and the other democratic—against each other, often with poor results. There are three possible outcomes of this contest: a reversion to the Gulf norms of absolutism, a transition to parliamentary democracy, and the continuation of the status quo stalemate.

Observers of Kuwaiti politics, and especially those who see Kuwaiti politics mostly in the context of the politics of other Gulf states, have long expected the al-Sabah to shut down the National Assembly, revise the constitution, and seize control of the political system. Instead, the al-Sabah have put up with the National Assembly. This suggests that the senior members of the ruling family either do not want to revert to Gulf norms or feel that they cannot successfully do so. Of the two possibilities, the latter seems the more likely. There are, of course, real liberals among the shaykhs of the al-Sabah, but other shaykhs are not. The current emir is not a liberal in the mold of Abdullah Salim, although he does not appear to desire to rule Kuwait through repression, which is what would be required to force Kuwait back toward ruling family absolutism. In 2009, in response to one of the many recent crises, the ruling family held a conclave and debated an unconstitutional dissolution of the National Assembly. There were supporters of this option, and there were opponents as well. The debate, according to reports in *al-Qabas*, focused on the ability of the ruling family to "control the streets" and whether Kuwaitis could be ruled "in this manner."[37] In the end, the shaykhs (and the emir) decided that Kuwait would simply be too hard to rule outside the bounds of the 1962 constitution. The Arab Spring confirmed the wisdom of this view.

37. Mubarak al-Abd al-Hadi, Ibrahim al-Saidi, and Tariq al-Aydan, "Al-hall al-aqall kulfatan su'ud al-Muhammad al-minasa" [The least costly solution is for al-Muhammad to take the stand], *al-Qabas*, March 5, 2009, 1; Muhammad Abd al-Qadir Al-Jasim, "Shatagul ya Nasir?" [What do you say, Nasir?], blog post, March 7, 2009, www.aljasem.org (accessed March 19, 2009).

The second possible path forward in Kuwait is one in which the opposition decisively wins its long battle with the ruling family and makes the National Assembly the strongest political actor in Kuwait. Since 2006, the National Assembly won significant concessions from the ruling family, moving Kuwait toward parliamentary control of the government. These concessions include redistricting in 2006, the first vote of confidence in a prime minister in 2009 (in which the ruling family admitted the principle that the authority of the government rests on the support of a majority in the National Assembly), and the forced resignation of the prime minister in 2011. Subsequently, however, the emir provoked an opposition boycott of the next two elections (in December 2012 and in the summer of 2013). The ruling family regained its footing and halted the slide toward parliamentarism. But this halt is unlikely to be permanent, and the odds are good that Kuwait, in a few years, will resume its fitful progress toward a stronger National Assembly.

Kuwait is a dynastic monarchy, in the sense that the ruling family forms an institution that controls the key posts in the state. I have argued elsewhere that these regimes are unusually resilient, and they are. They have avoided military coups, which are the preeminent threat to Middle Eastern monarchies. And they can survive street demonstrations of the sort seen in the Arab Spring. But the experience of Kuwait suggests that parliaments may be the Achilles' heel of dynastic monarchies. The dynastic monarchies emerged in Kuwait, and elsewhere, in a context in which the ruling families were the preeminent political institutions in their countries, without any effective competitors. Over the years, the National Assembly in Kuwait has emerged as a formidable institutional competitor to the ruling family, one that the ruling family cannot easily vanquish through its control of the state apparatus. The losses of the ruling family between 2006 and 2011 strongly suggest that the internal dynamics of the ruling family institution will not prevent concessions to the parliamentary opposition, and these concessions could someday include the loss of some of the key posts in the government—though one would expect the ministry of defense to be last.

Parliamentarism in Kuwait—that is to say, parliamentary appointment of the Council of Ministers—might alleviate the paralysis that currently besets the Kuwaiti political system. A prime minister selected by a parliamentary majority would have the support of that parliamentary majority in passing legislation, and ministers appointed by a majority coalition in the National Assembly could spend less time worrying about interpellations and more time implementing government policies. That said, it is also easy to imagine that parliamentary democracy in Kuwait could be a very factious affair with a multitude of parties and unstable governing coalitions. A prime minister selected by the National Assembly is not a panacea for the governance problems of

Kuwait—as is true, of course, of democracy in general, which does not always produce wise or efficient policies.

The two options discussed thus far amount to one side's winning the long struggle over control of the government—the National Assembly or the ruling family. This struggle, however, has been going on for several decades (it was joined in earnest in 1985, when the first opposition majority was elected to the National Assembly), and it could continue to go on for some time in the future. The emir's success in changing the electoral system and inducing the opposition to boycott in the November 2012 elections suggests that the status quo may linger for some time. If that turns out to be the case, we can expect to see more of the political crises for which Kuwait has become famous in the Gulf. In the middle to long term, however, a transition to parliamentarism—and thus democracy—is more likely than a reversion to absolutism.

Is democracy in Kuwait possible when only one-third of the residents are citizens? There is no doubt that a failure to include long-term residents would damage the quality of any Kuwait democracy that might someday emerge. The problem is not quite as bad as in the UAE where there are entire sectors of the economy in which citizens have very little role or presence except as business owners. There are fewer foreigners in Kuwait than in the UAE, and current trends do not point toward the immigration of millions more. So, the problem, although severe, is at least not becoming rapidly worse. In the long term, however, Kuwait cannot achieve full democracy without providing a path toward citizenship for long-term, permanent residents and reversing the demographic imbalance between citizens and expatriates.

Economic Diversification. The second challenge facing Kuwait is economic. Its economy today is almost completely dependent on hydrocarbons, and the government has made—as we have seen—little progress in diversifying the economy. In the short run Kuwait earns more money than it spends, and the state is able to provide the majority of Kuwaitis with a first-world standard of living. Eventually, however, the demands of citizens will overwhelm oil revenues and the days of plenty will come to an end.

When that day arrives, Kuwaiti citizens will need to find jobs in the private sector. If low-wage foreign labor is abundant, employers will hire expatriates instead of Kuwaitis, and Kuwaitis will not find the jobs they need. The only way to get less-skilled citizens into the private-sector labor market is to force employers to hire them. In chapter 1, I discussed a number of strategies to accomplish this; the ones that would work in this context are raising the cost of foreign labor and imposing quotas. The better of the two (except perhaps in the case of household labor) is to raise the cost of expatriate labor. The best way to do this is to limit supply, either through a hefty tax on foreign labor or by restricting immigration.

Given that we know the changes that Kuwait will need to make when spending outpaces oil revenues, the best way to prepare is clear: Kuwait should limit the supply and raise the cost of foreign labor. Any steps now made in this direction will make the eventual transition easier. By contrast, deepening the economy's reliance on cheap non-citizen labor will make it all that much harder to transition out of extreme rentierism in the future. Efforts should be concentrated on the less-skilled end of the labor market since it is here that problems will be most severe when Kuwait eventually loses the ability to offer graduates, as a matter of course, a job in the public sector.

Reforms should be gradual because sudden reforms would cause real harm to low-wage expatriates currently in Kuwait. A precipitous increase in the cost of foreign labor would also inconvenience Kuwaitis who have come to depend on expatriates for the provision of many services. Immediate and deep reforms are not likely to succeed for this reason. Put differently, the status quo exists for a reason, and changes are likely only in the margin. That said, it is important to have a clear picture of the goal: a Kuwait in which Kuwaitis do more work, and foreigners do less. It is also useful to have a clear understanding of what the goal is not, and the goal is not an imitation of Dubai, Doha, or Abu Dhabi. In the long run Kuwait needs to build an economy suited to its population of just over a million citizens (including the stateless *bidoon*). It does not need to compete with Gulf cities that have adopted an entirely different economic model. Attempts to imitate these cities would result in an increase in the number of expatriates in the labor force and a more difficult transition when the inevitable crisis in state finances arrives.

Reducing the amount of foreign labor in Kuwait would have a second benefit for Kuwaiti citizens. Kuwait spends immense sums on foreign labor. One obvious expense is salaries, but that is only the start. Foreigners consume highly-subsidized electricity, water, and fuel and require expensive state services. They add to traffic woes. Because expatriate labor exists almost entirely to provide services to Kuwaitis, the cost of the foreign population is paid for out of Kuwaiti oil wealth. Reducing—or at least not increasing—the size of the expatriate population would allow Kuwaiti citizens to conserve their country's wealth, postponing the day of reckoning when oil revenues no longer cover the public-sector salary bill.[38] A successful transition away from oil in Kuwait requires that Kuwaitis find goods and services to sell to the

38. Reducing the share of expatriates in the population also has a separate political benefit: Kuwait cannot be a full democracy when many long-term residents are excluded from the suffrage.

rest of the world. The sectors that produce these goods and services should employ mostly Kuwaitis, not foreigners—otherwise the problem is not solved. Developing these sectors now, and getting Kuwaitis to work in these sectors, is an immense challenge. (It will be easier when there is less oil money to go around.) That said, there are even today some promising industries. Kuwait already has a robust financial sector that employs citizens. Trade also offers prospects for growth, and Kuwait has a long history as an entrepôt. Finally Kuwait has had success with petrochemicals in the past. Even though the industry will not survive the complete exhaustion of oil reserves, this industry will still be viable when Kuwait makes a transition from extreme to middling rentierism. The petrochemical industry does not require a large number of expatriates (compared to tourism) or changes to Kuwaiti cultural norms.

Finally, Kuwait cannot reform its economy without a strong state led by a government that can make and implement decisions. Kuwait has made more progress toward the construction of a capable state than is usually thought, given that it started essentially from scratch a few generations in the past. But much more progress needs to be made. One hopes that the current talk about corruption in Kuwait leads to effective attacks on the problem rather than to a crippling cynicism.

In a perfect world Kuwait would today cut spending to a level that is sustainable in the long term, save more of its oil wealth, and put citizens to work doing the business of running the country rather than relying on foreigners. In the real world Kuwaitis elect deputies to the National Assembly who favor current consumption over long-term savings. As a result it seems inevitable now that Kuwait will spend much of its oil wealth over the course of a few generations. What Kuwait can do now is attempt to prepare as best it can for that future, given current political realities. Reducing its reliance on low-cost expatriate labor would help, as would nurturing the growth of a non-oil economy that employs citizens rather than foreigners. And, when fiscal crises arrive, a strong and capable state apparatus will help make the transition to a productive economy.

The Other Gulf Monarchies

Qatar. The current path of Qatar resembles that of the UAE. The chief difference between Qatar and the UAE is that Qatar is a unitary state with only one ruling family. There is no institution in Qatar that has a role equivalent to that of the Al Maktoum ruling family with its deep commitment to the creation of a business-oriented mega-city. Even so, the ruling family of Qatar has embraced elements of the Dubai model, especially the creation of an international brand. Qatar successfully bid for the 2022 World Cup in Doha, despite the high cost and questionable benefits for citizens of the emirate. The various foreign adventures of Qatar seem to have been driven more by the personal ambitions of a few members of the ruling family than by any specific security needs felt by a country that hosts one of the largest U.S. air bases outside U.S. territory.

Qatar has not yet diversified its economy to quite the same degree as the UAE, and its ruling family has not yoked its fate to expatriate-intensive business ventures to the same degree as have some of the ruling families of the UAE, particularly the Al Maktoum. That said, the Al Thani do have business interests that are likely to become more extensive in the future, and the family seems to have little compunction about welcoming a tsunami of foreigners to Qatar, creating a demographic imbalance almost as severe as that in the UAE.

If the senior members of the ruling family continue to encourage the growth of business in Qatar, and especially businesses staffed by and oriented toward foreigners, Qatar will wind up at the same place as the UAE—Qatari citizens will become a very small minority, marginalized politically, economically, and socially. The ruling family will be able to counter any citizen demands for democracy[39] with the foreign business and expatriate communities, which have no interest in the sorts of policies likely to be adopted by a parliament of citizens.

Bahrain. The Bahraini sectarian predicament engages issues that help reveal the dynamics of Gulf rentierism. In the middling rentiers, class politics revolves around tensions between capitalists and citizens over the composition of the workforce. Sunni Bahrainis have privileged access to state jobs, and the bulk of citizens who must find employment in the private sector—especially men with fewer skills—are Shi'i. This fact is reflected in the fate of efforts to reform the Bahraini labor market. The defeat of the moderate crown prince during the Arab Spring led to the abandonment of the labor market reforms he had advocated—reforms that had met with an angry backlash from business owners (mostly small business owners), many of whom were Sunni. The sectarian divide in Bahrain does not have an exact analog elsewhere in the Gulf; nevertheless, Bahraini politics do help us to see how the class politics affect the success or failure of efforts to reform labor markets in the middling rentiers.

Sectarian strife also helps to explain the growing demographic imbalance in Bahrain. The number of foreigners in Bahrain now exceeds the number of citizens. The foreign population exploded in recent years, rising from 38% in 2000 to 53.5% in 2010.[40] This is a remarkable result given that the Bahraini oil revenues

39. Al-Kuwari 2012a, 2012b.

40. The percentage of foreigners in the Bahraini population fell following the political turmoil of 2011 but remained above 50%. Central Bank of Bahrain, "Economic Indicators," March 2005 and June 2012, http://www.cbb.gov.bh/page-p-economic_indicators.htm; Sultanate of Oman 2011, table 1.2; [Saudi] Central Department of Statistics and Information, http://www.cdsi.gov.sa/socandpub/resd (accessed June 21, 2013).

per capita are in the same general range as those of Saudi Arabia and Oman and that in both of those countries the citizens still outnumber foreigners by a fair margin. Also remarkable is that Bahrain is the only Gulf monarchy that is currently naturalizing large numbers of its foreigners. This violates the logic of rentierism; the modest oil revenues of Bahrain must be divided among that many more citizens. The naturalizations, however, appear to be part of a ruling family strategy to alter the sectarian demography of the citizen population by giving citizenship to Sunnis. Many of these newly naturalized citizens hold jobs in the military, police, and security forces. The ruling family strategy thus serves the dual purpose of diluting the Shi'i majority while recruiting the security force personnel necessary to repress Shi'i dissent.

It is not hard to imagine some members of the Bahraini ruling family looking with some envy at the Dubai economic boom and demographic transformation. Economic growth in Bahrain would enrich the ruling family, and a true economic boom would lead to an influx of immigrants that would make the Shi'i population of the country a minority. The political problems of Bahrain, of course, render any such economic boom unlikely. Immigration, however, does offer the government an opportunity to transform the nature of the political community in a way that makes it easier for the ruling family to stay in power.

Oman and Saudi Arabia. None of the middling rentiers have the demographic imbalance seen in the UAE and Qatar, but the trends have been toward an increase in the expatriate percentage of the population. From 2003 to 2011, the foreign population in Oman rose by over 5%, reaching 29.4% of the population. From 2004 to 2012, the foreign population of Saudi Arabia also rose 5%, reaching 32% of the population. The steady increase of foreigners in Oman and Saudi Arabia is troubling (though not so troubling as the corresponding figures for Bahrain). The middling rentiers of the Gulf are at risk of creating societies in which an expatriate majority provides the bulk of the labor while citizens retreat into the public sector, reserved enclaves in the private sector, or unemployment. The situation in Oman and Saudi Arabia, however, has not gone nearly as far as in the other Gulf monarchies, and there are signs that the regimes in these two countries are uncomfortable with the increasing demographic imbalance and problems in their labor markets.

All told, Oman and Saudi Arabia reacted to the Arab Spring in a strikingly different fashion from the Bahraini regime, and this is a positive portent for the future direction of their politics. Even before 2011, the Saudi and Omani regimes had made efforts to try to force capitalists to hire citizens. After the Arab Spring, both redoubled these efforts. The Saudi regime in particular treated labor-market issues as a problem that bore on the survival of the regime itself. The regime sent hundreds of thousands of foreigners back home. The regime also imposed a tax on expatriate labor, levied on employers. Businesses mobilized against the tax but the regime did not back down. In fall 2013, construction companies reported that the levy was impacting their profits.[41] Despite close ties between the Saudi private sector and the regime, the regime decided that the need to create private sector jobs for citizens trumped the desires of Saudi employers for inexpensive labor. Nevertheless, some of the responses to the Arab Spring in Saudi Arabia and Oman exacerbated labor market distortions. The Al Saud, who had previously sought to limit the number and salaries of public-sector employees, surrendered their past restraint and gave out substantial raises to public-sector workers and created thousands of new public-sector jobs. The Omani regime also created state jobs in the immediate aftermath of the Arab Spring.[42]

The real measure of success for Oman and Saudi Arabia, over the coming decade, will be change in the percentage of foreigners in the total population. If these economies grow while at the same time keeping the percentage of expatriates in the population at today's level or lower, they will have found a sustainable path toward a productive society based on citizen labor. If the percentage of foreigners leaps (as it did in the 2000s in Bahrain), we may conclude that the regimes have decided to cater to the interests of capitalists at the expense of the long-term prospects for balanced political and economic development.

What are the prospects for greater political participation in Oman and Saudi Arabia? These two countries face better prospects than the other GCC monarchies, apart from Kuwait. The citizens, unlike in the UAE and Qatar, are still a majority in both Oman and Saudi Arabia. And although both have complicated identity and regional politics, neither faces the same identity predicament as Bahrain. There are only two paths these countries are likely to follow in the future. One of these is continued absolutism. Until spring 2011, this seemed by far the most likely outcome for the future. But the Arab Spring made the possibility of change in the monarchies real, if not imminent. When change does occur, the most obvious—and indeed the only really plausible—direction is toward the Kuwaiti model of constitutional reform. Of course, the princes of the Al Saud are notably resistant to even a hint of real political participation, much more so than

41. Habib Toumi, "Businessmen to Seek Clerics' Help against Levy," *Gulf News*, December 5, 2012, http://gulfnews.com/news/gulf/saudi-arabia/businessmen-to-seek-clerics-help-against-levy-1.1114555; "Saudi's Expat Worker Levy Hits Construction Profits," *Arabian Business*, September 12, 2013, http://www.arabianbusiness.com/saudi-s-expat-worker-levy-hits-construction-profits-517964.html.

42. Saleh al Shaibany, "Oman Will Up Spending by 9% to Create 80,000 Jobs," *The National* (Abu Dhabi), November 24, 2011, http://www.thenational.ae/news/world/middle-east/oman-will-up-spending-by-9-to-create-80-000-jobs.

the ruling family of Kuwait or of Oman. But, if we do see major protests in Saudi Arabia—and that is likely to happen eventually—the Kuwaiti model offers a path that may be more attractive than sheer repression. The Kuwaiti model gives the princes a way to retain—at least initially—some of their political power, much of their wealth, and their social status.

Prospects in Oman are, if anything, better than in Saudi Arabia. Sultan Qaboos has embraced a series of incremental reforms over the past two decades that has culminated in regular elections to a national representative assembly. The assembly needs to be granted more substantive powers. That might not happen soon, but it is a plausible direction of future change in Oman, especially if Omani citizens demand a greater voice in politics.

★ ★ ★

The obstacles facing the Gulf monarchies in creating productive democratic societies are perhaps not greater than those facing countries elsewhere in the world, but they are of a very distinctive sort—and this distinctiveness is created by rentierism, a tradition of importing foreign labor without allowing naturalization, and monarchical systems that potentially make the regime leaders the leading capitalists in their societies.

The Dubai model of development, with its dependence on cheap foreign labor, has some real virtues. It generates wealth and provides economic opportunities for many (mostly South Asian) expatriates. But in the end, the Dubai model creates a society with deep problems reconciling identity and citizenship, and this in turn makes it hard to imagine any clear path toward greater democracy, especially if the current economic and demographic trends continue. As a result, the UAE seems destined to become a caste society that includes entire economic sectors built on foreign labor, with much of that labor relegated to a permanently lower-caste status in a rigidly hierarchical society. The other Gulf rulers clearly are attracted to elements of the Dubai model, and as a result, the demography of Qatar today is as topsy-turvy as that of the UAE. The rulers of Bahrain, too, seem to be interested in encouraging immigration, although this is motivated by a straightforward animus directed at the Shi'i citizen majority.

In the other three Gulf states, however, the situation is better. Saudi Arabia and Oman do not suffer from an overwhelming demographic imbalance, and their regimes appear to be trying—if not entirely effectively—to create productive economies in which citizens work in the private sector. If they succeed in this, they will leave open a path toward political and economic development that will not feature a permanent caste system and an economy entirely built on low-cost noncitizen labor.

Kuwait is perhaps the hardest to understand from the outside. The country appears to be locked in interminable political conflict that saps its ability to diversify its economy. Yet Kuwaitis remain in control of their economic and political future. They are a minority in the population, but they have not built a diversified economy on low-cost expatriate labor. The problems of Kuwait, to be sure, are not small. The country needs to resolve the political paralysis generated by its monarchical political system. And Kuwait needs a strong state that can adapt to the eventual need to create productive private-sector jobs for its citizens when oil revenues decline. In the longer term, Kuwait needs to address its demographic imbalance. All this will not be easy to accomplish, especially the last. But Kuwaitis, at least, have in the National Assembly, an institution that gives them some measure of influence over the fate of their society and country.

References

Abdulla, Abdulkhaleq. 1984. "Political Dependency: The Case of the United Arab Emirates." PhD diss., Georgetown University.

—— 2006. "Dubai: Rihla madina arabiyya min al-mahalliyya ila al-'alamiya" [Dubai: Journey of an Arab city from localism to globalism]. *Al-Mustaqbal al-Arabi* 323 (January): 57–84.

Abdullah, Muhammad Morsy. 1978. *The United Arab Emirates: A Modern History*. London: Croom Helm.

Abu-Baker, Albadr S.S. 1995. "Political Economy of State Formation: The United Arab Emirates in Comparative Perspective." PhD diss., University of Michigan.

Abu Dhabi Government. 2012. *Statistical Yearbook of Abu Dhabi 2012*. Abu Dhabi: Statistics Centre. www.scad.ae.

Abu-Hakima, Ahmad Mustafa. 1965. *History of Eastern Arabia, 1750–1800: The Rise and Development of Bahrain and Kuwait*. Beirut: Khayats.

Acemoglu, Daron, and James A. Robinson. 2006. *Economic Origins of Dictatorship and Democracy*. Cambridge, UK: Cambridge University Press.

al-Abdallah, Yusuf Ibrahim. 2003. "Nash'at qatar wa tatawwurha hatta 'am 1868" [The emergence of Qatar and its development to 1868]. In *Tatawwur qatar al-siyasi: Min nash'at al-imarah hatta istiqlal al-dawla* [The political development of Qatar: From the emergence of the emirate to the independence of the state], edited by Ahmad al-Shalaq, Mustafa Aqil, and Yusuf Ibrahim al-Abdallah, 61–89.

al-Adsani, Khalid Sulayman. N.d. *Muthakkirat Khalid Sulayman al-Adsani, sikritir majlis al-umma al-tashri'i al-awl wa al-thani* [Memoirs of Khalid Sylayman al-Adsani, secretary of the first and second National Legislative Assemblies]. Unpublished manuscript, available at http://adsanee.8m.com/adsanee.html.

al-'Aqqad, Salah. 1992. *Al-Tayyarat al-siyasiyya fi al-khalij al-'arabi: min bidayyat al-'usur al-hadithah hatta azmat 1990–1991*. Cairo: Maktabat al-anjlu al-misriyya.

al-Astal, Ahmad Mahmoud. 2008. *Tajribat dawlat al-imarat al-'arabiyya al-muttahida fi majal qayyasat al-ra'y al-'amm: Mash li-asalib al-mumarasa wa-lil-ra'y al-'amm* [The experience of the UAE in the area of public opinion surveys: A review of techniques and of public opinion]. Abu Dhabi: The Emirates Center for Strategic Studies and Research.

al-Baghdadi, Ahmad. 1985. "Tajribat al-dimuqratiyya fi al-mujtama' al-kuwayti" [The democratic experience in Kuwaiti society]. *Al-Bahith* 38 ([year 7] 2): 9–38.

—— 1994. *Al-shaykh Abdallah al-Salim: Insanan . . . wa rajal dawla* [Shaykh Abdallah al-Salim: A man and a statesman]. Kuwait: Dar Qurtas.

al-Dayeen, Ahmad. 1999. *Waladat dustur al-kuwayt* [The birth of the Kuwaiti constitution]. Kuwait: Dar Qurtas.

Al-Dekhayel, Abdullkarim Hamoud. 1990. "The State and Political Legitimation in an Oil-Rentier Economy: Kuwait as a Case Study." PhD diss., University of Exeter.

Al-Ebraheem, Hassan A. 1975. *Kuwait: A Political Study*. Kuwait: Kuwait University.

Al-Fahad, Abdulaziz H. 2005. "Ornamental Constitutionalism: The Saudi Basic Law of Governance." *Yale Journal of International Law* 30: 375.

Al-Fahim, Mohammed. 1995. *From Rags to Riches: A Story of Abu Dhabi*. London: London Centre of Arab Studies.

Al-Fraih, Hamed Sulaiman. 1993. "Government Growth: The Case of Kuwait." PhD diss., University of Alabama.

Al-Ghazali, Essa Mohammad. 1989. "Human Resources Policies and the Welfare State Administration in Kuwait." PhD diss., University of Exeter.

al-Ghazali, Salah. 1985. *Al-hayat al-dimuqratiya fi al-kuwayt* [Democratic life in Kuwait]. Kuwait: Al-ittihad al-watani lil-talabat al-kuwayt.

al-Jasim, Najat Abd al-Qadir. 1980. *Baladiyyat al-kuwayt fi khamsiin 'aman* [The Kuwait municipality over fifty years]. Kuwait: Kuwait Municipality.

—— 1997. *Al-tatawwur al-siyasi wa al-iqtisadi lil-kuwayt bayn al-harbayn (1914–1939)* [The political and economic development of Kuwait between the wars]. 2nd ed.: n.p.: n.p.

al-Khatib, Ahmad. 2007. *Al-Duktur Ahmad al-Khatib yatadhakkir: Al-kuwayt min al-imara ila al-dawla* [Memoirs of Dr. Ahmad al-Khatib: Kuwait from Emirate to State]. Edited by Ghanim Al-Najjar. Casablanca, Morocco: al-Markaz al-Thaqafi al-Arabi.

Al-Kibsi, Gassan, Claus Benkert, and Jörg Schubert. 2007. "Getting Labor Policy to Work in the Gulf." *McKinsey Quarterly* (Special edition: Reappraising the Gulf States): 19–29.

Al-Kuwari, Ali Khalifa. 2011. "Halat al-dimuqratiyya fi Qatar: Qira'at dimuqratiyya fi dasatir al-duwal Al-'arabiyya" [The state of democracy in Qatar: Readings in democracy in the constitutions of the Arab states]. *Idafat* (13). http://www.caus.org.lb/Home/electronic_magazine.php?emagID=221&screen=1.

—— ed. 2012a. Al-sha'b yurid al-islah fi Qatar . . . aydan. Beirut: Muntada al-Ma'arif.

—— 2012b. "The People Want Reform . . . in Qatar, Too." Translated by Robin Moger. *Perspectives: Political Analysis and Commentary from the Middle East and North Africa* 4 (November). http://www.lb.boell.org/downloads/Perspectives_MENA_4_Qatar_Nov_2012_resized.pdf.

Allen, Calvin H. 1981. "The Indian Merchant Community of Masqaṭ." *Bulletin of the School of Oriental and African Studies, University of London* 44(1): 39–53.

—— 1987. *Oman: The Modernization of the Sultanate*. Boulder: Westview.

Al Maktoum, Mohammed bin Rashid. 2006. *Ru'yati: Al-tahaddiyyat fi sibaq al-tamayyuz* [My vision: Challenges in the race for excellence]. Beirut: al-Mu'assasa al-'arabiyya lil-dirasat wa al-nashr.

al-Nafisi, Abdallah. 1978. *Al-kuwayt: Al-ra'y al-akhar* [Kuwait: Another opinion]. London: Ta-Ha Advertising.

Al-Najjar, Ghanim. 2000. *Mudkhal lil-tatawwur al-siyasi fi al-kuwayt* [Introduction to political development in Kuwait]. 3rd ed. Kuwait: Dar Qurtas.

al-Qamis, Jasim, and Dhari al-Jatili. 2009. "Diwaniyyat al-ithnayn: Al-hadath laysa ba'idan wa la yumkin nisyanhu" [Monday Diwaniyas: Events not far in the past that it is not possible to forget]. *Al-Jarida* (Kuwait), March 2.

Al Rasheed, Madawi. 1992. "Durable and Non-Durable Dynasties: The Rashidis and Sa'udis in Central Arabia." *British Journal of Middle Eastern Studies* 19(2): 144–58.

—— 2005. "Circles of Power: Royals and Society in Saudi Arabia." In *Saudi Arabia in the Balance?: Political Economy, Society, Foreign Affairs*, edited by Paul Aarts and Gerd Nonneman, 185–213. New York: New York University Press.

al-Rifai, Yusuf Hashim. 1996. *Al-azma al-dusturiya al-ula fi hayat majlis al-umma al-kuwayti* [The first constitutional crisis in the history of Kuwait's Majlis al-Umma]. Kuwait: al-Rabiyan.

Al-Rokn, Mohammed Abdulla. 1991. "A Study of the United Arab Emirates Legislature under the 1971 Constitution with Special Reference to the Federal National Council (FNC)." PhD diss., University of Warwick.

Al Rumaihi, Mohamed. 1975. "Harakat 1938 al-islahiyya fi al-kuwayt wa al-bahrayn wa dubai" [The 1938 reform movement in Kuwait, Bahrain and Dubai]. *Dirasat al-Khalij wa al-Jazeera al-Arabiya* 1(4): 29–68.

al-Rumi, Fawzia Salih. 2005. *Tarikh nuzuh al-'a'ilat al-kuwaytiyya al-'ariqa ila al-kuwayt wa dawraha fi bina' al-dawla munthu nash'at al-kuwayt wa hata waqtna al-hadhir* [The history of the immigration of the ancient Kuwaiti families to Kuwait and their role in the building of the state since its founding and to the present time]. N.p.: n.p.

al-Rushayd, Abd al-Aziz. 1978. *Tarikh al-kuwayt* [History of Kuwait]. Tab'a munqaha. Beirut: Dar maktabat al-hayat. [Author's name is spelled "Rashid" in library catalogs.]

al-Sabah, Maymuna al-Khalifa. 2000. *Al-kuwayt fi zill al-himaya al-baritaniyya: Al-qarn al-'ishrin* [Kuwait under British protection: The twentieth century]. 3rd ed. Kuwait: Matabi' al-watan bi-al-kuwayt.

Al-Sabah, Youssif S. F. 1980. *The Oil Economy of Kuwait.* London: Kegan Paul International.

Al-Sagri, Saleh Hmad. 1988."Britain and the United Arab Emirates, 1820–1956, A Documentary Study." PhD diss., University of Kent at Canterbury.

al-Salama, Saad Said, and Amani Mubarak Al-Mubaraki. 2006. "B.O.T." Kuwait: State of Kuwait, Diwan al-Muhasaba [State Audit Bureau].

Al-Sayegh, Fatma. 1998. "Merchants' Role in a Changing Society: The Case of Dubai, 1900–90." *Middle Eastern Studies* 34(1): 87–102.

—— 2004. "Post-9/11 Changes in the Gulf: The Case of the UAE." *Middle East Policy* 11(2): 107.

al-Shahin, 'Abd al-Rahim 'Abd al-Latif. 1997. *Nizam al-hukm wa al-idarah fi al-imarat al-'arabiyya al-muttahidah* [The system of government and administration in the United Arab Emirates]. Ras al-Khaimah: Matba'at Jalfar.

Al-Shatti, Ismail. 2003. "Al-kuwayt wa tajribat al-intiqal ila al-dimuqratiyya" [Kuwait and the experience of transition to democracy]. *Al-Mustaqbal al-Arabi* 289: 115–39.

Alshayeji [Al-Shayeji], Abdullah Khalifah. 1988. "Democratization in Kuwait: The National Assembly as a Strategy for Political Survival." PhD diss., University of Texas at Austin.

Al-Shehabi, Omar Hisham. 2012. *Iqtila' al-judhur: Al-mashari' al-'aqariyya wa-tafaqum al-khalal al-sukkani fi majlis al-ta'awun li-duwal al-khalij al-'arabiyya* [Uprooting: Real estate projects and the aggravation of the population imbalance in the Arab states of the Gulf Cooperation Council]. Beirut: Markaz Dirasat al-Wahdah al-'Arabiyya.

al-Suwaidi, Abdulla. 2011. "The United Arab Emirates at 40: A Balance Sheet." *Middle East Policy* 18(4): 44–58.

al-Tabtabai, Adel. 1978. *Al-nizam al-ittihadi fi al-imarat al-arabiyya: Dirasa muqarana* [The federal system in the UAE: A comparative study]. N.p.: n.p.

—— 1985. *Al-sulta al-tashri'iyya fi duwal al-khalij al-'arabi: Nash'atha, tatawurrha, al-'awamil al-mu'aththira fi-ha* [Legislative power in the Arab Gulf states: Its emergence, its development, and the factors affecting it]. Kuwait: Majallat dirasat al-khalij wa al-jazira al-arabi.

—— 1988. "Al-nizam al-qanuni li-istighlal al-qasa'im al-sina'iyya" [The legal framework for the use of industrial parcels]. *Majallat al-Huquq* [Kuwait] 1988(1): 11–76.

—— ed. 1999. "Mahadhir ijtama'at lajnat al-dustur wa al-majlis al-ta'sisi" [Minutes of the Constitution Committee and the Founding Council]. *Majallat al-Huquq* [Kuwait] 23 (3 Suppl.).

Al-Tajir, Mahdi. 1987. *Bahrain, 1920–1945: Britain, the Shaikh, and the Administration.* London: Croom Helm.

al-Yousif, Yousif Khalifa. 2008. "'Andama tusbi' al-sulta ghanima: Halat majlis al-ta'awun al-khaliji [When the government becomes booty: The case of the Gulf].

al-Zayd, Khalid Sa'ud. 1981. "Jasim al-Qatami wa al-haraka al-wataniyya al-mu'asira fi al-kuwayt" [Jasim al-Qatami and the modern nationalist movement in Kuwait]. *Al-Bayan* 188 (November): 4–11.

Al-Zumai, Fahad. 2006. "Protection of Investors in Gulf Cooperation Council Stock Markets: A Case Study of Kuwait, Bahrain and the United Arab Emirates." PhD diss., School of Oriental and African Studies, University of London.

Andersen, Jørgen J., and Michael L. Ross. 2013. "The Big Oil Change: A Closer Look at the Haber-Menaldo Analysis." *Comparative Political Studies* (June 13). http://cps.sagepub.com/.

Anderson, Lisa. 1991. "Absolutism and the Resilience of Monarchy in the Middle East." *Political Science Quarterly* 106(1): 1–15.

Anscombe, Frederick F. 1997. *The Ottoman Gulf: The Creation of Kuwait, Saudi Arabia, and Qatar.* New York: Columbia University Press.

—— 2009. "The Ottoman Role in the Gulf." In *The Persian Gulf in History*, edited by Lawrence G. Potter. New York: Palgrave Macmillan.

Anthony, John Duke. 1975. *Arab States of the Lower Gulf: People, Politics, Petroleum.* Washington, DC: Middle East Institute.

Aslaksen, Silje. 2010. "Oil and Democracy: More than a Cross-Country Correlation?" *Journal of Peace Research* 47(4): 421–31.

Bahrain Center for Human Rights. 2009. "Bahrain: Dangerous Statistics and Facts about the National Security Apparatus." March 8. http://www.bahrainrights.org/en/node/2784.

Bahrain Independent Commission of Inquiry. 2011. "Report of the Bahrain Independent Commission of Inquiry." www.bici.org.bh.

Bahry, Louay. 1999. "Elections in Qatar: A Window of Democracy Opens in the Gulf." *Middle East Policy* 6(4): 118.

Barany, Zoltan. 2011. "The Role of the Military." *Journal of Democracy* 22(4): 24–35.

Baz, Ahmed Abdullah Saad. 1981. "Political Elite and Political Development in Kuwait." PhD diss., George Washington University.

Beckman, Ludvig. 2008. "Who Should Vote? Conceptualizing Universal Suffrage in Studies of Democracy." *Democratization* 15(1): 29–48.

Birdsall, Nancy, and Arvind Subramanian. 2004. "Saving Iraq from Its Oil." *Foreign Affairs* 83(4): 77.

Boghardt, Lori Plotkin. 2006. *Kuwait amid War, Peace, and Revolution: 1979–1991 and New Challenges*. New York: Palgrave Macmillan.

Boix, Carles. 2003. *Democracy and Redistribution*. Cambridge, UK: Cambridge University Press.

Bolt, Katharine, Mampite Matete, and Michael Clemens. 2002. "Manual for Calculating Adjusted Net Savings." Environment Department, World Bank. http://documents.worldbank.org/curated/en/2002/09/8228708/manual-calculating-adjusted-net-savings.

Brown, Nathan J. 2002. *Constitutions in a Nonconstitutional World: Arab Basic Laws and the Prospects for Accountable Government*. Albany: SUNY Press.

Brunnschweiler, Christa N., and Erwin H. Bulte. 2008. "The Resource Curse Revisited and Revised: A Tale of Paradoxes and Red Herrings." *Journal of Environmental Economics and Management* 55(3): 248–64.

Business Monitor International. 2007. *United Arab Emirates Business Forecast Report*. London: Business Monitor International.

Butti, Obaid A. 1992. "Imperialism, Tribal Structure, and the Development of the Ruling Elites: A Socioeconomic History of the Trucial States between 1892 and 1939." PhD diss., Georgetown University.

Card, David. 2012. "Comment: The Elusive Search for Negative Wage Impacts of Immigration." *Journal of the European Economic Association* 10(1): 211–15.

Carens, Joseph H. 2008. "Live-in Domestics, Seasonal Workers, and Others Hard to Locate on the Map of Democracy." *Journal of Political Philosophy* 16(4): 419–45.

Carter, Robert. 2005. "The History and Prehistory of Pearling in the Persian Gulf." *Journal of the Economic and Social History of the Orient* 48(2): 139–209.

Central Bank of Oman. 2011. *Annual Report 2010*. Economic Research and Statistics Department. June. N.p.

Chami, Ralph, Ahmed Al-Darwish, Serhan Cevik, Joshua Charap, Susan George, Borja Gracia, Simon Gray, and Sailendra Pattanayak. 2012. "Libya beyond the Revolution: Challenges and Opportunities," Middle East and Central Asia Departmental Paper 12/1. International Monetary Fund, Washington, DC.

Chorin, Ethan. 2010. "Articulating a 'Dubai Model' of Development: The Case of Djibouti." Report. Government of Dubai and Mohammed bin Rashid School of Government, Dubai UAE.

Colin Buchanan and Partners. 1970. *Studies for National Physical Plan and Master Plan for Urban Areas, First Report*. Kuwait: Mogahwi Press.

Collier, David, Henry E. Brady, and Jason Seawright. 2010. "Introduction to the Second Edition: A Sea Change in Political Methodology." In *Rethinking Social Inquiry: Diverse Tools, Shared Standards*, 2nd ed., edited by Henry E. Brady and David Collier, 1–10. Lanham, Md: Rowman & Littlefield.

Connell, John. 2006. "Nauru: The First Failed Pacific State?" *Round Table* 95 (383): 47–63.

Cordesman, Anthony H., Robert M. Shelala, and Omar Mohamed. 2013. *The Gulf Military Balance, Vol. 3: The Gulf and the Arabian Peninsula*. Washington, DC: Center for Strategic and International Studies.

Council of Economic Advisers. 2007. "Immigration's Economic Impact." June 20. http://georgewbush-whitehouse.archives.gov/cea/cea_immigration_062007.html (accessed June 24, 2013).

Crystal, Jill. 1990. *Oil and Politics in the Gulf: Rulers and Merchants in Kuwait and Qatar*. Cambridge, UK: Cambridge University Press.

Crystal, Jill, and Abdallah al-Shayeji. 1998. "The Pro-Democratic Agenda in Kuwait: Structures and Context." In *Political Liberalization and Democratization in the Arab World: Comparative Experiences*, edited by Rex Brynen, Bahgat Korany, and Paul Noble, 101–25. Boulder: Lynne Rienner.

Dahl, Robert Alan. 1998. *On Democracy*. New Haven: Yale University Press.

Darwiche, Fadwa. 1986. *The Gulf Stock Exchange Crash?: The Rise and Fall of the Souq Al-Manakh*. London: Croom Helm.

Davidson, Christopher M. 2005. *The United Arab Emirates: A Study in Survival*. Boulder: Lynne Rienner.

—— 2007a. "Arab Nationalism and British Opposition in Dubai, 1920–66." *Middle Eastern Studies* 43(6): 879–92.

—— 2007b. "The Emirates of Abu Dhabi and Dubai: Contrasting Roles in the International System." *Asian Affairs* 38(1): 33–48.

—— 2008. *Dubai: The Vulnerability of Success*. New York: Columbia University Press.

—— 2009. *Abu Dhabi: Oil and Beyond*. New York: Columbia University Press.

—— 2012. *After the Sheikhs: The Coming Collapse of the Gulf Monarchies*. London: Hurst & Co.

—— 2013. "Why the Sheikhs Will Fall." *Foreign Policy*. April 26. http://www.foreignpolicy.com/articles/2013/04/26/why_the_sheikhs_will_fall?page=0,2.

Davies, Charles. 1997. *The Blood-Red Arab Flag?: An Investigation into Qasimi Piracy, 1797–1820*. Exeter, UK: University of Exeter Press.

Delacroix, Jacques. 1980. "The Distributive State in the World System." *Studies in Comparative International Development* 15(3): 3–21.

Dickson, Harold R. P. 1956. *Kuwait and Her Neighbours*. London: Allen & Unwin.

Dresch, Paul. 2006. "Foreign Matter: The Place of Strangers in Gulf Society." In *Globalization and the Gulf*, edited by John W. Fox, Nada Mourtada-Sabbah, and Mohammed al-Mutawa, 200–222. London: Routledge.

Dudley, Dominic. 2012. "Expanding Nitaqat's Success." *MEED: Middle East Economic Digest* 56(41), October 12, 38–39.

Dunning, Thad. 2005. "Resource Dependence, Economic Performance, and Political Stability." *The Journal of Conflict Resolution* 49(4): 451–82.

—— 2008. *Crude Democracy: Natural Resource Wealth and Political Regimes*. Cambridge, UK: Cambridge University Press.

Edmonston, Barry, and James P. Smith. 1997. *The New Americans?: Economic, Demographic, and Fiscal Effects of Immigration.* Washington, DC: National Academy Press.

Ehteshami, Anoushiravan. 2003. "Reform from Above: The Politics of Participation in the Oil Monarchies." *International Affairs* 79(1): 53–75.

Ehteshami, Anoushiravan, and Steven Wright. 2007. "Political Change in the Arab Oil Monarchies: From Liberalization to Enfranchisement." *International Affairs* 83: 913–32.

England, James R. 2012. "Real Estate Investing in the Middle East: Foreign Ownership Restrictions in the GCC." Metropolitan Corporate Counsel, Mountainside, NJ. January 20, 42–43. http://www.metrocorpcounsel.com/articles/17520/real-estate-investing-middle-east-foreign-ownership-restrictions-gcc (accessed January 10, 2013).

Esposito, Frank. 2009. "Kuwait Ends Plans for Dow Joint Venture." *Plastics News,* January 5.

Eulau, Heinz H. F. 1942. "Early Theories of Parliamentarism." *Canadian Journal of Economics and Political Science* 8(1): 33–55.

Fagerberg, Jan, David C. Mowery, and Bart Verspagen. 2009. "The Evolution of Norway's National Innovation System." *Science & Public Policy* 36(6): 431–44.

Fasano, Ugo, and Rishi Goyal. 2004. "Emerging Strains in GCC Labor Markets." IMF Working Paper WP/04/71. International Monetary Fund, Washington, DC.

Flynn, Patrice. 2011. "The Saudi Arabian Labor Force: A Comprehensive Statistical Portrait." *Middle East Journal* 65(4): 575–86.

Foreign Policy. 2008. "The 2008 Global Cities Index." No. 169: 68–76.

Foreman, Colin. 2008. "Emirates Population to Exceed Forecasts." *MEED: Middle East Economic Digest* 52(10), March 7, 19.

—— 2011. "Abu Dhabi Imposes Cost Controls." *MEED: Middle East Economic Digest* 55(30), July 29, 20–21.

Freeman, Gus, and Siji Sudarsanan. 2012. "Impact of the Financial Crisis on the Housing Finance System of Kuwait." *Housing Finance International* (winter): 44–50.

Friedman, Milton. 1982. *Capitalism and Freedom.* Chicago: University of Chicago Press.

Frynas, Jedrzej George. 2004. "The Oil Boom in Equatorial Guinea." *African Affairs* 103(413): 527–46.

Gause, F. Gregory. 2000. "The Persistence of Monarchy in the Arabian Peninsula: A Comparative Analysis." In *Middle East Monarchies: The Challenge of Modernity*, edited by Joseph Kostiner. Boulder: Lynne Rienner.

Gavin, James. 2012. "Moving Forward with Nationalisation." *MEED: Middle East Economic Digest* 56(27), July 6, 38–41.

Gengler, Justin J. 2011. "Ethic Conflict and Political Mobilization in Bahrain and the Arab Gulf." PhD diss., University of Michigan.

—— 2013. "Royal Factionalism, the Khawalid, and the Securitization of 'the Shī'a Problem' in Bahrain." *Journal of Arabian Studies* 3(1): 53–79. doi:10.1080/21534764.2013.802944.

George, Alexander, and Andrew Bennett. 2005. *Case Studies and Theory Development in the Social Sciences.* Cambridge, MA: MIT Press.

Gerring, John. 2012. *Social Science Methodology: A Unified Framework.* 2nd ed. Cambridge, UK: Cambridge University Press.

Ghabbash, Ghanim Ubayd. 1990. *Fi al-siyasa wa-al-hayat* [In politics and life]. Beirut: Dar al-farabi.

Ghabra, Shafeeq. 1998. "Al-mu'assasat wa al-tanmiya al-siyasiyya al-'arabiyya: Halat al-kuwayt" [Arab political institutions and development: The case of Kuwait]. *Al-Mustaqbal al-Arabi* (229): 30–45.

Ghobash, Moza. 1996. *Al-tanmiyah al-bashariyya fi dawlat al-imarat, 1971–1994* [Population development in the UAE]. Abu Dhabi: Manshurat al-majma' al-thiqafi.

Ghubash, Hussein. 1999. *Al-imarat wa al-mustaqbal: Nahwa ru'yah wataniyya jadida wa-maqalat siyasiyya ukhra* [The emirates and the future: Toward a new national vision and other political articles]. Sharjah, UAE: Dar al-khalij lil-sahafa wa al-tiba'a wa al-nashr.

Goldstone, Jack A. 2003. "Comparative Historical Analysis and Knowledge Accumulation in the Study of Revolutions." In *Comparative Historical Analysis in the Social Sciences*, edited by James Mahoney and Dietrich Rueschemeyer, 41–90. Cambridge, UK: Cambridge University Press.

Goodman, James, and David Worth. 2008. "The Minerals Boom and Australia's 'Resource Curse.'" *Journal of Australian Political Economy* (61): 201–19.

Gorvett, Jon. 2005. "Abu Dhabi Takes the Property Plunge." *Middle East* (361): 40–41.

Haber, Stephen, and Victor Menaldo. 2011. "Do Natural Resources Fuel Authoritarianism? A Reappraisal of the Resource Curse." *American Political Science Review* 105(1): 1–26.

Hales, Mike, and Andres Mendoza Pena. 2012. "2012 Global Cities Index and Emerging Cities Outlook." ATKearney. http://www.atkearney.com/research-studies/global-cities-index.

Hall, Peter A. 2003. "Aligning Ontology and Methodology in Comparative Politics." In *Comparative Historical Analysis in the Social Sciences*, edited by James Mahoney and Dietrich Rueschemeyer, 373–404. Cambridge, UK: Cambridge University Press.

Halpern, Manfred. 1963. *The Politics of Social Change in the Middle East and North Africa*. Princeton: Princeton University Press.

Hamilton, Kirk, and Michael Clemens. 1999. "Genuine Savings Rates in Developing Countries." *World Bank Economic Review* 13(2): 333–56.

Hamzah, Rayya Yusuf. 2002. *Al-tajriba al-barlamaniyya al-ula fi al-bahrayn: Al-majlis al-ta'sisi wa al-majlis al-watani, 1972–1975* [The first parliamentary experience in Bahrain: The Constitutional Council and the National Assembly]. Bahrain: al-Mu'assasa al-'arabiya lil-tiba'ah wa al-nashr.

Hay, Rupert. 1959. *The Persian Gulf States*. Washington, DC: Middle East Institute.

Haydar, Faysal Ahmad Uthman. 1997. *Ruwwad al-dimuqratiya fi al-kuwayt: Min 'am 1921 hatta 'am 1996* [Pioneers of democracy in Kuwait from 1921 to 1996]. Kuwait: n.p.

Hazbun, Waleed. 2008. *Beaches, Ruins, Resorts?: The Politics of Tourism in the Arab World*. Minneapolis: University of Minnesota Press.

Heard-Bey, Frauke. 1999. "The United Arab Emirates: A Quarter Century of Federation." In *Middle East Dilemma: The Politics and Economics of Arab Integration*. New York: Columbia University Press.

—— 2004. *From Trucial States to United Arab Emirates: A Society in Transition*. Dubai, UAE: Motivate Publishing.

—— 2005. "The United Arab Emirates: Statehood and Nation-Building in a Traditional Society." *Middle East Journal* 59(3): 357–75.

Herb, Michael. 1999. *All in the Family: Absolutism, Revolution, and Democracy in the Middle Eastern Monarchies*. Albany: SUNY Press.

—— 2002. "Emirs and Parliaments in the Gulf." *Journal of Democracy* 13(4): 41–47.

—— 2004. "Princes and Parliaments in the Arab World." *Middle East Journal* 58(3): 367–84.

—— 2005. "No Representation without Taxation? Rents, Development and Democracy." *Comparative Politics* 37(3): 297–316.

—— 2009. "A Nation of Bureaucrats: Political Participation and Economic Diversification in Kuwait and the United Arab Emirates." *International Journal of Middle East Studies* 41(3): 375–95.

—— 2013. "Kuwait's Endless Elections: The Opposition in Retreat." Policy Brief. Project on Middle East Democracy (POMED). http://pomed.org/herb2013/.

Hertog, Steffen. 2010a. "Defying the Resource Curse: Explaining Successful State-Owned Enterprises in Rentier States." *World Politics* 62(2): 261–301.

—— 2010b. *Princes, Brokers, and Bureaucrats: Oil and the State in Saudi Arabia.* Ithaca: Cornell University Press.

—— 2010c. "The Sociology of the Gulf Rentier Systems: Societies of Intermediaries." *Comparative Studies in Society and History* 52(2): 282–318.

Hicks, Neil, and Ghanim Al-Najjar. 1995. "The Utility of Tradition: Civil Society in Kuwait." In *Civil Society in the Middle East*, edited by Augustus R. Norton, 186–213. Leiden: Brill.

Holes, Clive. 2005. "Dialect and National Identity: The Cultural Politics of Self-Representation in Bahraini." In *Monarchies and Nations: Globalisation and Identity in the Arab States of the Gulf*, edited by Paul Dresch and James P. Piscatori, 52–72. London: I. B. Tauris.

Hopper, Matthew S. 2010. "Globalization and the Economics of African Slavery in Arabia in the Age of Empire." *Journal of African Development* 12(1): 155–84.

Human Rights Watch. 2006. "Building Towers, Cheating Workers: Exploitation of Migrant Construction Workers in the United Arab Emirates," 18, No. 8. Human Rights Watch, New York.

—— 2010. "Slow Reform: Protection of Migrant Domestic Workers in Asia and the Middle East." Human Rights Watch, New York.

Hvidt, Martin. 2009. "The Dubai Model: An Outline of Key Development-Process Elements in Dubai." *International Journal of Middle East Studies* 41(3): 397–418.

—— 2011. "Economic and Institutional Reforms in the Arab Gulf Countries." *Middle East Journal* 65(1): 85–102.

International Crisis Group. 2005. "Bahrain's Sectarian Challenge." Middle East Report no. 40. http://www.crisisgroup.org/en/regions/middle-east-north-africa/iraq-iran-gulf/bahrain/040-bahrains-sectarian-challenge.aspx.

—— 2011a. "Popular Protest in North Africa and the Middle East (III): The Bahrain Revolt." MENA Report no. 105. http://www.crisisgroup.org/en/regions/middle-east-north-africa/iraq-iran-gulf/bahrain/105-popular-protests-in-north-africa-and-the-middle-east-iii-the-bahrain-revolt.aspx.

—— 2011b. "Popular Protest in North Africa and the Middle East (VIII): Bahrain's Rocky Road to Reform." Middle East Report no. 111. http://www.crisisgroup.org/en/regions/middle-east-north-africa/iraq-iran-gulf/bahrain/111-popular-protest-in-north-africa-and-the-middle-east-viii-bahrains-rocky-road-to-reform.aspx.

International Monetary Fund (IMF). 1998. *United Arab Emirates: Recent Economic Developments.* Country Report no. 98/134. Washington, DC: International Monetary Fund.

—— 2003. *United Arab Emirates: Selected Issues and Statistical Appendix*. Country Report no. 03/67. Washington, DC: International Monetary Fund.

—— 2005a. *United Arab Emirates: Selected Issues and Statistical Appendix*. Country Report no. 05/268. Washington, DC: International Monetary Fund.

—— 2005b. *United Arab Emirates: 2005 Article IV Consultation*. Country Report no. 5/269. Washington, DC: International Monetary Fund.

—— 2007. *United Arab Emirates: Statistical Appendix*. Country Report no. 07/348. Washington, DC: International Monetary Fund.

—— 2008. *Qatar: 2007 Article IV Consultation*. Country Report no. 08/5. Washington, DC: International Monetary Fund.

—— 2009a. *Kuwait: 2009 Article IV Consultation*. Country Report no. 09/152. Washington, DC: International Monetary Fund.

—— 2009b. *Qatar: Statistical Appendix*. Country Report no. 09/32. Washington, DC: International Monetary Fund.

—— 2010a. *Kuwait: 2010 Article IV Consultation*. Country Report no. 10/236. Washington, DC: International Monetary Fund.

—— 2010b. *United Arab Emirates: 2009 Article IV Consultation*. Country Report no. 10/42. Washington, DC: International Monetary Fund.

—— 2011a. *Kuwait: Statistical Appendix*. Country Report no. 11/219. Washington, DC: International Monetary Fund.

—— 2011b. *United Arab Emirates: Selected Issues and Statistical Appendix*. Country Report no. 11/112. Washington, DC: International Monetary Fund.

—— 2012a. *Kuwait: Selected Issues and Statistical Annex*. Country Report no. 12/151. Washington, DC: International Monetary Fund.

—— 2012b. *Saudi Arabia: Selected Issues*. Country Report no. 12/272. Washington, DC: International Monetary Fund.

—— 2012c. *United Arab Emirates: 2012 Article IV Consultation*. Country Report 12/116. Washington, DC: International Monetary Fund.

—— 2012d. *United Arab Emirates: Selected Issues and Statistical Annex*. Country Report no. 12/136. Washington, DC: International Monetary Fund.

—— 2013. *Republic of Equatorial Guinea: 2012 Article IV Consultation*. Country Report no. 13/83. Washington, DC: International Monetary Fund.

James, Ed. 2005. "Balanced on a Knife Edge." *MEED: Middle East Economic Digest* 49(22), June 3, 41–44.

—— 2008a. "Kuwait Picks Winners for Al-Zour Refinery." *MEED: Middle East Economic Digest* 52(16), April 18, 11.

—— 2008b. "Wealth Masks Economic Stagnation." *MEED: Middle East Economic Digest* 52(13), March 28, n.p.

Janardhan, N. 2011. *Boom amid Gloom: The Spirit of Possibility in the 21st Century Gulf*. Reading, UK: Ithaca Press.

Jarman, Robert L. 2002. *Sabah al-Salim Al-Sabah: Amir of Kuwait, 1965–77*. London: London Centre of Arab Studies.

Jonas, Andrew E. G., and David Wilson. 1999. *The Urban Growth Machine: Critical Perspectives Two Decades Later*. Albany: SUNY Press.

Jones, Jeremy, and Nicholas Ridout. 2005. "Democratic Development in Oman." *Middle East Journal* 59(3): 376–92.

Jum'ah, Salwa Sha'rawi. 1993. "Al-tajriba al-barlamaniyya fi al-kuwayt: Dirasa fi al-'awamil al-dakhiliyya" [Kuwait's parliamentary experience: A study of domestic factors]. In *Al-tahawwulat al-dimuqratiya fi al-watan al-'arabi* [Democratic transformation in the Arab nation], edited by Nivin 'abd al-Mun'im Mus'ad. Cairo: University of Cairo.

Kamrava, Mehran. 2009. "Royal Factionalism and Political Liberalization in Qatar." *Middle East Journal* 63(3): 401–20.

—— 2013. *Qatar: Small State, Big Politics*. Ithaca: Cornell University Press.

Kanna, Ahmed. 2011. *Dubai, the City as Corporation*. Minneapolis: University of Minnesota Press.

Kapiszewski, Andrzej. 2001. *Nationals and Expatriates: Population and Labour Dilemmas of the Gulf Cooperation Council States*. Reading, UK: Ithaca Press.

—— 2006. "Elections and Parliamentary Activity in the GCC States: Broadening Political Participation in the Gulf Monarchies." In *Constitutional Reform and Political Participation in the Gulf*, edited by Abdulhadi Khalaf and Giacomo Luciani, 88–131. Dubai: Gulf Research Center.

Karl, Terry Lynn. 1997. *The Paradox of Plenty: Oil Booms and Petro-States*. Berkeley: University of California Press.

Kéchichian, Joseph A. 2004. "Democratization in Gulf Monarchies: A New Challenge to the GCC." *Middle East Policy* 11(4): 37–57.

Khalaf, 'Abd ul-Hadi. 1985. "Labor Movements in Bahrain." *MERIP Reports* (132) (May): 24–29. doi:10.2307/3011059.

Khalifa, Ali Abd al-Latif. c2002. *'Uqdat al-dhamm wa azmat Qasim 'am 1961* [The problem of annexation and the crisis of Qasim in 1961]. N.p.: n.p. [Kuwait University library.]

Khuri, Fuad I. 1980. *Tribe and State in Bahrain: The Transformation of Social and Political Authority in an Arab State*. Chicago: University of Chicago Press.

Kingdom of Saudi Arabia. N.d. *Al-kitab al-ihsa'i al-sanawi li-wizarat al-'amal 2012* [Statistical yearbook of the Ministry of Labor 2012] Ministry of Labor. Kropf, Annika. 2010. "Resource Abundance vs. Resource Dependence in Cross-Country Growth Regressions." *OPEC Energy Review* 34(2): 107–30.

Kurzman, Charles. 2004. *The Unthinkable Revolution in Iran*. Cambridge, MA: Harvard University Press.

Kuwait Chamber of Commerce and Industry (KCCI). 2005. "Al-takhsis bi-nizam al-bina' wa al-tashgil wa al-tahwil B.O.T." [Privatization via the build, operate and transfer B.O.T. mechanism]. Report presented to the minister of finance at his request. http://www.kuwaitchamber.org.kw.

—— 2007. "Waqfa taqim ma'a 'mashru' qanun bi-ta'dil ahkam al-marsum raqam 105 li-sana 1980 fi sha'n nizam amlak al-dawla'" [Assessment of the "bill to amend provisions of the decree number 105 of the year 1980 concerning the public property system"]. http://www.kuwaitchamber.org.kw.

—— 2009. "Aliyyat al-'amal wa al-khatwat al-mustaqbaliyya lil-qata' al-khass fi siyaq tanfith al-istratijiyya al-wataniya lil-siyaha" [Methods of action and future steps for the private sector in the context of implementing the National Strategy for Tourism]. http://www.kuwaitchamber.org.kw.

Kuwait Financial Centre (Markaz). "Kuwait Real Estate: Commentary and Analysis," February 2008. http://www.markaz.com (accessed July 3, 2008).

Kuwait News Agency (KUNA). 1999. *Masirat al-dimuqratiyya fi al-kuwayt* [The path of democracy in Kuwait]. Kuwait: Kuwait News Agency.

—— 2005. "Bi-raghba min al-majlis al-'ala lil-murur wa naffatha ba'da barmaja tawqit al-isharat al-duw'iyya taqsim al-dawam li-fatratayn" [According to the wishes of the High Council for Traffic, and implemented after the program of timing traffic signals, hours of work are divided into two periods]. November 9, Kuwait.

Lacher, Wolfram. 2011. "Families, Tribes and Cities in the Libyan Revolution." *Middle East Policy* 18(4): 140–54.

Lienhardt, Peter. 1975. "The Authority of Shaykhs in the Gulf: An Essay in Nineteenth-Century History." *Arabian Studies* 2: 61–75.

Listhaug, Ola. 2005. "Oil Wealth Dissatisfaction and Political Trust in Norway: A Resource Curse?" *West European Politics* 28(4): 834–51.

Logan, John R., and Harvey Luskin Molotch. 1987. *Urban Fortunes?: The Political Economy of Place.* Berkeley: University of California Press.

Longva, Anh Nga. 2005. "Neither Autocracy nor Democracy but Ethnocracy: Citizens, Expatriates and the Socio-Political System in Kuwait." In *Monarchies and Nations: Globalisation and Identity in the Arab States of the Gulf*, edited by Paul Dresch and James Piscatori, 114–35. London: I. B. Tauris.

—— 2006. "Nationalism in Pre-Modern Guise: The Discourse on Hadhar and Badu in Kuwait." *International Journal of Middle East Studies* 38(2): 171–87.

Lopez-Guerra, Claudio. 2005. "Should Expatriates Vote?" *Journal of Political Philosophy* 13(2): 216–34.

Lorimer, John G. 1908a. *Gazetteer of the Persian Gulf, Oman, and Central Arabia, Vol. 2A: Geographical and Statistical.* Calcutta: Superintendent of Government Printing.

—— 1908b. *Gazetteer of the Persian Gulf, Oman, and Central Arabia, Vol. 2B: Geographical and Statistical.* Calcutta: Superintendent of Government Printing.

Lucas, Russell E. 2004. "Monarchical Authoritarianism: Survival and Political Liberalization in a Middle Eastern Regime Type." *International Journal of Middle East Studies* 36(1): 103–19.

Luciani, Giacomo. 1990. "Allocation vs. Production States: A Theoretical Framework." In *The Arab State,* edited by Giacomo Luciani, 65–84. Berkeley: University of California Press.

Lynch, Marc. 2012. *The Arab Uprising: The Unfinished Revolutions of the New Middle East.* New York: PublicAffairs.

Mahoney, James, Erin Kimball, and Kendra L. Koivu. 2009. "The Logic of Historical Explanation in the Social Sciences." *Comparative Political Studies* 42(1): 114–46.

Marr, Phebe. 1985. *The Modern History of Iraq.* Boulder: Westview.

Martin, Matthew. 2013. "Foreign Workforce on the Way Out." *MEED: Middle East Economic Digest* 57(21), May 24, 18–19.

McClenaghan, Gregor. 2007. "Demand Drives Up Land Prices." *MEED: Middle East Economic Digest* 51(45), November 9, 57–61.

McSherry, Brendan. 2006. "The Political Economy of Oil in Equatorial Guinea." *African Studies Quarterly* 8(3): 23–45.

Middle East Journal. 1961. "Chronology June 16, 1961–September 15, 1961." *Middle East Journal* 15(4): 416–44.

—— 1962. "Chronology September 16, 1961—December 15, 1961." *Middle East Journal* 16(1): 60–85.

—— 1963. "Chronology September 16, 1962–March 15, 1963." *Middle East Journal* 17 (1–2): 104–43.

Mirza, Adal. 2012. "Getting It Right the Third Time." *MEED: Middle East Economic Digest* 56(18), May 4, 22–23.

Molotch, Harvey. 1976. "The City as a Growth Machine: Toward a Political Economy of Place." *American Journal of Sociology* 82(2): 309–32.

Monitor Group and Cambridge Energy Research Associates. 2006. *National Economic Strategy: An Assessment of the Competitiveness of the Libyan Arab Jamahiriya.* Tripoli: General Planning Council of Libya. http://www.isc.hbs.edu/.

Moore, Pete W. 2004. *Doing Business in the Middle East: Politics and Economic Crisis in Jordan and Kuwait.* Cambridge, UK: Cambridge University Press.

Morgan, Stephen L. 2007. *Counterfactuals and Causal Inference: Methods and Principles for Social Research.* Analytical Methods for Social Research. New York: Cambridge University Press.

Musa, Husayn. 1987. *Al-nidhal al-watani al-dimuqrati al-sha'b al-bahrayn (1920–1981)* [The modern national and democratic struggle in Bahrain]. N.p.: Al-haqiqa.

Nagy, Sharon. 1997. "Social and Spatial Process: An Ethnographic Study of Housing in Qatar." PhD diss., University of Pennsylvania.

Nakhleh, Emile A. 1976. *Bahrain?: Political Development in a Modernizing Society.* Lexington, MA: Lexington Books.

—— 1980. "Political Participation and the Constitutional Experiments in the Gulf: Bahrain and Qatar." In *Social and Economic Development in the Arab Gulf,* edited by Tim Niblock, 161–76. London: Croom Helm.

Nation of Brunei Department of Economic Planning and Development. 2010. *Brunei Darussalam Statistical Yearbook 2010.* Brunei Darussalam: Department of Statistics, Prime Minister's Office.

Nelson, Caren. 2004. "UAE National Women at Work in the Private Sector: Conditions and Constraints." TANMIA Labour Market Study no. 20. National Human Resource and Employment Authority, Centre for Labour Market Research and Information (CLMRI), Dubai, UAE

Niethammer, Katja. 2006. "Voices in Parliament, Debates in Majalis, and Banners on Streets: Avenues of Political Participation in Bahrain," EUI RSCAS Working Paper no. 2006/27. Robert Schuman Centre for Advanced Studies, European University Institute, Firenze, Italy.

Nonneman, Gerd. 2006. "Political Reform in the Gulf Monarchies: From Liberalisation to Democratisation: A Comparative Perspective." Durham Middle East Papers, Sir William Luce Fellowship Paper no. 6. Institute for Middle Eastern and Islamic Studies, Durham University, Durham, UK.

O'Grady, Paul, Michael Meyer-Resende, Ibrahim Hadban, and Homoud Alenezi. 2008. "Assessment of the Electoral Framework, Final Report: Kuwait." Democracy Reporting International (DRI) and the Kuwaiti Transparency Society, Berlin.

Onley, James, and Sulayman Khalaf. 2006. "Shaikhly Authority in the Pre-Oil Gulf: An Historical-Anthropological Study." *History & Anthropology* 17(3): 189–208.

Ottaviano, Gianmarco I. P., and Giovanni Peri. 2012. "Rethinking the Effect of Immigration on Wages." *Journal of the European Economic Association* 10(1): 152–97.

Oxford Business Group. 2006. "Global Citizen: OBG Talks to Crown Prince Sheikh Mohammed Bin Zayed Al Nahyan." In *Emerging Abu Dhabi 2006,* 18–19. London: Oxford Business Group.

—— 2008. "Country Business Intelligence Reports: Kuwait." http://www.oxfordbusinessgroup.com/publication.asp?country=33 (accessed July 1, 2013).

Parolin, Gianluca Paolo. 2006. "Generations of Gulf Constitutions: Paths and Perspectives." In *Constitutional Reform and Political Participation in the Gulf*, edited by Abdulhadi Khalaf and Giacomo Luciani, 51–87. Dubai: Gulf Research Center.

Partrick, Neil. 2009. "Nationalism in the Gulf States," Kuwait Programme on Development, Governance and Globalisation in the Gulf States, Center for the Study of Global Governance, London School of Economics.

Pierson, Paul. 2004. *Politics in Time: History, Institutions, and Social Analysis.* Princeton: Princeton University Press.

Pierson, Paul, and Theda Skocpol. 2002. "Historical Institutionalism in Contemporary Political Science." In *Political Science: State of the Discipline*, edited by Ira Katznelson and Helen V. Milner, 693–721. New York: W. W. Norton and American Political Science Association.

Przeworski, Adam. 1985. *Capitalism and Social Democracy.* Cambridge, UK: Cambridge University Press.

Qatar National Bank. N.d. *Annual Report 2006.* www.qnb.com.qa.

Rabi, Uzi. 2006. "Oil Politics and Tribal Rulers in Eastern Arabia: The Reign of Shakhbut (1928–1966)." *British Journal of Middle Eastern Studies* 33(1): 37–50.

Raghu, Mandagolathur R., and Layla Jasem Al-Ammar. 2012. "Investment Sector: Too Important to Be Left, Policy Options." Kuwait Financial Centre (Markaz Research), Kuwait.

Raghu, Mandagolathur R., Layla Jasem Al-Ammar, and Madhu Soothanan. 2011. "Markaz Sector Report: GCC Asset Management—2011." Kuwait Financial Centre (Markaz Research, Kuwait. http://www.markaz.com (accessed December 11. 2011).

Ragin, Charles C. 2008. *Redesigning Social Inquiry: Fuzzy Sets and Beyond.* Chicago: University of Chicago Press.

Ramady, Mohamed A. 2005. *The Saudi Arabian Economy?: Policies, Achievements and Challenges.* New York: Springer.

Randeree, Kasim. 2012. "Workforce Nationalization in the Gulf Cooperation Council States." Occasional Paper no. 9. Center for International and Regional Studies, Georgetown University School of Foreign Service in Qatar.

Redfern, Bernadette. 2008. "Investors Spoilt for Choice." *MEED: Middle East Economic Digest* 52(9), February 29: 32–33.

Roscoe, Andrew. 2011. "Delays Stall Tourism Ambitions." *MEED: Middle East Economic Digest* 55(44), November 4, 13–14.

Rosenfeld, Henry. 1965. "The Social Composition of the Military in the Process of State Formation in the Arabian Desert." *Journal of the Royal Anthropological Institute of Great Britain and Ireland* 95(1): 75–86.

Ross, Michael L. 2001. "Does Oil Hinder Democracy?" *World Politics* 53(April): 325–61.

—— 2004. "What Do We Know about Natural Resources and Civil War?" *Journal of Peace Research* 41(3): 337–56.

—— 2008. "Oil, Islam, and Women." *American Political Science Review* 102(1): 107–23.

—— 2012. *The Oil Curse: How Petroleum Wealth Shapes the Development of Nations*. Princeton: Princeton University Press.

Ruggles-Brise, Olivia, and Eva Aimable. 2012. "Travel & Tourism Economic Impact 2012: United Arab Emirates," World Travel & Tourism Council. http://www.wttc.org/site_media/uploads/downloads/united_arab_emirates2012.pdf.

Sachs, Jeffrey D., and Andrew M Warner. 1995. "Natural Resource Abundance and Economic Growth." NBER Working Paper no. 5398. National Bureau of Economic Research, Cambridge, MA.

Said (Zahlan), Rosemarie J. 1970. "The 1938 Reform Movement in Dubai." *Al-Abhath* (December): 247–318.

Saleh, Hassan Mohammed Abdulla. 1991. "Labor, Nationalism and Imperialism in Eastern Arabia: Britain, the Shaikhs and the Gulf Oil Workers in Bahrain, Kuwait and Qatar, 1932–1956." PhD diss., University of Michigan.

Salem, Paul. 2007. "Kuwait: Politics in a Participatory Emirate." *The Carnegie Papers* 3.

Salih, Kamal Osman. 1991. "Kuwait: Political Consequences of Modernization, 1750–1986." *Middle Eastern Studies* 27(1): 46–66.

—— 2006. "Parliamentary Control of the Executive: Evaluation of the Interpellation Mechanism, Case Study Kuwait National Assembly, 1992–2004." *Journal of South Asian and Middle Eastern Studies* 29(3): 36–69.

Salisbury, Peter. 2009. "Political Disputes Hold Back Kuwait." *MEED: Middle East Economic Digest* 53(3), January 16: 18–19.

—— 2010a. "A Reputation to Rebuild." *MEED: Middle East Economic Digest* 54(11), March 12: 37–38.

—— 2010b. "State Enters an Era of Change." *MEED: Middle East Economic Digest* 54(10), March 5: 2021.

Sampler, Jeffrey L, and Saeb Eigner. 2008. *Sand to Silicon—Going Global: Rapid Growth Lessons from Dubai*. Dubai, UAE: Motivate Publishing.

Saudi Arabian Monetary Agency (SAMA). 2012. *Forty Eighth Annual Report 2012*. Research and Statistics Department. Riyadh. N.p.

Schumpeter, Joseph A. 1954. "The Crisis of the Tax State." *International Economic Papers* 4: 5–38.

Sell, Christopher. 2008. "A Welcome Development to Kuwait's BOT Law." *MEED: Middle East Economic Digest* 52(13), March 28, 37–40.

Shambayati, Hootan. 1994. "The Rentier State, Interest Groups, and the Paradox of Autonomy: State and Business in Turkey and Iran." *Comparative Politics* 26(3): 307–31.

Silverstein, Ken. 2002. "U.S. Oil Politics in the 'Kuwait of Africa.'" *The Nation,* April 22, 11–20.

Slot, Ben J. 1998. *The Origins of Kuwait*. 2nd ed. Kuwait: Center for Research and Studies on Kuwait.

—— 2005. *Mubarak Al-Sabah: Founder of Modern Kuwait 1896–1915*. London: Arabian Publishing.

Smith, Benjamin B. 2004. "Oil Wealth and Regime Survival in the Developing World, 1960–1999." *American Journal of Political Science* 48(2): 232–46.

—— 2007. *Hard Times in the Lands of Plenty: Oil Politics in Iran and Indonesia.* Ithaca: Cornell University Press.

Smith, Benjamin B., and Joseph Kraus. 2005. "Democracy Despite Oil: Transition and Consolidation in Latin America and Africa." Paper presented at the Annual Meeting of the American Political Science Association, Washington, DC.

Smith, Benjamin B., and David Waldner. In press. "Rentier States and State Transformations." In *The Oxford Handbook of Transformations of the State*, edited by Stephan Leibfried, Frank Nullmeier, Evelyne Huber, Matthew Lange, Jonah Levy, and John D. Stephens. Oxford: Oxford University Press.

Smith, Simon C. 1999. *Kuwait, 1950–1965: Britain, the al-Sabah, and Oil.* Oxford: Oxford University Press.

—— 2004. *Britain's Revival and Fall in the Gulf: Kuwait, Bahrain, Qatar, and the Trucial States, 1950–71.* London: RoutledgeCurzon.

Speece, Mark. 1989. "Aspects of Economic Dualism in Oman, 1830–1930." *International Journal of Middle East Studies* 21(4): 495–515.

St. John, Ronald Bruce. 2008. "The Changing Libyan Economy: Causes and Consequences." *Middle East Journal* 62(1): 75–91.

Stasz, Cathleen, Eric R. Eide, and Francisco Martorell. 2007. *Post-Secondary Education in Qatar: Employer Demand, Student Choice, and Options for Policy.* Santa Monica, CA: Rand-Qatar Policy Institute.

State of Kuwait. 2009. *Annual Statistical Abstract 2008.* Central Statistical Bureau. Kuwait.

—— 2010. "Al-khitta al-inma'iya mutawassita al-'ajl lil-sanwat 2010/2011—2013/2014" [The medium-term development plan for the years 2010/2011–2013/2014]. Al-'amana al-'ama lil-majlis al-'ala lil-takhtit wa al-tanmiya [General Secretariat of the Supreme Council for Planning and Development]. Kuwait.

—— 2012a. *Annual Statistical Abstract 2011.* Central Statistical Bureau. Kuwait. http://www.csb.gov.kw.

—— 2012b. "Statistics on Employees in the Government Sector as of 30/6/2012." Central Statistical Bureau. Kuwait. http://www.csb.gov.kw.

—— 2013a. "Government Finance Statistics 2007/2008–2011/2012." Central Statistical Bureau, Kuwait. May. http://www.csb.gov.kw.

—— 2013b. *Statistical Review 2013.* Central Statistical Bureau. Kuwait.

State of Qatar. 2010a. *Annual Abstract 2010,* Statistics Authority. http://www.qsa.gov.qa (accessed December 27, 2012).

—— 2010b. *The General Census of Population and Housing and Establishment.* Qatar Statistics Authority, April. http://www.qsa.gov.qa.

—— 2011. *Qatar: Social Trends 1998–2010.* Qatar Statistics Authority, October. http://www.qsa.gov.qa.

Statistics Denmark. 2011. *Statistical Yearbook 2011.* Copenhagen.

Statistics Norway. 2011. *Statistical Yearbook of Norway 2011.* Oslo.

Statistics Sweden. 2012. *Statistical Yearbook of Sweden 2012.* Stockholm.

Stijns, Jean-Philippe C. 2001. "Natural Resource Abundance and Economic Growth Revisited." Berkeley Economics Dissertations-in-Progress Series 25127. University of California, Berkeley. http://ideas.repec.org/p/ags/ucbeed/25127.html.

Sultanate of Oman. 2011. *Statistical Yearbook 2011.* Ministry of the National Economy. www.ncsi.gov.om/viewPublication.aspx?id=878 (accessed June 4, 2013). [Data is for 2010].

Sweet, Louise E. 1964. "Pirates or Polities? Arab Societies of the Persian or Arabian Gulf, 18th Century." *Ethnohistory* 11(3): 262–80.

Taryam, Abdullah Omran. 1987. *The Establishment of the United Arab Emirates, 1950–85.* London: Croom Helm.

Taylor, Richard, and Kiki Thoma. 1985. "Mortality Patterns in the Modernized Pacific Island Nation of Nauru." *American Journal of Public Health* 75(2): 149–55.

Tétreault, Mary Ann. 2000. *Stories of Democracy: Politics and Society in Contemporary Kuwait.* New York: Columbia University Press.

Thomas, Karen. 2007. "The Boom Spreads North." *MEED: Middle East Economic Digest* 51, December 14: 46–51.

Timmons, Jeffrey F. 2010. "Taxation and Representation in Recent History." *Journal of Politics* 72: 191.

Tomlinson, Hugh. 2007. "Job Seeking." *MEED: Middle East Economic Digest* 51(11), March 16, 4–6.

—— 2009. "Abu Dhabi's Cultural Centre." *MEED: Middle East Economic Digest* (Suppl.) November 6, 8–10.

Tony Blair Associates. 2009. "Vision Kuwait 2030 Final Report," Prepared for the Emiri Diwan. Tony Blair Associates, London.

Trinidad and Tobago. 2012. *Trinidad and Tobago 2011 Population and Housing Census Demographic Report.* Central Statistical Office.

United Arab Emirates. 2006. *Preliminary Results of Population, Housing and Establishments Census 2005.* Ministry of the Economy.

—— 2008a. *Al-nata'ij al-ra'isiyya li'mash nafaqat wa dakhl al-usra 2007–2008* [Official results of the survey on household income and expenditure], Central Statistical Department, Ministry of the Economy.

—— 2008b. *Taqrir bil-nata'ij al-'awaliya li-masa' al-quwa al-'amila 2008* [Report on the early results of the labor force survey 2008]. Central Statistical Department, Ministry of the Economy.

—— 2009. *U.A.E. in Figures 2008.* Ministry of the Economy. http://www.economy.ae/Arabic/EconomicAndStatisticReports/StatisticReports/Pages/UAEinNumbers.aspx (accessed June 20, 2009).

—— 2010a. *Statistical Abstract 2008.* National Bureau of Statistics. http://www.uaestatistics.gov.ae (accessed September 8, 2012).

—— 2010b. *U.A.E. in Figures 2007.* National Bureau of Statistics. http://www.uaestatistics.gov.ae.

—— 2011. "Population Estimates 2006–2010." National Bureau of Statistics. March 31. http://www.uaestatistics.gov.ae.

—— 2012. *U.A.E. in Figures 2011.* National Bureau of Statistics. http://www.uaestatistics.gov.ae.

United Nations. 1963. *Yearbook of the United Nations 1961.* New York: UN Office of Public Information. http://unyearbook.un.org.

—— 1965. *Yearbook of the United Nations 1963.* New York: UN Office of Public Information. http://unyearbook.un.org.

—— 1974. *Yearbook of the United Nations 1971*. New York: UN Office of Public Information. http://unyearbook.un.org.

US Department of State. 2011. *2010 Human Rights Report: Equatorial Guinea*. Washington, DC.

Valeri, Marc. 2006. "Liberalization from Above: Political Reforms and Sultanism in Oman." In *Constitutional Reform and Political Participation in the Gulf*, edited by Abdulhadi Khalaf and Giacomo Luciani, 187–210. Dubai: Gulf Research Center.

—— 2009. *Oman: Politics and Society in the Qaboos State*. New York: Columbia University Press.

Van der Meulen, Hendrik. 1997. "The Role of Tribal and Kinship Ties in the Politics of the United Arab Emirates." PhD diss., Tufts University.

Vora, Neha. 2008. "Producing Diasporas and Globalization: Indian Middle-Class Migrants in Dubai." *Anthropological Quarterly* 81(2): 377–406.

Wajdi, Ahmad. 2004. "Nizam al-tawzif al-markazi bi-dawlat al-kuwayt" [The central employment system in the state of Kuwait]. State of Kuwait, Civil Service Commission, Technical Office.

Wilkinson, John Craven. 1987. *The Imamate Tradition of Oman*. Cambridge, UK: Cambridge University Press.

Wilson, D. 1833. "Memorandum Respecting the Pearl Fisheries in the Persian Gulf." *Journal of the Royal Geographical Society of London* 3: 283–86.

Winckler, Onn. 2008. "The Surprising Results of the Saudi Arabian 2004 Demographic Census." *International Journal of Middle East Studies* 40(1): 12–15.

Wood, Geoffrey. 2004. "Business and Politics in a Criminal State: The Case of Equatorial Guinea." *African Affairs* 103(413): 547–67.

World Bank. 2011. The Changing Wealth of Nations: Measuring Sustainable Development in the New Millennium. Washington, DC: World Bank.

Worrall, James. 2012. "Oman: The 'Forgotten' Corner of the Arab Spring." *Middle East Policy* 19(3): 98–115. doi:10.1111/j.1475-4967.2012.00550.x.

Wright, Gavin, and Jesse Czelusta. 2004. "The Myth of the Resource Curse." *Challenge* 47(2): 6–38.

Wright, Steven. 2008. "Fixing the Kingdom: Political Evolution and Socio-Economic Challenges in Bahrain." Occasional Paper no. 3. Center for International and Regional Studies, Georgetown University School of Foreign Service in Qatar.

Yom, Sean L. 2011. "Oil, Coalitions, and Regime Durability: The Origins and Persistence of Popular Rentierism in Kuwait." *Studies in Comparative International Development* 46(2): 217–41.

Yom, Sean L., and F. Gregory Gause III. 2012. "Resilient Royals: How Arab Monarchies Hang On." *Journal of Democracy* 23(4): 74–88.

Al-Yousif, Yousif Khalifa. 2008. "'Andama tusbi' al-sulta ghanima: Halat majlis al-ta'awun al-khaliji [When the government becomes booty: The case of the Gulf Cooperation Council]." *Al-Mustaqbal al-Arabi* 351(April/May): 70–87.

Zahlan, Rosemarie Said. 1978. *The Origins of the United Arab Emirates: A Political and Social History of the Trucial States*. New York: St. Martin's Press.

—— 1980. "Hegemony, Dependence and Development in the Gulf." In *Social and Economic Development in the Arab Gulf*, edited by Tim Niblock, 61–79. London: Croom Helm.

—— 1998. *The Making of the Modern Gulf States: Kuwait, Bahrain, Qatar, the United Arab Emirates, and Oman*. Reading, UK: Ithaca Press.

Index